Copyright © 2019 By Jenniffer Jones   All Rights Reserved

The information contained in this book and its contents is not designed to replace or take the place of any form of medical or professional advice; and is not meant to replace the need for independent medical, financial, legal or other professional advice or services, as may be required. The content and information in this book has been provided for educational and entertainment purposes only.

The content and information contained in this book has been compiled from sources deemed reliable, and it is accurate to the best of the Author's knowledge, information and belief. However, the Author cannot guarantee its accuracy and validity and cannot be held liable for any errors and/or omissions. Further, changes are periodically made to this book as and when needed. Where appropriate and/or necessary, you must consult a professional (including but not limited to your doctor, attorney, financial advisor or such other professional advisor) before using any of the suggested remedies, techniques, or information in this book.

ISBN-13: 978-1095251539

Table of Content

Introduction 1
Chapter 1 What You Need to Know About Air Frying 2
    The Benefits of Air Frying 2
    Best Practices When Air Frying....................... 3
    Air Fryer Accessories Advantages.................. 4
        Skewers on Double Layer Rack 4
        Grill Pan 5
        Baking Dish.................................... 5
    Tips on Cleaning... 6
    Air Fryer Cooking Chart................................... 7
    Measurement Conversion Charts 10
Chapter 2 Air Fryer Seafood Recipes........11
    Air Fried Cod with Basil Vinaigrette 11
    Almond Flour Coated Crispy Shrimps 11
    Another Crispy Coconut Shrimp Recipe...... 11
    Apple Slaw Topped Alaskan Cod Filet 12
    Baked Cod Fillet Recipe From Thailand...... 13
    Baked Scallops with Garlic Aioli 13
    Basil 'n Lime-Chili Clams............................... 13
    Bass Filet in Coconut Sauce........................... 14
    Beer Battered Cod Filet 14
    Buttered Baked Cod with Wine..................... 15
    Buttered Garlic-Oregano on Clams 15
    Butterflied Prawns with Garlic-Sriracha 16
    Cajun Seasoned Salmon Filet........................ 16
    Cajun Spiced Lemon-Shrimp Kebabs 16
    Cajun Spiced Veggie-Shrimp Bake 17
    Celery Leaves 'n Garlic-oil Grilled Turbot ... 17
    Char-Grilled Drunken Halibut 18
    Clams with Herbed Butter in Packets 18
    Cocktail Prawns in Air Fryer 18
    Cornmeal 'n Old Bay Battered Fish 19
    Crisped Flounder Filet with Crumb Tops.... 19
    Crispy Coconut Covered Shrimps................. 20
    Crispy Fish Fingers with Lemon-Garlic....... 20
    Crispy Fried Fish-Paprika Nuggets 21
    Crispy Lemon-Parsley Fish Cakes 21
    Crispy Shrimps The Cajun Way 22

Crispy Spicy-Lime Fish Filet.......................... 22
Cumin, Thyme 'n Oregano Herbed Shrimps 22
Crispy and Spicy Hot Shrimps....................... 23
Dijon Mustard 'n Parmesan Crusted Tilapia 23
Drunken Skewered Shrimp............................ 24
Easy 'n Crispy Cod Nuggets 24
Easy Battered Lemony Fillet.......................... 25
Easy Lobster Tail with Salted Butter 25
Easy Crispy Catfish Filet................................. 25
Egg Frittata with Smoked Trout.................... 26
Fennel Salad Topped with Roast Salmon 26
Fried Shrimps with Sweet Chili Sauce.......... 27
Garlic-Cilantro Over Salmon Steak............... 27
Gingery Cod Filet Recipe from Hong Kong . 28
Grilled Bacon 'n Scallops................................ 28
Grilled Scallops with Pesto............................. 28
Grilled Shrimp with Chipotle-Orange Seasoning.. 29
Grilled Squid with Aromatic Sesame Oil..... 29
Healthy and Easy to Make Salmon 29
Honey-Ginger Soy Sauce Over Grilled Tuna 30
Jamaican-Jerk Seasoned Salmon 30
Kashmiri Chili Powder 'n Garlic Shrimp BBQ 31
Lemony-Parsley Linguine with Grilled Tuna 31
Lemon Tuna 'n Buttered Rice Puff................ 32
Lemon-Basil on Cod Filet............................... 33
Lemon-Garlic on Buttered Shrimp Fry 33
Lemon-Paprika Salmon Filet......................... 34
Lemon-Pepper Red Mullet Fry...................... 34
Lemony Grilled Halibut 'n Tomatoes 35
Lemony Tuna-Parsley Patties........................ 35
Lemony-Sage on Grilled Swordfish 36
Lime 'n Chat masala Rubbed Snapper 36
Lime, Oil 'n Leeks on Grilled Swordfish....... 37
Lobster-Spinach Lasagna Recipe from Maine 37
Mango Salsa on Fish Tacos 38

Miso Sauce Over Grilled Salmon (Japanese) 38
Old Bay 'n Dijon Seasoned Crab Cakes 39
Orange Roughie with Caesar & Cheese Dressing... 39
Oregano & Cumin Flavored Salmon Grill.... 39
Outrageous Crispy Fried Salmon Skin 40
Pesto Basted Shrimp on the Grill.................. 40
Pesto Sauce Over Fish Filet 41
Pina Colada Sauce Over Coconut Shrimps.. 41
Quick 'n Easy Tuna-Mac Casserole............... 42
Salad Niçoise With Peppery Halibut 42
Salmon Topped with Creamy Avocado-Cashew Sauce................................... 43
Salted Tequila 'n Lime Shrimp...................... 43
Savory Bacalao Tapas Recipe from Portugal 43
Shrimp, Mushroom 'n Rice Casserole 44
Soy-Orange Flavored Squid........................... 45
Spiced Coco-Lime Skewered Shrimp 45
Sweet Honey-Hoisin Glazed Salmon............ 46
Sweet-Chili Sauce Dip 'n Shrimp Rolls 46
Tartar Sauce 'n Crispy Cod Nuggets 47
Tomato 'n Onion Stuffed Grilled Squid 47
Tortilla-Crusted with Lemon Filets 47
Turmeric Spiced Salmon with Soy Sauce 48
Very Easy Lime-Garlic Shrimps..................... 48

Chapter 3 Air Fryer Vegetarian Recipes ...49

Almond Flour Battered 'n Crisped Onion Rings 49
Almond Flour Battered Wings 49
Baby Corn in Chili-Turmeric Spice............... 50
Baked Cheesy Eggplant with Marinara........ 50
Baked Polenta with Chili-Cheese.................. 51
Baked Portobello, Pasta 'n Cheese................ 51
Baked Potato Topped with Cream Cheese... 52
Baked Zucchini Recipe from Mexico............ 53
Banana Pepper Stuffed with Tofu 53
Bell Pepper Wrapped in Tortilla 54
Black Bean Burger with Garlic-Chipotle...... 54
Brown Rice, Spinach Frittata 55
Brussels Sprouts with Balsamic Oil.............. 55
Buttered Carrot-Zucchini with Mayo 56
Cauliflower Steak with Thick Sauce............. 56
Cheddar 'n Zucchini Casserole 57
Cheesy BBQ Tater Tot..................................... 57
Chives 'n Thyme Spiced Veggie Burger 58
Coconut Battered Cauliflower Bites............. 58
Creamy 'n Cheese Broccoli Bake 59
Creole Seasoned Vegetables........................... 60
Crisped Baked Cheese Stuffed Chile Pepper 60
Crisped Noodle Salad Chinese Style 61
Crisped Tofu with Paprika 61
Crispy Avocado Fingers.................................. 62
Crispy Savory Spring Rolls............................. 62
Crispy Asparagus Dipped in Paprika............ 63
Crispy Fry Green Tomatoes 63
Crispy Onion Seasoned with Paprika 'n Cajun 64
Crispy Vegetarian Ravioli............................... 64
Crispy Vegie Tempura Style 65
Crispy Wings with Lemony Old Bay Spice... 65
Curry 'n Coriander Spiced Bread Rolls......... 66
Easy Baked Root Veggies 66
Easy Fry Portobello Mushroom..................... 67
Egg-Less Spinach Quiche 67
Fried Broccoli Recipe from India.................. 68
Fried Chickpea-Fig on Arugula 68
Fried Falafel Recipe from the Middle East .. 69
Fried Tofu Recipe from Malaysia.................. 69
Garlic 'n Basil Crackers................................... 70
Garlic-Wine Flavored Vegetables.................. 70
Grilled 'n Glazed Strawberries....................... 71
Grilled Tomatoes on Garden Salad............... 71
Grilled Drunken Mushrooms......................... 72
Grilled Eggplant with Cumin-Paprika Spice 72
Grilled Olive-Tomato with Dill-Parsley Oil . 73
Healthy Apple-licious Chips 73
Healthy Breakfast Casserole 74
Herby Veggie Cornish Pasties........................ 75
Herby Zucchini 'n Eggplant Bake.................. 75
Hollandaise Topped Grilled Asparagus........ 76
Italian Seasoned Easy Pasta Chips................ 77
Jackfruit-Cream Cheese Rangoon................. 77

Jalapeno Stuffed with Bacon 'n Cheeses...... 77
Layered Tortilla Bake 78
Loaded Brekky Hash Browns 78
Melted Cheese 'n Almonds on Tomato 79
Minty Green Beans with Shallots................... 79
Mushroom 'n Bell Pepper Pizza 80
Mushrooms Marinated in Garlic Coco-Aminos 80
Mushrooms Stuffed with Cream Cheese-Pesto 81
Open-Faced Vegan Flatbread........................ 81
Orange Glazed Fried Tofu............................... 82
Pineapple with Butter Glaze........................... 82
Pita 'n Tomato Pesto Casserole 83
Pull-Apart Bread With Garlicky Oil.............. 83
Quinoa Bowl with Lime-Sriracha 84
Roasted Bell Peppers 'n Onions in a Salad .. 84
Roasted Broccoli with Salted Garlic 85
Roasted Chat-Masala Spiced Broccoli.......... 85
Roasted Mushrooms in Herb-Garlic Oil...... 86
Rosemary Olive-Oil Over Shrooms n Asparagus... 86
Salted 'n Herbed Potato Packets 86
Salted Beet Chips 87
Salted Garlic Zucchini Fries........................... 87
Salted Potato-Kale Nuggets 87
Savory Zucchini-Bell Pepper Medley 88
Scrumptiously Healthy Chips........................ 88
Shallots 'n Almonds on French Green Beans 89
Shepherd's Pie Vegetarian Approved........... 89
Skewered Corn in Air Fryer 90
Spicy Veggie Recipe from Thailand 90
Spinach Balls Spiced with Garlic 'n Pepper. 91
Sweet 'n Nutty Marinated Cauliflower-Tofu 91
Tender Butternut Squash Fry........................ 92
Tofu Bites Soaked in Chili-Ginger Peanut Butter... 92
Twice-Fried Cauliflower Tater Tots.............. 93
Vegetarian Sushi Rice Bowl 93
Veggie Wontons with Chili-Oil Seasoning... 94
Vegie Grill Recipe with Tandoori Spice........ 94
Your Traditional Mac 'n Cheese 95
Zucchini garlic-Sour Cream Bake 95
Zucchini Topped with Coconut Cream 'n Bacon... 96

Chapter 4 Air Fryer Meat Recipes 97
3-Cheese Meatball and Pasta......................... 97
Air Fried Grilled Steak.................................... 98
Air Fried Roast Beef.. 98
Air Fried Steak... 98
Air Fryer Beef Casserole 99
Almond Flour 'n Egg Crusted Beef................ 99
Another Easy Teriyaki BBQ Recipe 99
Apricot Glazed Pork Tenderloins 100
Baby Back Rib Recipe from Kansas City 100
Bacon, Spinach & Feta Quiche..................... 101
Bacon-Cheeseburger Casserole 102
Baked Cheese 'n Pepperoni Calzone 102
Balsamic Glazed Pork Chops 103
Beef Brisket Recipe from Texas.................... 103
Beef Recipe Texas-Rodeo Style 104
Beef Roast in Worcestershire-Rosemary ...104
Beefy 'n Cheesy Spanish Rice Casserole..... 105
Beefy Bell Pepper 'n Egg Scramble 105
Beefy Steak Topped with Chimichurri Sauce 106
Bourbon-BBQ Sauce Marinated Beef BBQ 106
Buttered Garlic-Thyme Roast Beef............. 107
Cajun 'n Coriander Seasoned Ribs.............. 107
Cajun Sweet-Sour Grilled Pork.................... 108
Capers 'n Olives Topped Flank Steak 108
Caraway, Sichuan 'n Cumin Lamb Kebabs 109
Champagne-Vinegar Marinated Skirt Steak 109
Char-Grilled Skirt Steak with Fresh Herbs 109
Charred Onions 'n Steak Cube BBQ............110
Cheddar Cheese 'n Bacon Stuffed Pastry Pie 110
Cheesy Ground Beef 'n Mac Taco Casserole 111
Cheesy Herbs Burger Patties 111

Cheesy Potato Casserole the Amish Way... 112
Cheesy Sausage 'n Grits Bake From Down South.. 112
Chili-Espresso Marinated Steak.................. 113
Chives on Bacon & Cheese Bake 113
Cilantro-Mint Pork BBQ Thai Style............ 113
Coriander Lamb with Pesto 'n Mint Dip.... 114
Coriander, Mustard 'n Cumin Rubbed Flank Steak 114
Cornbread, Ham 'n Eggs Frittata................ 115
Country Style Sausage & Hash Browns...... 116
Creamy Burger & Potato Bake..................... 116
Crispy Fried Pork Chops the Southern Way 117
Crispy Roast Garlic-Salt Pork...................... 117
Cumin 'n Chili Rubbed Steak Fajitas.......... 117
Cumin-Paprika Rubbed Beef Brisket 118
Cumin-Sichuan Lamb BBQ with Dip 118
Curry Pork Roast in Coconut Sauce 119
Eastern Chunky Shish Kebabs 120
Easy & The Traditional Beef Roast Recipe 120
Easy Corn Dog Bites 121
Egg Noodles, Ground Beef & Tomato Sauce Bake 121
Eggs 'n Bacon on Biscuit Brekky................. 122
Fat Burger Bombs 122
Flatiron Steak Grill on Parsley Salad.......... 123
Fried Pork with Sweet and Sour Glaze....... 123
Garlic Lemon-Wine on Lamb Steak 124
Garlic-Cumin 'n Orange Juice Marinated Steak 124
Garlicky Buttered Chops............................... 125
Garlic-Mustard Rubbed Roast Beef............ 125
Garlic-Rosemary Lamb BBQ 126
Garlic-Rosemary Rubbed Beef Rib Roast.. 126
Ginger Soy Beef Recipe from the Orient.... 126
Ginger, Garlic 'n Pork Dumplings................ 127
Ginger-Orange Beef Strips............................ 127
Gravy Smothered Country Fried Steak 128
Grilled Beef with Grated Daikon Radish ... 129
Grilled Prosciutto Wrapped Fig 129
Grilled Sausages with BBQ Sauce 129
Grilled Spicy Carne Asada............................ 130
Grilled Steak on Tomato-Olive Salad 130
Grilled Tri Tip over Beet Salad 131
Ground Beef on Deep Dish Pizza 131
Ground Beef, Rice 'n Cabbage Casserole.... 132
Hanger Steak in Mole Rub 132
Hickory Smoked Beef Jerky......................... 133
Italian Beef Roast 133
Italian Sausage & Tomato Egg Bake 134
Keto-Approved Cheeseburger Bake............ 134
Maple 'n Soy Marinated Beef....................... 135
Maras Pepper Lamb Kebab Recipe from Turkey... 135
Meat Balls with Mint Yogurt Dip From Morocco 136
Meatballs 'n Parmesan-Cheddar Pizza....... 136
Meatloaf with Sweet-Sour Glaze 137
Meaty Pasta Bake from the Southwest....... 137
Monterey Jack 'n Sausage Brekky Casserole 138
Mustard 'n Italian Dressing on Flank Steak 138
Mustard 'n Pepper Roast Beef 139
New York Steak with Yogurt-Cucumber Sauce 139
Onion 'n Garlic Rubbed Trip Tip................. 139
Oregano-Paprika on Breaded Pork............. 140
Paprika Beef 'n Bell Peppers Stir Fry.......... 140
Peach Puree on Ribeye 141
Pickling 'n Jerk Spiced Pork 141
Pineapple, Mushrooms & Beef Kebabs....... 142
Pineapple-Teriyaki Beef Skewer.................. 143
Pork Belly Marinated in Onion-Coconut Cream.. 143
Pork Belly with Sweet-Sour Sauce 143
Pork Chops Crusted in Parmesan-Paprika 144
Pork Chops Marinate in Honey-Mustard... 144
Pork Chops On the Grill Simple Recipe 145
Pork Stuffed with Gouda 'n Horseradish ... 145
Pork with Balsamic-Raspberry Jam 145

Pureed Onion Marinated Beef 146	Tri-Tip Skewers Hungarian Style 163
Rib Eye Steak Recipe from Hawaii 146	Very Tasty Herbed Burgers 163
Rib Eye Steak Seasoned with Italian Herb 147	**Chapter 5 Air Fryer Poultry Recipes 164**
Roast Beef with Balsamic-Honey Sauce 147	Air Fried Chicken Tenderloin 164
Roast Beef with Buttered Garlic-Celery 148	Almond Flour Battered Chicken Cordon Bleu 164
Roasted Ribeye Steak with Rum 148	Almond Flour Coco-Milk Battered Chicken 165
Saffron Spiced Rack of Lamb 148	
Sage Sausage 'n Chili-Hot Breakfast 149	Bacon 'n Egg-Substitute Bake 165
Salt and Pepper Pork Chinese Style 150	Baked Rice, Black Bean and Cheese 166
Salted 'n Peppered Scored Beef Chuck 150	Basil-Garlic Breaded Chicken Bake 166
Salted Corned Beef with Onions 150	BBQ Chicken Recipe from Greece 167
Salted Porterhouse with Sage 'n Thyme Medley 151	BBQ Pineapple 'n Teriyaki Glazed Chicken 168
Salted Steak Pan Fried Steak 151	BBQ Turkey Meatballs with Cranberry Sauce 168
Sausage 'n Cauliflower Frittata 152	Blueberry Overload French Toast 169
Sausage 'n Rice Bake from Mexico 152	Broccoli-Rice 'n Chees Casserole 170
Scallion Sauce on Lemongrass-Chili Marinated Tri-Tip 153	Buffalo Style Chicken Dip 170
Seasoned Ham 'n Mushroom Egg Bake 153	Buttered Spinach-Egg Omelet 171
Shepherd's Pie Made of Ground Lamb 154	Caesar Marinated Grilled Chicken 171
Sherry 'n Soy Garlicky Steak 155	Cheese Stuffed Chicken 172
Simple Garlic 'n Herb Meatballs 155	Cheesy Potato, Broccoli 'n Ham Bake 172
Simple Herbs de Provence Pork Loin Roast 155	Cheesy Turkey-Rice with Broccoli 173
Simple Lamb BBQ with Herbed Salt 156	Chestnuts 'n Mushroom Chicken Casserole 173
Simple Salt and Pepper Skirt Steak 156	Chicken BBQ on Kale Salad 174
Sirloin with Yogurt 'n Curry-Paprika 156	Chicken BBQ Recipe from Italy 174
Skirt Steak BBQ Recipe from Korea 157	Chicken BBQ Recipe from Peru 175
Smoked Brisket with Dill Pickles 157	Chicken BBQ with Sweet 'n Sour Sauce 175
Smoked Sausage 'n Shrimp Jambalaya 158	Chicken Fry Recipe from the Mediterranean 176
Sriracha-Hoisin Glazed Grilled Beef 158	Chicken Grill Recipe from California 176
Tasty Beef Pot Pie 159	Chicken in Packets Southwest Style 177
Tasty Stuffed Gyoza 159	Chicken Kebab with Aleppo 'n Yogurt 177
Tomato Salsa Topped Grilled Flank Steak 160	Chicken Meatballs with Miso-Ginger 178
Top Loin Beef Strips with Blue Cheese 160	Chicken Pot Pie with Coconut Milk 178
Top Round Roast with Mustard-Rosemary-Thyme Blend 161	Chicken Roast with Pineapple Salsa 179
Traditional Beef 'n Tomato Stew 161	Chicken Strips with Garlic 179
Traditional Beefy Spaghetti 162	Chicken Tikka Masala Kebab 180
Tri-Tip in Agave Nectar & Red Wine Marinade 162	Chicken with Ginger-Cilantro Coconut 180
	Chicken with Peach Glaze 181

Chicken-Parm, Broccoli 'n Mushroom Bake 181
Chicken-Penne Pesto 182
Chicken-Veggie Fusilli Casserole 182
Chili, Lime & Corn Chicken BBQ 183
Chinese Five Spiced Marinated Chicken.... 184
Chipotle Chicken ala King 184
Chipotle-Garlic Smoked Wings 185
Chives, Eggs 'n Ham Casserole 186
Chorizo-Oregano Frittata 186
Cilantro-Lime 'n Liquid Smoke Chicken Grill 187
Coco Milk -Oregano Marinated Drumsticks 187
Copycat KFC Chicken Strips 188
Creamy Chicken 'n Pasta Tetrazzini 188
Creamy Chicken 'n Rice 189
Creamy Chicken Breasts with crumbled Bacon 189
Creamy Chicken-Veggie Pasta 190
Creamy Coconut Egg 'n Mushroom Bake .. 190
Creamy Scrambled Eggs with Broccoli 191
Creamy Turkey Bake 191
Crispy 'n Salted Chicken Meatballs 192
Crispy Fried Buffalo Chicken Breasts 192
Crispy Tender Parmesan Chicken 193
Curried Rice 'n Chicken Bake 193
Curry-Peanut Butter Rubbed Chicken 194
Dijon-Garlic Thighs 194
Drunken Chicken Jerk Spiced 195
Easy Chicken Fried Rice 195
Easy Fried Chicken Southern Style 196
Easy How-To Hard Boil Egg in Air Fryer .. 196
Eggs 'n Turkey Bake 196
Eggs Benedict on English Muffins 197
Eggs, Cauliflower 'n Broccoli Brekky 197
French Toast with Apples 'n Raisins 198
Garam Masala 'n Yogurt Marinated Chicken 198
Garlic Paprika Rubbed Chicken Breasts 199
Garlic Rosemary Roasted Chicken 199

Ginger Garam Masala Rubbed Chicken 200
Greens 'n Turkey sausage Frittata 200
Grilled Chicken Pesto 201
Grilled Chicken Recipe From Jamaica 201
Grilled Chicken Recipe from Korea 201
Grilled Chicken Recipe from Morocco 202
Grilled Chicken Wings with Curry-Yogurt . 202
Grilled Thighs with Honey Balsamic 203
Healthy Turkey Shepherd's Pie 203
Honey & Sriracha Over Chicken 204
Honey, Lime, And Garlic Chicken BBQ 205
Honey-Balsamic Orange Chicken 205
Lebanese Style Grilled Chicken 206
Leftovers 'n Enchilada Bake 206
Lemon-Aleppo Chicken 207
Lemon-Butter Battered Thighs 208
Lemon-Oregano Chicken BBQ 208
Lemon-Parsley Chicken Packets 208
Malaysian Chicken Satay with Peanut Sauce 209
Meat-Covered Boiled Eggs 210
Middle Eastern Chicken BBQ with Tzatziki Sauce 210
Mixed Vegetable Breakfast Frittata 211
Mushroom 'n Coconut Cream Quiche 211
Naked Cheese, Chicken Stuffing 212
Non-Fattening Breakfast Frittata 212
Orange-Tequila Glazed Chicken 213
Oregano-Thyme Rubbed Thighs 213
Over the Top Chicken Enchiladas 214
Paprika-Cumin Rubbed Chicken Tenderloin 215
Pasta with Turkey-Basil Red Sauce 215
Pepper-Salt Egg 'n Spinach Casserole 216
Peppery Lemon-Chicken Breast 216
Pineapple Juice-Soy Sauce Marinated Chicken 216
Quick 'n Easy Brekky Eggs 'n Cream 217
Quick 'n Easy Garlic Herb Wings 217
Radish Hash Browns with Onion-Paprika Spice 218

Reuben Style Chicken Roll-up 218
Roast Chicken Recipe from Africa 219
Salsa on Chicken-Rice Bake 219
Salsa Verde Over Grilled Chicken 220
Salted Meaty Egg Frittata 220
Savory Chives 'n Bacon Frittata 221
Shishito Pepper Rubbed Wings 221
Soy-Honey Glaze Chicken Kebabs 221
Spinach 'n Bacon Egg Cups 222
Spinach-Egg with Coconut Milk Casserole 222
Sriracha-Ginger Chicken 223
Sriracha-vinegar Marinated Chicken 223
Sticky-Sweet Chicken BBQ 224
Sweet Lime 'n Chili Chicken Barbecue 224
Teriyaki Glazed Chicken Bake 224
Tomato, Cheese 'n Broccoli Quiche 225
Tomato, Eggplant 'n Chicken Skewers 225
Turmeric and Lemongrass Chicken Roast. 226

Chapter 6 Air Fryer Dessert Recipes 227
Angel Food Cake 227
Apple Pie in Air Fryer 227
Apple-Toffee Upside-Down Cake 228
Banana-Choco Brownies 228
Blueberry & Lemon Cake 229
Bread Pudding with Cranberry 229
Cherries 'n Almond Flour Bars 230
Cherry-Choco Bars 230
Chocolate Chip in a Mug 231
Choco-Peanut Mug Cake 231
Coco-Lime Bars 231
Coconut 'n Almond Fat Bombs 232
Coconutty Lemon Bars 232
Coffee 'n Blueberry Cake 233
Coffee Flavored Cookie Dough 233
Coffee Flavored Doughnuts 234
Crisped 'n Chewy Chonut Holes 234
Crispy Good Peaches 235
Easy Baked Chocolate Mug Cake 235
Hot Coconut 'n Cocoa Buns 236
Keto-Friendly Doughnut Recipe 236
Lava Cake in A Mug 237

Leche Flan Filipino Style 237
Lusciously Easy Brownies 238
Maple Cinnamon Buns 238
Melts in Your Mouth Caramel Cheesecake 239
Mouth-Watering Strawberry Cobbler 240
Oriental Coconut Cake 240
Pecan-Cranberry Cake 241
Poppy Seed Pound Cake 241
Pound Cake with Fresh Apples 242
Quick 'n Easy Pumpkin Pie 242
Raspberry-Coco Desert 243
Raspberry-Coconut Cupcake 243
Strawberry Pop Tarts 244
Strawberry Shortcake Quickie 244
Vanilla Pound Cake 245
Yummy Banana Cookies 245
Zucchini-Choco Bread 246

Introduction

Admit it. You love your comfort foods as much as the next guy. Unfortunately, most comfort foods are fried, and while eating fried food is convenient and can calm the senses, it can cause a lot of health problems.

Consuming too much fat can have long-term detrimental effects on the body. When you eat fried foods, saturated fats can clog arteries that can lead to problems like high blood pressure, stroke, heart attack, and Alzheimer's disease. Studies have also found that eating fried foods can trigger inflammatory responses in the body. Thus it puts you at high risk for obesity.

Although fried foods are dangerous to your body, it does not mean that you should stop or feel guilty eating your favorite comfort foods. The thing is that there is a way for you to enjoy fried foods without the need to feel guilty. But how? This is where the air fryer comes in.
.

The air fryer is a very valuable kitchen appliance that allows you to recreate your favorite fried comfort foods without using any oil at all! This means that you can cook fried foods with no worries, and you don't need to deprive yourself of eating your favorite dishes.

Preparing your favorite dishes with the air fryer is also easy. In fact, you don't need to have excellent kitchen prowess when making delicious oil-less fried recipes. With this Air Fryer Cookbook, you will be able to prepare delicious recipes without the need to sacrifice your health.

Even if you are a novice, preparing healthy air fried food is very convenient as the recipes are very easy to follow. You will never feel guilty about cooking and eating your favorite dishes. So go ahead and start air frying your foods and enjoy the benefits that it gives your body

Chapter 1 What You Need to Know About Air Frying

Fried foods are the ultimate comfort foods. But with recent studies linking greasy foods to heart attacks, obesity, and diabetes, many are now staying away from enjoying them completely. However, completely avoiding fried foods can be difficult, especially if you love munching these little snacks. Now, you don't have to worry because you can always enjoy your favorite fried foods without the need to use any grease. How? Through air frying, of course!

Air frying has become the latest craze in making greasy comfort foods healthier. It is done in a kitchen appliance-an air fryer-that cooks food by circulating hot air of up to 390 °F (200 °C) at high speed around it to create a crispy layer much like you are cooking with oil. Health conscious people who still don't want to give up their favorite fried foods can take advantage of air fryer-ed foods.

The Benefits of Air Frying

Besides providing us comfort and satisfaction, eating fried foods provide little benefits. But with an air fryer, anyone can whip up healthy and satisfying foods minus any guilt. There are many benefits of air frying food instead of cooking them in a conventional deep fryer. Below are the benefits of why you should air fry your foods more often.

- **Versatile:** An air fryer is not only a fryer, so you can use it to cook different types of foods. You can use it to bake bread, make popcorn, or even make roasted vegetables.

- **Cost effective:** Since you don't use any oil in cooking your food, you can save a lot of money from buying cooking oil.

- **Easy to cook:** Never mind if you are a kitchen novice. Since air fryers are digital, it requires less skill so you can cook delicious dishes even if you are not good at cooking.

- **Fewer calories**: Since you do not add any oil to cook your food compared to traditional frying methods, you don't add a few calories to cook your food. Remember that a cup of oil is already equivalent to 800 calories alone, so deep frying increases the calorie value of your food to a dangerously high level.

The thing is that there are many benefits of air frying and if you decide to make a simple change in your diet by only eating fried foods that are cooked in an air fryer, you will be able to enjoy a healthier and more convenient life.

Best Practices When Air Frying

While it is easy to use an air fryer, using it for the first time can present some challenges. But this should not scare you from air frying your foods. After all, you get more health benefits than actual frying your food in oil. Below are the best practices and tips that you can do to successfully air fry your favorite foods.

- **Shake the basket**: To distribute the ingredients within the basket, you can shake the basket a few times while cooking.
- **Spray a little amount of oil**: If you are not satisfied with how brown your food is, you can spray oil halfway through the cooking process. Make sure that you spray the food lightly and not lather it with oil. Preheat the air fryer before you place your food inside: Just like cooking in an oven, you need to preheat your air fryer so that your food will cook properly. Turn the air fryer on and preheat for at least three minutes.
- **Never put too many foods inside the basket**: While it is very tempting to cook more food at a time, overcrowding your air fryer prevents the hot air from circulating properly within the fryer thus you end up with food that is not evenly brown or crispy.
- **Add water to the air fryer drawer**: If you are cooking greasy foods, add water to the air fryer drawer located under the

basket. This prevents the grease from getting too hot and causing it to smoke.
- **Hold your food properly**: Since air fryers have strong fans that can blow off light food particles, secure them in place using toothpicks. If food gets stuck on the fan or the heating element of the fryer, they might get burned and will cause smoke to form during the cooking process. Flip your food: Halfway through the cooking time, flip your food over just as you would when cooking on a grill. This will ensure that the food will brown evenly on all sides.
- **Press the breading on your food firmly**: An air fryer has a strong fan that can blow off parts of your food thus if you are putting breading on your food, make sure that you press it firmly to help it stay in place while you are cooking.
- **Use oven-safe accessories**: When cooking with an air fryer, use oven-safe accessories like small baking pans or tins where you can place your food. Oven-safe accessories can withstand extremely high temperatures, so they don't get damaged once you are cooking your food.

Air Fryer Accessories Advantages

Air fryer accessories come in different shapes and functions. Air fryer accessories can take your air fryer into the next level as you can prepare all kinds of foods aside from frying them. There are many types of air fryer accessories that you can get, and they will help you create meals that you would never think possible that you can make in an air fryer. These include baked goodies, grilled, and even barbecued meats.

So, here is a quick list and description of each air fryer accessory available in the market. It also includes how to use it and when best to use it.

Skewers on Double Layer Rack

The double layer rack accessory allows you to maximize the cooking space within the fryer. You can bake, fry, or grill fish, chicken, pork, or beef on the bottom rack while cook another type of food on the upper rack such as burgers and sausages. This accessory also comes with four skewers so that you can make kabobs, meat on skewers, and grill.

All there is to it is to put all the food on the rack and slide the entire thing–rack, food, and all–and cook according to cooking instructions. This is a great accessory for expanding the usefulness of your air fryer and also in making combos at a lesser amount of time. You will be surprised by how much food will fit in your air fryer using this accessory.

The rack is dishwasher safe, thus clean-up is a breeze as it is dishwasher-friendly. It is also compatible with most air fryer models but makes sure that you ask the store where you are buying it if it is compatible with the brand and model of air fryer that you have.

Grill Pan

The grill pan comes with a rapid air technology design thanks to the perforated surface that makes it ideal for the air to flow throughout the food while grilling. Air fryers are not only good for frying food without oil. Use the air fryer grill pan so that you can make perfectly grilled fish, meat, and vegetables. It is not only used for grilling but also searing and browning foods.

Since the grill pan is placed at the bottom of the air fryer, it comes with an Easy Click removable handle so that you can place the grill pan in the air fryer or take them out to clean. The perforations on the surface of the grill pan also allow the extra fat to drip away so that you can make the perfect grilled surface on the meat. Moreover, the surface of the grill pan is non-stick so that you can easily remove the food from the pan. It also has a very large enough surface so that you can grill a big steak fish, a whole fillet of fish, and a generous amount of vegetables.

Baking Dish

The air fryer baking dish or pan does not only help you cook baked goodies such as cakes and bread, but you can also cook quiche, lasagna, shepherd's pie, and other deep-dish recipes that you usually cook in an oven. It comes with a non-stick surface, thus clean-up is effortless as it is also dishwasher safe. The non-stick surface also ensures that you can easily take out your food, so you get perfect results all the time.

The air fryer baking dish allows you to use your air fryer as an oven to bake cakes, muffins, and bread. The baking dish While some people use heat-proof dishes for their air fryers, using the right baking dish for your air fryer ensures that you can cook your recipes properly as they are designed to ensure that proper air flow is distributed within the air fryer to cook the food evenly.

As there are so many brands of air fryers available in the market, it is important to choose an air fryer accessory that will be compatible with your air fryer. Thus, it is crucial to check with the store whether the air fryer accessory that you want to buy is compatible with the brand and model of the air fryer that you have.

Tips on Cleaning

Cleaning the air fryer is easy, and it does not require you to do a lot of complicated tasks. The first thing that you need to do is to unplug the air fryer before cleaning to prevent electrocution. The basket is dishwasher-friendly, so you can take it out from the fryer's chamber and clean them in the sink or the dishwasher.

Once you remove the fryer basket, give extra attention to the base of the fryer where most of the drippings from the food have collected and dried. Make sure that you remove the browning that has accumulated at the base as this can lead to burning in future cooking. You can remove the browning by spraying it with warm soapy water and allowing it to soak for at least an hour. This will soften the browning, so you can easily wipe it clean. Aside from taking care of the inside of the air fryer, it is also important to clean the exterior using a warm moist cloth.

Air Fryer Cooking Chart

Over time, many manufacturers have tweaked the cooking settings of the air fryer to suit their different inventions. However, you will have many recipes falling along the time and temperature patterns as the chart below.

It is essential to read your manufacturer's time and temperature instructions and then, you can adjust both to fit the recipe in question to ensure that you have well-cooked meals. Also, work with a food thermometer to aid you in reaching the accurate internal temperature of meats and seafood for safe consumption.

Vegetables

	Temp (°F)	Time (mins)		Temp (°F)	Time (mins)
Asparagus (1-inch slices)	400 °F	5	Onions (quartered)	400 °F	11
Beets (whole)	400 °F	40	Parsnips (½-inch chunks)	380 °F	15
Bell Peppers (1-inch chunks)	400 °F	15	Pearl Onions	400 °F	10
Broccoli (florets)	400 °F	6	Potatoes (whole baby pieces)	400 °F	15
Broccoli Rabe (chopped)	400 °F	6	Potatoes (1-inch chunks)	400 °F	12
Brussel Sprouts (halved)	380 °F	15	Potatoes (baked whole)	400 °F	40
Cabbage (diced)	380 °F	15	Pumpkin (½-inch chunks)	380 °F	13
Carrots (halved)	380 °F	15	Radishes	380 °F	15
Cauliflower (florets)	400 °F	12	Squash (½-inch chunks)	400 °F	12
Collard Greens	250 °F	12	Sweet Potato (baked)	380 °F	30 to 35
Corn on the cob	390 °F	6	Tomatoes (halves)	350 °F	10
Cucumber (½-inch slices)	370 °F	4	Tomatoes (cherry)	400 °F	4
Eggplant (2-inch cubes)	400 °F	15	Turnips (½-inch chunks)	380 °F	15
Fennel (quartered)	370 °F	15	Zucchini (½-inch sticks)	400 °F	12

Green Beans	400 °F	5	Mushrooms (¼-inch slices)	400 °F	5
Kale (halved)	250 °F	12			

Chicken

	Temp (°F)	Time (mins)		Temp (°F)	Time (mins)
Breasts, bone in (1 ¼ lb.)	370 °F	25	Legs, bone-in (1 ¾ lb.)	380 °F	30
Breasts, boneless (4 oz)	380 °F	12	Thighs, boneless (1 ½ lb.)	380 °F	18 to 20
Drumsticks (2 ½ lb.)	370 °F	20	Wings (2 lb.)	400 °F	12
Game Hen (halved 2 lb.)	390 °F	20	Whole Chicken	360 °F	75
Thighs, bone-in (2 lb.)	380 °F	22	Tenders	360 °F	8 to 10

Beef

	Temp (°F)	Time (mins)		Temp (°F)	Time (mins)
Beef Eye Round Roast (4 lb.s.)	400 °F	45 to 55	Meatballs (1-inch)	370 °F	7
Burger Patty (4 oz.)	370 °F	16 to 20	Meatballs (3-inch)	380 °F	10
Filet Mignon (8 oz.)	400 °F	18	Ribeye, bone-in (1-inch, 8 oz)	400 °F	10 to 15
Flank Steak (1.5 lb.s)	400 °F	12	Sirloin steaks (1-inch, 12 oz)	400 °F	9 to 14
Flank Steak (2 lb.s)	400 °F	20 to 28			

Pork & Lamb

	Temp (°F)	Time (mins)		Temp (°F)	Time (mins)
Bacon (regular)	400 °F	5 to 7	Pork Tenderloin	370 °F	15
Bacon (thick cut)	400 °F	6 to 10	Sausages	380 °F	15
Pork Loin (2 lb.)	360 °F	55	Lamb Loin Chops (1-inch thick)	400 °F	8 to 12
Pork Chops, bone in (1-inch, 6.5 oz)	400 °F	12	Rack of Lamb (1.5 – 2 lb.)	380 °F	22

Fish & Seafood

	Temp (°F)	Time (mins)		Temp (°F)	Time (mins)
Calamari (8 oz)	400 °F	4	Tuna Steak	400 °F	7 to 10
Fish Fillet (1-inch, 8 oz)	400 °F	10	Scallops	400 °F	5 to 7
Salmon, fillet (6 oz)	380 °F	12	Shrimp	400 °F	5
Swordfish steak	400 °F	10			

Frozen Foods

	Temp (°F)	Time (mins)		Temp (°F)	Time (mins)
Breaded Shrimp	400 °F	9	French Fries (thick - 17 oz)	400 °F	18
Chicken Nuggets (12 oz)	400 °F	10	Mozzarella Sticks (11 oz)	400 °F	8
Fish Sticks (10 oz.)	400 °F	10	Onion Rings (12 oz)	400 °F	8
Fish Fillets (½-inch, 10 oz)	400 °F	14	Pot Stickers (10 oz)	400 °F	8
French Fries (thin - 20 oz)	400 °F	14			

Measurement Conversion Charts

Volume Equivalents (Liquid)

US STANDARD	US STANDARD (OUNCES)	METRIC (APPROXIMATE)
2 TABLESPOONS	1 fl.oz.	30 mL
1/4 CUP	2 fl.oz.	60 mL
1/2 CUP	4 fl.oz.	120 mL
1 CUP	8 fl.oz.	240 mL
1 1/2 CUP	12 fl.oz.	355 mL
2 CUPS OR 1 PINT	16 fl.oz.	475 mL
4 CUPS OR 1 QUART	32 fl.oz.	1 L
1 GALLON	128 fl.oz.	4 L

Volume Equivalents (DRY)

US STANDARD	METRIC (APPROXIMATE)
1/8 TEASPOON	0.5 mL
1/4 TEASPOON	1 mL
1/2 TEASPOON	2 mL
3/4 TEASPOON	4 mL
1 TEASPOON	5 mL
1 TABLESPOON	15 mL
1/4 CUP	59 mL
1/2 CUP	118 mL
3/4 CUP	177 mL
1 CUP	235 mL
2 CUPS	475 mL
3 CUPS	700 mL
4 CUPS	1 L

Weight Equivalents

US STANDARD	METRIC (APPROXIMATE)
1/2 OUNCE	15g
1 OUNCE	30g
2 OUNCE	60g
4 OUNCE	115g
8 OUNCE	225g
12 OUNCE	340g
16 OUNCES OR 1 POUND	455g

Temperatures Equivalents

FAHRENHEIT (F)	CELSIUS (C) (APPROXIMATE)
250	121
300	149
325	163
350	177
375	190
400	205
425	218
450	232

Chapter 2 Air Fryer Seafood Recipes

Air Fried Cod with Basil Vinaigrette

Serves: 4, Cooking Time: 15 minutes

Ingredients

- ¼ cup olive oil
- 4 cod fillets
- A bunch of basil, torn
- Juice from 1 lemon, freshly squeezed
- Salt and pepper to taste

Instructions

1) Preheat the air fryer for 5 minutes.
2) Season the cod fillets with salt and pepper to taste.
3) Place in the air fryer and cook for 15 minutes at 350°F.
4) Meanwhile, mix the rest of the ingredients in a bowl and toss to combine.
5) Serve the air fried cod with the basil vinaigrette.

Nutrition information:
Calories per serving: 235; Carbohydrates: 1.9g; Protein: 14.3g; Fat: 18.9g

Almond Flour Coated Crispy Shrimps

Serves: 4, Cooking Time: 10 minutes

Ingredients

- ½ cup almond flour
- 1 tbsp. yellow mustard
- 1-pound raw shrimps, peeled and deveined
- 3 tbsps. olive oil
- Salt and pepper to taste

Instructions

1) Place all ingredients in a Ziploc bag and give a good shake.
2) Place in the air fryer and cook for 10 minutes at 400°F.

Nutrition information:
Calories per serving: 206; Carbohydrates: 1.3g; Protein: 23.5g; Fat: 11.9g

Another Crispy Coconut Shrimp Recipe

Serves: 4, Cooking Time: 20 minutes

Ingredients

- ½ cup flour
- ½ stick cold butter, cut into cubes
- ½ tbsp. lemon juice
- 1 egg yolk, beaten
- 1 green onion, chopped
- 1-pound salmon fillets, cut into small cubes
- 3 tbsps. whipping cream

- 4 eggs, beaten
- Salt and pepper to taste

Instructions
1) Preheat the air fryer to 390°F.
2) Season salmon fillets with lemon juice, salt and pepper.
3) In another bowl, combine the flour and butter. Add cold water gradually to form a dough. Knead the dough on a flat surface to form a sheet.
4) Place the dough on the baking dish and press firmly on the dish.
5) Beat the eggs and egg yolk and season with salt and pepper to taste.
6) Place the salmon cubes on the pan lined with dough and pour the egg over.
7) Cook for 15 to 20 minutes.
8) Garnish with green onions once cooked.

Nutrition information:
Calories per serving: 483; Carbs: 5.2g; Protein: 45.2g; Fat: 31.2g

Apple Slaw Topped Alaskan Cod Filet

Serves: 3, Cooking Time: 15 minutes

Ingredients
- ¼ cup mayonnaise
- ½ red onion, diced
- 1 ½ pounds frozen Alaskan cod
- 1 box whole wheat panko bread crumbs
- 1 granny smith apple, julienned
- 1 tbsp. vegetable oil
- 1 tsp. paprika
- 2 cups Napa cabbage, shredded
- Salt and pepper to taste

Instructions
1) Preheat the air fryer to 390°F.
2) Place the grill pan accessory in the air fryer.
3) Brush the fish with oil and dredge in the breadcrumbs.
4) Place the fish on the grill pan and cook for 15 minutes. Make sure to flip the fish halfway through the cooking time.
5) Meanwhile, prepare the slaw by mixing the remaining Ingredients in a bowl.
6) Serve the fish with the slaw.

Nutrition information:
Calories per serving: 316; Carbs: 13.5g; Protein: 37.8g; Fat: 12.2g

Baked Cod Fillet Recipe From Thailand

Serves: 4, Cooking Time: 20 minutes

Ingredients

- ¼ cup coconut milk, freshly squeezed
- 1 tbsp. lime juice, freshly squeezed
- 1-pound cod fillet, cut into bite-sized pieces
- Salt and pepper to taste

Instructions

1) Preheat the air fryer for 5 minutes.
2) Place all ingredients in a baking dish that will fit in the air fryer.
3) Place in the air fryer.
4) Cook for 20 minutes at 325°F.

Nutrition information:
Calories per serving: 844; Carbohydrates: 2.3g; Protein: 21.6g; Fat: 83.1g

Baked Scallops with Garlic Aioli

Serves: 4, Cooking Time: 10 minutes

Ingredients

- 1 cup bread crumbs
- 1/4 cup chopped parsley
- 16 sea scallops, rinsed and drained
- 2 shallots, chopped
- 3 pinches ground nutmeg
- 4 tbsps. olive oil
- 5 cloves garlic, minced
- 5 tbsps. butter, melted
- salt and pepper to taste

Instructions

1) Lightly grease baking pan of air fryer with cooking spray.
2) Mix in shallots, garlic, melted butter, and scallops. Season with pepper, salt, and nutmeg.
3) In a small bowl, whisk well olive oil and bread crumbs. Sprinkle over scallops.
4) For 10 minutes, cook on 390°F until tops are lightly browned.
5) Serve and enjoy with a sprinkle of parsley.

Nutrition information:
Calories per Serving: 452; Carbs: 29.8g; Protein: 15.2g; Fat: 30.2g

Basil 'n Lime-Chili Clams

Serves: 3, Cooking Time: 15 minutes

Ingredients

- ½ cup basil leaves
- ½ cup tomatoes, chopped
- 1 tbsp. fresh lime juice
- 25 littleneck clams
- 4 cloves of garlic, minced
- 6 tbsps. unsalted butter

- Salt and pepper to taste

Instructions
1) Preheat the air fryer to 390°F.
2) Place the grill pan accessory in the air fryer.
3) On a large foil, place all ingredients. Fold over the foil and close by crimping the edges.
4) Place on the grill pan and cook for 15 minutes.
5) Serve with bread.

Nutrition information:
Calories per serving: 163; Carbs: 4.1g; Protein: 1.7g; Fat: 15.5g

Bass Filet in Coconut Sauce

Serves: 4, Cooking Time: 15 minutes

Ingredients
- ¼ cup coconut milk
- ½ pound bass fillet
- 1 tbsp. olive oil
- 2 tbsps. jalapeno, chopped
- 2 tbsps. lime juice, freshly squeezed
- 3 tbsps. parsley, chopped
- Salt and pepper to taste

Instructions
1) Preheat the air fryer for 5 minutes
2) Season the bass with salt and pepper to taste
3) Brush the surface with olive oil.
4) Place in the air fryer and cook for 15 minutes at 350°F.
5) Meanwhile, place in a saucepan, the coconut milk, lime juice, jalapeno and parsley.
6) Heat over medium flame.
7) Serve the fish with the coconut sauce.

Nutrition information:
Calories per serving: 139; Carbohydrates: 2.7g; Protein: 8.7g; Fat: 10.3

Beer Battered Cod Filet

Serves: 2, Cooking Time: 15 minutes

Ingredients
- ½ cup all-purpose flour
- ¾ tsp. baking powder
- 1 ¼ cup lager beer
- 2 cod fillets
- 2 eggs, beaten
- Salt and pepper to taste

Instructions
1) Preheat the air fryer to 390°F.
2) Pat the fish fillets dry then set aside.
3) In a bowl, combine the rest of the Ingredients to create a batter.

4) Dip the fillets on the batter and place on the double layer rack.
5) Cook for 15 minutes.

Nutrition information:
Calories per serving: 229; Carbs: 33.2g; Protein: 31.1g; Fat: 10.2g

Buttered Baked Cod with Wine

Serves: 2, Cooking Time: 12 minutes

Ingredients
- 1 tbsp. butter
- 1 tbsp. butter
- 2 tbsps. dry white wine
- 1/2 pound thick-cut cod loin
- 1-1/2 tsps. chopped fresh parsley
- 1-1/2 tsps. chopped green onion
- 1/2 lemon, cut into wedges
- 1/4 sleeve buttery round crackers (such as Ritz®), crushed
- 1/4 lemon, juiced

Instructions
1) In a small bowl, melt butter in microwave. Whisk in crackers.
2) Lightly grease baking pan of air fryer with remaining butter. And melt for 2 minutes at 390°F.
3) In a small bowl whisk well lemon juice, white wine, parsley, and green onion.
4) Coat cod filets in melted butter. Pour dressing. Top with butter-cracker mixture.
5) Cook for 10 minutes at 390°F.
6) Serve and enjoy with a slice of lemon.

Nutrition information:
Calories per Serving: 266; Carbs: 9.3g; Protein: 20.9g; Fat: 16.1g

Buttered Garlic-Oregano on Clams

Serves: 4, Cooking Time: 5 minutes

Ingredients
- ¼ cup parmesan cheese, grated
- ¼ cup parsley, chopped
- 1 cup breadcrumbs
- 1 tsp. dried oregano
- 2 dozen clams, shucked
- 3 cloves of garlic, minced
- 4 tbsps. butter, melted

Instructions
1) In a medium bowl, mix together the breadcrumbs, parmesan cheese, parsley, oregano, and garlic. Stir in the melted butter.
2) Preheat the air fryer to 390°F.
3) Place the baking dish accessory in the air fryer and place the clams.
4) Sprinkle the crumb mixture over the clams.
5) Cook for 5 minutes.

Nutrition information:
Calories per serving: 160; Carbs: 6.3g; Protein: 2.9g; Fat: 13.6g

Butterflied Prawns with Garlic-Sriracha

Serves: 2, Cooking Time: 15 minutes

Ingredients
- 1 tbsp. lime juice
- 1 tbsp. sriracha
- 1-pound large prawns, shells removed and cut lengthwise or butterflied
- 1tsp. fish sauce
- 2 tbsps. melted butter
- 2 tbsps. minced garlic
- Salt and pepper to taste

Instructions
1) Preheat the air fryer to 390°F.
2) Place the grill pan accessory in the air fryer.
3) Season the prawns with the rest of the ingredients.
4) Place on the grill pan and cook for 15 minutes. Make sure to flip the prawns halfway through the cooking time.

Nutrition information:
Calories per serving: 443; Carbs:9.7 g; Protein: 62.8g; Fat: 16.9g

Cajun Seasoned Salmon Filet

Serves: 1, Cooking Time: 15 minutes

Ingredients
- 1 salmon fillet
- 1 tsp. juice from lemon, freshly squeezed
- 3 tbsps. extra virgin olive oil
- A dash of Cajun seasoning mix
- Salt and pepper to taste

Instructions
1) Preheat the air fryer for 5 minutes.
2) Place all ingredients in a bowl and toss to coat.
3) Place the fish fillet in the air fryer basket.
4) Bake for 15 minutes at 325°F.
5) Once cooked drizzle with olive oil

Nutrition information:
Calories per serving: 523; Carbohydrates: 4.6g; Protein: 47.9g; Fat: 34.8g

Cajun Spiced Lemon-Shrimp Kebabs

Serves: 2, Cooking Time: 10 minutes

Ingredients
- 1 tsp cayenne
- 1 tsp garlic powder
- 1 tsp kosher salt
- 1 tsp onion powder
- 1 tsp oregano
- 1 tsp paprika
- 12 pcs XL shrimp
- 2 lemons, sliced thinly crosswise

- 2 tbsp olive oil

Instructions
1) In a bowl, mix all Ingredients except for sliced lemons. Marinate for 10 minutes.
2) Thread 3 shrimps per steel skewer.
3) Place in skewer rack.
4) Cook for 5 minutes at 390°F.
5) Serve and enjoy with freshly squeezed lemon.

Nutrition information:
Calories per Serving: 232; Carbs: 7.9g; Protein: 15.9g; Fat: 15.1g

Cajun Spiced Veggie-Shrimp Bake

Serves: 4, Cooking Time: 20 minutes

Ingredients
- 1 Bag of Frozen Mixed Vegetables
- 1 Tbsp Gluten Free Cajun Seasoning
- Olive Oil Spray
- Season with salt and pepper
- Small Shrimp Peeled & Deveined (Regular Size Bag about 50-80 Small Shrimp)

Instructions
1) Lightly grease baking pan of air fryer with cooking spray. Add all Ingredients and toss well to coat. Season with pepper and salt, generously.
2) For 10 minutes, cook on 330°F. Halfway through cooking time, stir.
3) Cook for 10 minutes at 330°F.
4) Serve and enjoy.

Nutrition information:
Calories per Serving: 78; Carbs: 13.2g; Protein: 2.8g; Fat: 1.5g

Celery Leaves 'n Garlic-oil Grilled Turbot

Serves: 2, Cooking Time: 20 minutes

Ingredients
- ½ cup chopped celery leaves
- 1 clove of garlic, minced
- 2 tbsps. olive oil
- 2 whole turbot, scaled and head removed
- Salt and pepper to taste

Instructions
1) Preheat the air fryer to 390°F.
2) Place the grill pan accessory in the air fryer.
3) Season the turbot with salt, pepper, garlic, and celery leaves.
4) Brush with oil.
5) Place on the grill pan and cook for 20 minutes until the fish becomes flaky.

Nutrition information:
Calories per serving: 269; Carbs: 3.3g; Protein: 66.2g; Fat: 25.6g

Char-Grilled Drunken Halibut

Serves: 6, Cooking Time: 20 minutes

Ingredients
- 1 tbsp. chili powder
- 2 cloves of garlic, minced
- 3 pounds halibut fillet, skin removed
- 4 tbsps. dry white wine
- 4 tbsps. olive oil
- Salt and pepper to taste

Instructions
1) Place all ingredients in a Ziploc bag.
2) Allow to marinate in the fridge for at least 2 hours.
3) Preheat the air fryer to 390°F.
4) Place the grill pan accessory in the air fryer.
5) Grill the fish for 20 minutes making sure to flip every 5 minutes.

Nutrition information:
Calories per serving: 385; Carbs: 1.7g; Protein: 33g; Fat: 40.6g

Clams with Herbed Butter in Packets

Serves: 2, Cooking Time: 20 minutes

Ingredients
- ½ cup unsalted butter, diced
- 1 tbsp. dill, chopped
- 1 tbsp. fresh lemon juice
- 1 tbsp. parsley, chopped
- 24 littleneck clams, scrubbed clean
- Lemon wedges
- Salt and pepper to taste

Instructions
1) Preheat the air fryer to 390°F.
2) Place the grill pan accessory in the air fryer.
3) On a large foil, place the clams and the rest of the ingredients.
4) Fold the foil and crimp the edges.
5) Place on the grill pan and cook for 15 to 20 minutes or until all clams have opened.

Nutrition information:
Calories per serving: 384; Carbs: 6g; Protein: 18g; Fat: 32g

Cocktail Prawns in Air Fryer

Serves: 1, Cooking Time: 8 minutes

Ingredients
- ½ tsp. black pepper
- ½ tsp. sea salt
- 1 tbsp. ketchup
- 1 tbsp. white wine vinegar
- 1 tsp. chili flakes
- 1 tsp. chili powder
- 12 prawns, shelled and deveined

Instructions

1) Preheat the air fryer to 390°F.
2) Place the shrimps in a bowl.
3) Stir in the rest of the Ingredients until the shrimps are coated with the sauce.
4) Place the shrimps on the double layer rack and cook for 8 minutes.
5) Serve with mayonnaise if desired.

Nutrition information:
Calories per serving: 148; Carbs: 9.8g; Protein: 21.9g; Fat: 2.3g

Cornmeal 'n Old Bay Battered Fish

Serves: 6, Cooking Time: 15 minutes

Ingredients
- ¼ cup flour
- ½ tsp. garlic powder
- ¾ cup fine cornmeal
- 1 tsp. paprika
- 2 tsps. old bay seasoning
- 6 fish fillets cut in half
- Salt and pepper to taste

Instructions
1) Preheat the air fryer to 330°F.
2) Place the cornmeal, flour, and seasonings in a Ziploc bag.
3) Add the fish fillets and shake until the fish is covered in flour.
4) Place on the double layer rack and cook for 15 minutes.

Nutrition information:
Calories per serving: 239; Carbs: 10.1g; Protein:22.9g; Fat: 11.8g

Crisped Flounder Filet with Crumb Tops

Serves: 4, Cooking Time: 15 minutes

Ingredients
- 1 cup dry bread crumbs
- 1 egg beaten
- 1 lemon, sliced
- 4 pieces of flounder fillets
- 5 tbsps. vegetable oil

Instructions
1) Brush flounder fillets with vegetable oil before dredging in bread crumbs.
2) Preheat the air fryer to 390°F.
3) Place the fillets on the double layer rack.
4) Cook for 15 minutes.

Nutrition information:
Calories per serving: 277; Carbs: 22.5g; Protein: 26.9g; Fat: 17.7g

Crispy Coconut Covered Shrimps

Serves: 6, Cooking Time: 6 minutes

Ingredients
- ½ cup almond flour
- 1 cup dried coconut
- 1 cup egg white
- 12 large shrimps, peeled and deveined
- 4 tbsps. butter
- Salt and pepper to taste

Instructions
1) Season the shrimps with salt and pepper.
2) Place all ingredients in a Ziploc bag and shake until well combined.
3) Place the ingredients in the air fryer basket.
4) Close and cook for 6 minutes 400°F.

Nutrition information:
Calories per serving:272; Carbohydrates:6.1g; Protein: 15.3g; Fat: 18.7g

Crispy Fish Fingers with Lemon-Garlic

Serves: 1, Cooking Time: 10 minutes

Ingredients
- ¼ tsp. baking soda
- ½ pound fish, cut into fingers
- ½ tsp. crushed black pepper
- ½ tsp. red chili flakes
- ½ tsp. salt
- ½ tsp. turmeric powder
- 1 cup bread crumbs
- 1 tsp. ginger garlic paste
- 2 eggs, beaten
- 2 tbsps. lemon juice
- 2 tsps. corn flour
- 2 tsps. garlic powder
- Oil for brushing

Instructions
1) Preheat the air fryer to 390°F.
2) Season the fish fingers with salt, lemon juice, turmeric powder, chili flakes, garlic powder, black pepper, and garlic paste. Add the corn flour, eggs, and baking soda.
3) Dredge the seasoned fish in breadcrumbs and brush with cooking oil.
4) Place on the double layer rack.
5) Cook for 10 minutes.

Nutrition information:
Calories per serving: 773; Carbs: 32.7g; Protein: 64.9g; Fat: 42.5g

Crispy Fried Fish-Paprika Nuggets

Serves: 6, Cooking Time: 25 minutes

Ingredients

- 1 ½ pounds fresh fish fillet, chopped finely
- 1 cup almond flour
- 1 tbsp. lemon juice
- 1 tbsp. olive oil
- 1 tsp. chili powder
- 1 tsp. smoked paprika
- 2 cloves of garlic, minced
- 2 eggs, beaten
- Salt and pepper to taste

Instructions

1) Place all ingredients in a bowl and mix until well-combined.
2) Form small nuggets using your hands. Place in the fridge to set for 2 hours.
3) Preheat the air fryer for 5 minutes.
4) Carefully place the nuggets in the fryer basket.
5) Cook for 25 minutes at 350ºF.

Nutrition information:
Calories per serving: 359; Carbohydrates: 21.7g; Protein: 19.1g; Fat: 21.7g

Crispy Lemon-Parsley Fish Cakes

Serves: 3, Cooking Time: 20 minutes

Ingredients

- ½ cup dried coconut flakes
- 1 cup almond flour
- 1 cup cooked salmon, shredded
- 1 tbsp. chopped parsley
- 1 tbsp. lemon juice
- 2 eggs, beaten
- 3 tbsps. coconut oil
- Salt and pepper to taste

Instructions

1) Mix the salmon, almond flour, eggs, salt, pepper, lemon juice and parsley in a bowl.
2) Form small balls using your hands and dredge in coconut flakes.
3) Brush the surface of the balls with coconut oil.
4) Place in the air fryer basket and cook in a preheated air fryer for 20 minutes at 325ºF.
5) Halfway through the cooking time, give the fryer basket a shake.

Nutrition information:
Calories per serving: 490; Carbohydrates: 9.9g; Protein: 35.5g; Fat: 34.2g

Crispy Shrimps The Cajun Way

Serves: 3, Cooking Time: 8 minutes

Ingredients
- ¼ tsp. cayenne pepper
- ¼ tsp. smoked paprika
- ½ pound tiger shrimps,
- ½ tsp. old bay seasoning
- 3 tbsps. olive oil
- A pinch of salt

Instructions
1) Preheat the air fryer for 5 minutes.
2) Toss all ingredients in a bowl that will fit the air fryer.
3) Place the shrimps in the air fryer basket and cook for 8 minutes at 390°F.

Nutrition information:
Calories per serving: 213; Carbohydrates: 0.3g; Protein: 15.4g; Fat: 16.7g

Crispy Spicy-Lime Fish Filet

Serves: 4, Cooking Time: 15 minutes

Ingredients
- 1 egg white, beaten
- 1 tbsp. lime juice, freshly squeezed
- 1 tsp. lime zest
- 2 fish fillets, cut into pieces
- 2 tbsp. olive oil
- 5 tbsps. almond flour
- A dash of chili powder
- Salt and pepper to taste

Instructions
1) Preheat the air fryer.
2) Place all ingredients in a Ziploc bag and shake until all ingredients are well combined.
3) Place in the air fryer basket.
4) Cook for 15 minutes at 400°F.

Nutrition information:
Calories per serving: 192; Carbohydrates: 9.63g; Protein: 8.14g; Fat: 13.14g

Cumin, Thyme 'n Oregano Herbed Shrimps

Serves: 4, Cooking Time: 6 minutes

Ingredients
- ¼ tsp. cayenne pepper
- ¼ tsp. red chili flakes
- 1 tsp. cumin
- 1 tsp. oregano
- 1 tsp. salt
- 1 tsp. thyme
- 2 tbsps. coconut oil
- 2 tsps. cilantro
- 2 tsps. onion powder
- 2 tsps. smoked paprika
- 20 jumbo shrimps, peeled and deveined

Instructions
1) Preheat the air fryer to 390°F.
2) Season the shrimps with all the Ingredients.

3) Place the seasoned shrimps in the double layer rack.
4) Cook for 6 minutes.

Nutrition information:
Calories per serving: 220; Carbs: 2.5g; Protein: 34.2g; Fat: 8.1g

Crispy and Spicy Hot Shrimps

Serves: 6, Cooking Time: 5 minutes

Ingredients
- ½ tsp. ground black pepper
- ½ tsp. salt
- 1 tsp. chili flakes
- 1 tsp. chili powder
- 12 fresh prawns, peeled and deveined
- 4 tbsps. olive oil

Instructions
1) Preheat the air fryer for 5 minutes.
2) Toss all ingredients in a bowl that will fit the air fryer.
3) Place the shrimps in the air fryer basket and cook for 5 minutes at 400°F.

Nutrition information:
Calories per serving: 156; Carbohydrates: 0.8g; Protein: 15.3g; Fat: 10.2g

Dijon Mustard 'n Parmesan Crusted Tilapia

Serves: 2, Cooking Time: 15 minutes

Ingredients
- 1 tbsp. lemon juice
- 1 tsp. prepared horseradish
- 1/4 cup dry bread crumbs
- 2 tbsps. grated Parmesan cheese, divided
- 2 tsps. butter, melted
- 2 tsps. Dijon mustard
- 2 tilapia fillets (5 ounces each)
- 3 tbsps. reduced-fat mayonnaise

Instructions
1) Lightly grease baking pan of air fryer with cooking spray. Place tilapia in a single layer.
2) In a small bowl, whisk well mayo, lemon juice, mustard, 1 tbsp. cheese and horseradish. Spread on top of fish.
3) In another bowl, mix remaining cheese, melted butter, and bread crumbs. Sprinkle on top of fish.
4) For 15 minutes, cook on 390°F.
5) Serve and enjoy.

Nutrition information:
Calories per Serving: 212; Carbs: 7.0g; Protein: 28.0g; Fat: 8.0g

Drunken Skewered Shrimp

Serves: 6, Cooking Time: 20 minutes

Ingredients

- 1/2 tsp. dried crushed red pepper
- 1/2 tsp. freshly ground black pepper
- 12 1-inch-long pieces andouille or other fully cooked smoked sausage
- 12 2-layer sections of red onion wedges
- 12 cherry tomatoes
- 12 uncooked extra-large shrimp (13 to 15 per pound), peeled, deveined
- 2 tbsps. chopped fresh thyme
- 3/4 cup olive oil
- 3/4 tsp. salt
- 4 large garlic cloves, pressed
- 4 tsps. Sherry wine vinegar
- 5 tsps. smoked paprika*
- Nonstick vegetable oil spray

Instructions

1) In medium bowl, mix well red pepper, black pepper, salt, wine vinegar, smoked paprika, thyme, garlic, and oil. Transfer half to a small bowl for dipping.
2) Thread alternately sausage and shrimp in skewers. Place on skewer rack on air fryer and baste with the paprika glaze. Cook in batches.
3) For 10 minutes, cook on 360°F. Halfway through cooking time, baste and turnover skewers.
4) Serve and enjoy with the reserved dip on the side.

Nutrition information:
Calories per Serving: 329; Carbs: 9.8g; Protein: 8.5g; Fat: 28.4g

Easy 'n Crispy Cod Nuggets

Serves: 6, Cooking Time: 20 minutes

Ingredients

- ½ cup almond flour
- 1 ½ pound cod fillet cut into big chunks
- 1 egg, beaten
- 3 tbsps. olive oil
- Salt and pepper to taste

Instructions

1) Preheat the air fryer for 5 minutes.
2) Season the cod fillets with salt and pepper to taste.
3) Add the eggs and mix to combine.
4) Dredge individual cod chunks into the almond flour and set aside on a plate.
5) Brush all sides with olive oil.
6) Place in the fryer basket and cook for 20 minutes at 375°F.

Nutrition information:
Calories per serving: 170; Carbohydrates: 0.9 g; Protein: 18.2g; Fat: 10.4g

Easy Battered Lemony Fillet

Serves: 4, Cooking Time: 15 minutes

Ingredients
- ½ cup almond flour
- 1 egg, beaten
- 1 lemon
- 4 fish fillets
- 4 tbsps. vegetable oil
- Salt and pepper to taste

Instructions
1) Season the fish fillets with lemon, salt, and pepper.
2) Soak in the beaten egg and dredge in almond flour.
3) Place in the air fryer basket.
4) Cook for 15 minutes at 400°F.

Nutrition information:
Calories per serving: 469; Carbohydrates: 17.6g; Protein: 15.8g; Fat: 37.3g

Easy Lobster Tail with Salted Butter

Serves: 4, Cooking Time: 6 minutes

Ingredients
- 2 tbsps. melted butter
- 4 lobster tails
- Salt and pepper to taste

Instructions
1) Preheat the air fryer to 390°F.
2) Place the grill pan accessory.
3) Cut the lobster through the tail section using a pair of kitchen scissors.
4) Brush the lobster tails with melted butter and season with salt and pepper to taste.
5) Place on the grill pan and cook for 6 minutes.

Nutrition information:
Calories per serving: 170; Carbs: 1.1g; Protein: 25.7g; Fat: 6.9g

Easy Crispy Catfish Filet

Serves: 4, Cooking Time: 15 minutes

Ingredients
- ¼ cup almond flour
- 1 egg, beaten
- 4 catfish fillets
- 4 tbsps. olive oil
- Salt and pepper to taste

Instructions
1) Preheat the air fryer for 5 minutes
2) Season the catfish fillets with salt and pepper to taste.

3) Soak in the beaten eggs and dredge in almond flour.
4) Brush the surface with olive oil
5) Place in the air fryer and cook for 15 minutes at 350°F.

Nutrition information:
Calories per serving:308; Carbohydrates: 1.3g; Protein: 28.4g; Fat: 20.6g

Egg Frittata with Smoked Trout

Serves: 6, Cooking Time: 15 minutes

Ingredients
- 1 onion, chopped
- 2 fillets smoked trout, shredded
- 2 tbsps. coconut oil
- 2 tbsps. olive oil
- 6 eggs, beaten
- Salt and pepper to taste

Instructions
1) Preheat the air fryer for 5 minutes.
2) Place all ingredients in a mixing bowl until well-combined.
3) Pour into a baking dish that will fit in the air fryer.
4) Cook for 15 minutes at 400°F.

Nutrition information:
Calories per serving: 254; Carbohydrates: 3.4g; Protein: 14.2g; Fat:20.4g

Fennel Salad Topped with Roast Salmon

Serves: 4, Cooking Time: 10 minutes

Ingredients
- 1 clove of garlic, grated
- 1 tsp. fresh thyme, chopped
- 1 tsp. salt
- 2 tbsps. chopped dill
- 2 tbsps. olive oil
- 2 tbsps. orange juice
- 2 tsps. chopped parsley
- 2/3 cup Greek yogurt
- 4 pieces salmon fillets
- 4 cups sliced fennel

Instructions
1) Preheat the air fryer to 390°F.
2) Season the salmon fillets with parsley, thyme, salt, and olive oil. Rub the spices on the salon.
3) Place the grill pan accessory in the air fryer.
4) Place the fish and cook for 10 minutes.
5) Flip the fish halfway through the cooking time to brown all sides evenly.
6) While the fish is cooking, prepare the salad by combining the rest of the rest of the ingredients in a bowl.
7) Serve the fish with the salad.

Nutrition information:
Calories per serving: 458; Carbs: 9g; Protein: 38g; Fat: 30g

Fried Shrimps with Sweet Chili Sauce

Serves: 1, Cooking Time: 6 minutes

Ingredients
- ½ cup flour
- ½ cup sweet chili sauce
- ½ pound raw shrimps, peeled and deveined
- 1 egg, beaten
- 1 tsp. chili powder
- Salt and pepper to taste

Instructions
1) Mix together the shrimps and eggs in a bowl. Season with salt and pepper to taste.
2) In another bowl, mix the chili powder and flour.
3) Dredge the shrimps in the flour mixture.
4) Preheat the air fryer to 330°F.
5) Place the shrimps on the double layer rack.
6) Cook for 6 minutes.
7) Serve with chili sauce.

Nutrition information:
Calories per serving: 719; Carbs: 81.3g; Protein: 66.4g; Fat: 14.2g

Garlic-Cilantro Over Salmon Steak

Serves: 2, Cooking Time: 15 minutes

Ingredients
- ½ cup Greek yogurt
- 1 cup cilantro leaves
- 1 tsp. honey
- 2 cloves of garlic, minced
- 2 salmon steaks
- 2 tbsps. vegetable oil
- Salt and pepper to taste

Instructions
1) Preheat the air fryer to 390°F.
2) Place the grill pan accessory in the air fryer.
3) Season the salmon steaks with salt and pepper. Brush with oil.
4) Grill for 15 minutes and make sure to flip halfway through the cooking time.
5) In a food processor, mix the garlic, cilantro leaves, yogurt and honey. Season with salt and pepper to taste. Pulse until smooth.
6) Serve the salmon steaks with the cilantro sauce.

Nutrition information:
Calories per serving: 485; Carbs: 6.3g; Protein: 47.6g; Fat: 29.9g

Gingery Cod Filet Recipe from Hong Kong

Serves: 2, Cooking Time: 15 minutes

Ingredients

- 2 cod fish fillets
- 250 mL water
- 3 tbsps. coconut aminos
- 3 tbsps. coconut oil
- 5 slices of ginger
- A dash of sesame oil
- Green onions for garnish

Instructions

1) Preheat the air fryer for 5 minutes
2) Place all ingredients except for the green onions in a baking dish.
3) Place in the air fryer and cook for 15 minutes at 400°F.
4) Garnish with green onions.

Nutrition information:

Calories per serving: 571; Carbohydrates: 4.3g; Protein: 22.3g; Fat: 51.6g

Grilled Bacon 'n Scallops

Serves: 2, Cooking Time: 12 minutes

Ingredients

- 1 tsp. smoked paprika
- 6 bacon strips
- 6 large scallops

Instructions

1) Wrap one bacon around one scallop and thread in a skewer ensuring that it will not unravel. Repeat until all ingredients are used.
2) Season with paprika.
3) Place on skewer rack in air fryer.
4) For 12 minutes, cook on 390°F. Halfway through cooking time, turnover skewers.
5) Serve and enjoy.

Nutrition information:

Calories per Serving: 72; Carbs: 2.4g; Protein: 1.9g; Fat: 6.0g

Grilled Scallops with Pesto

Serves: 3, Cooking Time: 15 minutes

Ingredients

- ½ cup prepared commercial pesto
- 12 large scallops, side muscles removed
- Salt and pepper to taste

Instructions

1) Place all ingredients in a Ziploc bag and allow the scallops to marinate in the fridge for at least 2 hours.
2) Preheat the air fryer to 390°F.
3) Place the grill pan accessory in the air fryer.
4) Grill the scallops for 15 minutes.
5) Serve on pasta or bread if desired.

Nutrition information:

Calories per serving: 137; Carbs: 7.7g; Protein:15.3 g; Fat: 5g

Grilled Shrimp with Chipotle-Orange Seasoning

Serves: 2, Cooking Time: 24 minutes

Ingredients

- 3 tbsps. minced chipotles in adobo sauce
- salt
- ½-pound large shrimps
- juice of 1/2 orange
- 1/4 cup barbecue sauce

Instructions

1) In a small shallow dish, mix well all Ingredients except for shrimp. Save ¼ of the mixture for basting.
2) Add shrimp in dish and toss well to coat. Marinate for at least 10 minutes.
3) Thread shrimps in skewers. Place on skewer rack in air fryer.
4) For 12 minutes, cook on 360°F. Halfway through cooking time, turnover skewers and baste with sauce. If needed, cook in batches.
5) Serve and enjoy.

Nutrition information:
Calories per Serving: 179; Carbs: 24.6g; Protein: 16.6g; Fat: 1.5g

Grilled Squid with Aromatic Sesame Oil

Serves: 3, Cooking Time: 10 minutes

Ingredients

- 1 ½ pounds squid, cleaned
- 2 tbsp. toasted sesame oil
- Salt and pepper to taste

Instructions

1) Preheat the air fryer to 390°F.
2) Place the grill pan accessory in the air fryer.
3) Season the squid with sesame oil, salt and pepper.
4) Grill the squid for 10 minutes.

Nutrition information:
Calories per serving: 220; Carbs: 0.9g; Protein: 27g; Fat: 12g

Healthy and Easy to Make Salmon

Serves: 2, Cooking Time: 10 minutes

Ingredients

- ½ of lemon
- 2 tsps. avocado oil
- 2 tsps. paprika
- 2 wild caught salmon fillets
- Salt and pepper to taste

Instructions

1) Preheat the air fryer to 390°F.
2) Season the salmon fillets with avocado oil, paprika, salt, and pepper. Drizzle with lemon juice on both sides.
3) Place the grill pan accessory in the air fryer.
4) Place the salmon fillets and cook for 10 minutes.
5) Be sure to flip the fillets halfway through the cooking time.

Nutrition information:
Calories per serving: 382; Carbs: 2.2g; Protein: 66.1g; Fat: 12g

Honey-Ginger Soy Sauce Over Grilled Tuna

Serves: 3, Cooking Time: 20 minutes

Ingredients
- 1 ½ pounds tuna, thick slices
- 1 serrano chili, seeded and minced
- 2 tbsps. grated fresh ginger
- 2 tbsps. honey
- 2 tbsps. peanut oil
- 2 tbsps. rice vinegar
- 2 tbsps. soy sauce

Instructions
1) Place all ingredients in a Ziploc bag.
2) Allow to marinate in the fridge for at least 2 hours.
3) Preheat the air fryer to 390°F.
4) Place the grill pan accessory in the air fryer.
5) Grill the fish for 15 to 20 minutes.
6) Flip the fish halfway through the cooking time.
7) Meanwhile, pour the marinade in a saucepan and allow to simmer for 10 minutes until the sauce thickens.
8) Brush the tuna with the sauce before serving.

Nutrition information:
Calories per serving: 357; Carbs:14.8 g; Protein: 44.9g; Fat: 13.1g

Jamaican-Jerk Seasoned Salmon

Serves: 2, Cooking Time: 12 minutes

Ingredients
- 1 ½ tbsps. mayonnaise
- 1 tsp. grated lime zest
- 1/4 cup sour cream
- 1/4 cup sweetened shredded coconut, toasted
- 2 salmon fillets (6 ounces each)
- 2 tsps. Caribbean jerk seasoning
- 4 tbsp cream of coconut
- 4 tbsp cup lime juice

Instructions
1) Lightly grease baking pan of air fryer with cooking spray. Add salmon with skin side down.

Spread mayo on top and season with Caribbean jerk.
2) For 12 minutes, cook on 330°F.
3) On medium low fire, place a pan and bring lime juice, lime zest, cream of coconut, and sour cream to a simmer. Mix well. Transfer to a bowl for dipping.
4) Serve and enjoy.

Nutrition information:
Calories per Serving: 490; Carbs: 16.0g; Protein: 30.0g; Fat: 34.0g

Kashmiri Chili Powder 'n Garlic Shrimp BBQ

Serves: 4, Cooking Time: 10 minutes

Ingredients
- 1 fresh red Chile (such as Fresno), seeds removed, finely grated
- 1 tbsp. coarsely ground pepper
- 1 tbsp. fresh lime juice
- 1-pound large shrimp, peeled, deveined
- 2 tbsps. vegetable oil, plus more for grill
- 3 garlic cloves, finely grated
- Kosher salt
- Lime wedges and Kashmiri chili powder or paprika (for serving)

Instructions
1) In a large bowl, mix well oil, lime juice, pepper, garlic, and Chile. Add shrimp and marinate for at least 10 minutes. Season with salt.
2) Thread shrimp into steel skewers.
3) Place in skewer rack.
4) Cook for 5 minutes at 390°F.
5) Serve and enjoy with chili powder and lime wedges.

Nutrition information:
Calories per Serving: 144; Carbs: 2.2g; Protein: 15.6g; Fat: 8.0g

Lemony-Parsley Linguine with Grilled Tuna

Serves: 2, Cooking Time: 20 minutes

Ingredients
- 1 tbsp. capers, chopped
- 1 tbsp. olive oil
- 12 ounces linguine, cooked according to package Instructions
- 1-pound fresh tuna fillets
- 2 cups parsley leaves, chopped
- Juice from 1 lemon
- Salt and pepper to taste

Instructions
1) Preheat the air fryer to 390°F.
2) Place the grill pan accessory in the air fryer.
3) Season the tuna with salt and pepper. Brush with oil.
4) Grill for 20 minutes.

5) Once the tuna is cooked, shred using forks and place on top of cooked linguine. Add parsley and capers. Season with salt and pepper and add lemon juice.

Nutrition information:
Calories per serving: 520; Carbs: 60.6g; Protein: 47.7g; Fat: 9.6g

Lemon Tuna 'n Buttered Rice Puff

Serves: 6, Cooking Time: 60 minutes

Ingredients
- 1 tsp. salt
- 2 egg yolks1 (12 ounce) can tuna, undrained
- 2 tbsps. grated onion
- 1 tbsp. lemon juice
- 2 egg whites
- 1 1/2 cups milk
- 1 1/3 cups water
- 1/3 cup butter
- 1/4 cup all-purpose flour
- 1/4 tsp. ground black pepper
- 2/3 cup uncooked white rice

Instructions
1) In a saucepan bring water to a boil. Stir in rice, cover and cook on low fire until liquid is fully absorbed, around 20 minutes.
2) In another saucepan over medium fire, melt butter. Stir in pepper, salt, and flour. Cook for 2 minutes. Whisking constantly, slowly add milk. Continue cooking and stirring until thickened.
3) In medium bowl, whisk egg yolks. Slowly whisk in half of the thickened milk mixture. Add to pan of remaining milk and continue cooking and stirring for 2 more minutes. Stir in lemon juice, onion, tuna, and rice.
4) Lightly grease baking pan of air fryer with cooking spray. And transfer rice mixture.
5) Beat egg whites until stiff peak forms. Slowly fold into rice mixture.
6) Cover pan with foil.
7) For 20 minutes, cook on 360°F.
8) Cook for 15 minutes at 390°F until tops are lightly browned and the middle has set.
9) Serve and enjoy.

Nutrition information:
Calories per Serving: 302; Carbs: 24.1g; Protein: 20.6g; Fat: 13.6g

Lemon-Basil on Cod Filet

Serves: 4, Cooking Time: 15 minutes

Ingredients

- ¼ cup olive oil
- 4 cod fillets
- A bunch of basil, torn
- Juice from 1 lemon, freshly squeezed
- Salt and pepper to taste

Instructions

1) Preheat the air fryer for 5 minutes.
2) Season the cod fillets with salt and pepper to taste. Place on lightly greased air fryer baking pan.
3) Mix the rest of the ingredients in a bowl and toss to combine. Pour over fish.
4) Cook for 15 minutes at 330°F.
5) Serve and enjoy.

Nutrition information:
Calories per serving: 235; Cars: 1.9g; Protein: 14.3g; Fat: 18.9g

Lemon-Garlic on Buttered Shrimp Fry

Serves: 4, Cooking Time: 15 minutes

Ingredients

- 1 tbsp. chopped chives or 1 tsp. dried chives
- 1 tbsp. lemon juice
- 1tbsp. minced basil leaves plus more for sprinkling or 1 tsp. dried basil
- 1 tbsp. minced garlic
- 1-lb defrosted shrimp (21-25 count)
- 2 tbsps. chicken stock (or white wine)
- 2 tsps. red pepper flakes
- 4 tbsps. butter

Instructions

1) Lightly grease baking pan of air fryer with cooking spray. Melt butter for 2 minutes at 330°F. Stir in red pepper flakes and garlic. Cook for 3 minutes.
2) Add remaining Ingredients in pan and toss well to coat.
3) Cook for 5 minutes at 330°F. Stir and let it stand for another 5 minutes.
4) Serve and enjoy.

Nutrition information:
Calories per Serving: 213; Carbs: 1.0g; Protein: 23.0g; Fat: 13.0g

Lemon-Paprika Salmon Filet

Serves: 2, Cooking Time: 15 minutes

Ingredients
- 1 tbsp. butter, melted
- 1 tbsp. minced fresh thyme or 1 tsp. dried thyme
- 1 tsp. grated lemon zest
- 1/2 tsp. salt
- 1/4 tsp. lemon-pepper seasoning
- 1/4 tsp. paprika
- 1-1/2 cups soft bread crumbs
- 2 garlic cloves, minced
- 2 salmon fillets (6 ounces each)
- 2 tbsps. minced fresh parsley

Instructions
1) In a medium bowl mix well bread crumbs, fresh parsley thyme, garlic, lemon zest, salt, lemon-pepper seasoning, and paprika.
2) Lightly grease baking pan of air fryer with cooking spray. Add salmon filet with skin side down. Evenly sprinkle crumbs on tops of salmon.
3) For 10 minutes, cook on 390°F. Let it rest for 5 minutes.
4) Serve and enjoy.

Nutrition information:
Calories per Serving: 331; Carbs: 9.0g; Protein: 31.0g; Fat: 19.0g

Lemon-Pepper Red Mullet Fry

Serves: 4 , Cooking Time: 15 minutes

Ingredients
- 1 tbsp. olive oil
- 4 whole red mullets, gutted and scales removed
- Juice from 1 lemon
- Salt and pepper to taste

Instructions
1) Preheat the air fryer to 390°F.
2) Place the grill pan accessory in the air fryer.
3) Season the red mullet with salt, pepper, and lemon juice.
4) Brush with olive oil.
5) Grill for 15 minutes per batch.

Nutrition information:
Calories per serving: 152; Carbs: 0.9g; Protein: 23.1g; Fat: 6.2g

Lemony Grilled Halibut 'n Tomatoes

Serves: 4, Cooking Time: 15 minutes

Ingredients
- ½ cup hearts of palm, rinse and drained
- 1 cup cherry tomatoes
- 2 tbsps. oil
- 4 halibut fillets
- Juice from 1 lemon
- Salt and pepper to taste

Instructions
1) Preheat the air fryer to 390°F.
2) Place the grill pan accessory in the air fryer.
3) Season the halibut fillets with lemon juice, salt and pepper. Brush with oil.
4) Place the fish on the grill pan.
5) Arrange the hearts of palms and cherry tomatoes on the side and sprinkle with more salt and pepper.
6) Cook for 15 minutes.

Nutrition information:
Calories per serving: 208; Carbs: 7g; Protein: 21 g; Fat: 11g

Lemony Tuna-Parsley Patties

Serves: 4, Cooking Time: 10 minutes

Ingredients
- ½ cup panko bread crumbs
- 1 egg, beaten
- 1 tbsp. lemon juice
- 2 cans of tuna in brine
- 2 tbsps. chopped parsley
- 2 tsps. Dijon mustard
- 3 tbsps. olive oil
- A drizzle Tabasco sauce

Instructions
1) Drain the liquid from the canned tuna and put in a bowl.
2) Mix the tuna and season with mustard, bread crumbs, lemon juice, and parsley.
3) Add the egg and Tabasco sauce. Mix until well combined.
4) Form patties using your hands and place in the fried to set for at least 2 hours.
5) Preheat the air fryer to 390°F.
6) Place the grill pan accessory.
7) Brush the patties with olive oil and place on the grill pan.
8) Cook for 10 minutes.
9) Make sure to flip the patties halfway through the cooking time for even browning.

Nutrition information:
Calories per serving: 209; Carbs: 2.9g; Protein: 18.8g; Fat: 13.5g

Lemony-Sage on Grilled Swordfish

Serves: 2, Cooking Time: 16 minutes

Ingredients
- ½ lemon, sliced thinly in rounds
- 1 tbsp lemon juice
- 1 tsp parsley
- 1 zucchini, peeled and then thinly sliced in lengths
- 1/2-pound swordfish, sliced into 2-inch chunks
- 2 tbsp olive oil
- 6-8 sage leaves
- salt and pepper to taste

Instructions
1) In a shallow dish, mix well lemon juice, parsley, and sliced swordfish. Toss well to coat and generously season with pepper and salt. Marinate for at least 10 minutes.
2) Place one length of zucchini on a flat surface. Add one piece of fish and sage leaf. Roll zucchini and then thread into a skewer. Repeat process to remaining Ingredients.
3) Brush with oil and place on skewer rack in air fryer.
4) For 8 minutes, cook on 390°F. If needed, cook in batches.
5) Serve and enjoy with lemon slices.

Nutrition information:
Calories per Serving: 297; Carbs: 3.7g; Protein: 22.8g; Fat: 21.2g

Lime 'n Chat masala Rubbed Snapper

Serves: 2, Cooking Time: 25 minutes

Ingredients
- 1/3 cup chat masala
- 1-1/2 pounds whole fish, cut in half
- 2 tbsps. olive oil
- 3 tbsps. fresh lime juice
- Salt to taste

Instructions
1) Preheat the air fryer to 390°F.
2) Place the grill pan accessory in the air fryer.
3) Season the fish with salt, chat masala and lime juice.
4) Brush with oil
5) Place the fish on a foil basket and place inside the grill.
6) Cook for 25 minutes.

Nutrition information:
Calories per serving: 308 ; Carbs: 0.7g; Protein: 35.2g; Fat: 17.4g

Lime, Oil 'n Leeks on Grilled Swordfish

Serves: 4, Cooking Time: 20 minutes

Ingredients
- 2 tbsps. olive oil
- 3 tbsps. lime juice
- 4 medium leeks, cut into an inch long
- 4 swordfish steaks
- Salt and pepper to taste

Instructions
1) Preheat the air fryer to 390ºF.
2) Place the grill pan accessory in the air fryer.
3) Season the swordfish with salt, pepper and lime juice.
4) Brush the fish with olive oil
5) Place fish fillets on grill pan and top with leeks.
6) Grill for 20 minutes.

Nutrition information:
Calories per serving: 611; Carbs: 14.6g; Protein: 48g; Fat: 40g

Lobster-Spinach Lasagna Recipe from Maine

Serves: 6, Cooking Time: 50 minutes

Ingredients
- 1 (16 ounce) jar Alfredo pasta sauce
- 1 cup shredded Cheddar cheese
- 1 egg
- 1 pound cooked and cubed lobster meat
- 1 tbsp. chopped fresh parsley
- 1/2 (15 ounce) container ricotta cheese
- 1/2 cup grated Parmesan cheese
- 1/2 cup shredded mozzarella cheese
- 1/2 medium onion, minced
- 1/2 tsp. freshly ground black pepper
- 1-1/2 tsps. minced garlic
- 5-ounce package baby spinach leaves
- 8 no-boil lasagna noodles

Instructions
1) Mix well half of Parmesan, half of mozzarella, half of cheddar, egg, and ricotta cheese in a medium bowl. Stir in pepper, parsley, garlic, and onion.
2) Lightly grease baking pan of air fryer with cooking spray.
3) On bottom of pan, spread ½ of the Alfredo sauce, top with a single layer of lasagna noodles. Followed by 1/3 of lobster meat, 1/3 of ricotta cheese mixture, 1/3 of spinach. Repeat layering process until all ingredients are used up.
4) Sprinkle remaining cheese on top. Shake pan to settle lasagna and burst bubbles. Cover pan with foil.
5) For 30 minutes, cook on 360ºF.
6) Remove foil and cook for 10 minutes at 390ºF until tops are lightly browned.
7) Let it stand for 10 minutes.

8) Serve and enjoy.
Nutrition information:
Calories per Serving: 558; Carbs: 20.4g; Protein: 36.8g; Fat: 36.5g

Mango Salsa on Fish Tacos

Serves: 4, Cooking Time: 10 minutes
Ingredients
- ½ cup mango salsa of your choice
- 1 cup corn kernels
- 1 cup mixed greens
- 1 red bell pepper, seeded and diced
- 1 yellow onion, peeled and diced
- 4 large burrito-size tortillas
- 4 pieces fish fillets
- Juice from ½ lemon
- Salt and pepper to taste

Instructions
1) Preheat the air fryer to 330°F.
2) Season the fish with lemon juice, salt and pepper.
3) Place seasoned fish on the double layer rack.
4) Cook for 10 minutes.
5) Assemble the taco wraps by laying the tortillas on a flat surface and add fish fillet together with the onions, pepper, corn kernels, and mixed greens.
6) This makes 4 tortilla wraps
7) Serve with mango salsa.

Nutrition information:
Calories per serving: 378; Carbs: 36g; Protein: 26.8g; Fat: 14g

Miso Sauce Over Grilled Salmon(Japanese)

Serves: 4, Cooking Time: 16 minutes
Ingredients
- 1 1/4 pounds skinless salmon fillets, thinly sliced
- 2 tsps. superfine sugar
- 2 tbsps. mirin (Japanese rice wine)
- 2 tsps. dashi powder
- 1/4 cup yellow miso paste
- Amaranth leaves (optional), to serve
- Chili pepper, to serve

Instructions
1) In a bowl mix well sugar, mirin, dashi powder, and miso.
2) Thread salmon into skewers. Baste with miso paste and chili pepper. Place on skewer rack in air fryer. Cook in batches for 8 minutes at 360°F. Halfway through cooking time, turnover and baste with leaves.
3) Serve and enjoy.

Nutrition information:
Calories per Serving: 281; Carbs: 7.6g; Protein: 39.8g; Fat: 10.1g

Old Bay 'n Dijon Seasoned Crab Cakes

Serves: 2, Cooking Time: 10 minutes

Ingredients
- ¼ cup chopped green onion
- ½ cup panko
- 1 ½ tsp. old bay seasoning
- 1 tsp. Dijon mustard
- 1 tsp. Worcestershire sauce
- 1-pound lump crab meat
- 2 large eggs
- Salt and pepper to taste

Instructions
1) Preheat the air fryer to 390°F.
2) Place the grill pan in the air fryer.
3) In a mixing bowl, combine all Ingredients until everything is well-incorporated.
4) Use your hands to form small patties of crab cakes.
5) Place on the grill pan and cook for 10 minutes.
6) Flip the crab cakes halfway through the cooking time for even browning.

Nutrition information:
Calories per serving: 129; Carbs: 4.3g; Protein: 16.2g; Fat: 5.1g

Orange Roughie with Caesar & Cheese Dressing

Serves: 2, Cooking Time: 15 minutes

Ingredients
- 2 orange roughie fillets (4 ounces each)
- 1/2 cups crushed butter-flavored crackers
- 1/2 cup shredded cheddar cheese
- 1/4 cup creamy Caesar salad dressing

Instructions
1) Lightly grease baking pan of air fryer with cooking spray. Add filet on bottom of pan. Drizzle with dressing, sprinkle crumbled crackers and cook for 10 minutes at 390°F.
2) Sprinkle cheese and let it stand for 5 minutes.
3) Serve and enjoy.

Nutrition information:
Calories per Serving: 341; Carbs: 5.0g; Protein: 32.6g; Fat: 21.1g

Oregano & Cumin Flavored Salmon Grill

Serves: 4, Cooking Time: 15 minutes

Ingredients
- 2 tbsps. chopped fresh oregano
- 1 1/2 pounds skinless salmon fillet (preferably wild), cut into 1" pieces
- 2 tsps. sesame seeds
- 1 tsp. ground cumin
- 1 tsp. kosher salt

- 1/4 tsp. crushed red pepper flakes
- 2 lemons, very thinly sliced into rounds
- 2 tbsps. olive oil

Instructions
1) In a small bowl, mix well oregano, sesame seeds, cumin, salt, and pepper flakes.
2) Thread salmon and folded lemon slices in a skewer. Brush with oil and sprinkle with spice.
3) Place skewers on air fryer skewer rack and cook for 5 minutes at 360°F. If needed, cook in batches.
4) Serve and enjoy.

Nutrition information:
Calories per Serving: 313; Carbs: 2.3g; Protein: 34.3g; Fat: 18.5g

Outrageous Crispy Fried Salmon Skin

Serves: 4, Cooking Time: 10 minutes

Ingredients
- ½ pound salmon skin, patted dry
- 4 tbsps. coconut oil
- Salt and pepper to taste

Instructions
1) Preheat the air fryer for 5 minutes.
2) In a large bowl, combine everything and mix well.
3) Place in the fryer basket and close.
4) Cook for 10 minutes at 400°F.
5) Halfway through the cooking time, give a good shake to evenly cook the skin.

Nutrition information:
Calories per serving: 221; Carbohydrates: 1.1g; Protein: 15.2g; Fat: 16.9g

Pesto Basted Shrimp on the Grill

Serves: 4, Cooking Time: 16 minutes

Ingredients
- 1 cup pesto
- 1/4 cup chopped fresh basil
- 1-lb extra-large shrimp, peeled and deveined
- bamboo skewers, soaked in water
- Extra-virgin olive oil, for drizzling
- Freshly ground black pepper

Instructions
1) Thread shrimp into skewers and place on skewer rack. Drizzle with oil, season with pepper and salt and cook for 8 minutes at 360°F.
2) Halfway through cooking time, turnover skewers and baste with pesto.
3) Serve and enjoy with a garnish of fresh basil.

Nutrition information:
Calories per Serving: 544; Carbs: 9.6g; Protein: 7.0g; Fat: 53.0

Pesto Sauce Over Fish Filet

Serves: 3, Cooking Time: 20 minutes

Ingredients
- 1 bunch fresh basil
- 1 cup olive oil
- 1 tbsp. parmesan cheese, grated
- 2 cloves of garlic,
- 2 tbsps. pine nuts
- 3 white fish fillets
- Salt and pepper to taste

Instructions

1) In a food processor, combine all ingredients except for the fish fillets.
2) Pulse until smooth.
3) Place the fish in a baking dish and pour over the pesto sauce.
4) Place in the air fryer and cook for 20 minutes at 400°F.

Nutrition information:
Calories per serving: 191; Carbohydrates: 9.5g; Protein: 8.2g; Fat: 13.3g

Pina Colada Sauce Over Coconut Shrimps

Serves: 4, Cooking Time: 6 minutes

Ingredients
- 1 ½ pounds jumbo shrimps, peeled and deveined
- ½ cup cornstarch
- 2/3 cup coconut milk
- 2 tbsps. honey
- ¾ cups panko bread crumbs
- 1 cup shredded coconut flakes
- ¼ cup pineapple chunks, drained
- 1/3 cup light coconut milk
- 1/3 cup non-fat Greek yogurt
- Salt and pepper to taste
- Toasted coconut meat for garnish

Instructions

1) Preheat the air fryer to 390°F.
2) Place the shrimps and cornstarch in a Ziploc bag and give a good shake.
3) In a bowl, stir in coconut milk and honey. Set aside.
4) In another bowl, mix the coconut flakes and bread crumbs. Set aside.
5) Dip the shrimps in the milk mixture then dredge in the bread crumbs.
6) Place in the double layer rack and cook for 6 minutes.
7) Meanwhile, combine the rest of the Ingredients to create the dipping sauce.

Nutrition information:
Calories per serving: 493; Carbs: 21.4g; Protein: 38.9g; Fat: 27.9g

Quick 'n Easy Tuna-Mac Casserole

Serves: 4, Cooking Time: 20 minutes

Ingredients
- 1/2 (10.75 ounce) can condensed cream of chicken soup
- 1-1/2 cups cooked macaroni
- 1/2 (5 ounce) can tuna, drained
- 1/2 cup shredded Cheddar cheese
- 3/4 cup French fried onions

Instructions
1) Lightly grease baking pan of air fryer with cooking spray.
2) Mix soup, tuna, and macaroni in pan. Sprinkle cheese on top.
3) For 15 minutes, cook on 360°F.
4) Remove basket and toss the mixture a bit. Sprinkle fried onions.
5) Cook for another 5 minutes.
6) Serve and enjoy.

Nutrition information:
Calories per Serving: 411; Carbs: 37.1g; Protein: 11.5g; Fat: 28.5g

Salad Niçoise With Peppery Halibut

Serves: 6, Cooking Time: 15 minutes

Ingredients
- 1 ½ pounds halibut fillets
- 1 cup cherry tomatoes, halved
- 2 pounds mixed vegetables
- 2 tbsps. olive oil
- 4 cups torn lettuce leaves
- 4 large hard-boiled eggs, peeled and sliced
- Salt and pepper to taste

Instructions
1) Preheat the air fryer to 390°F.
2) Place the grill pan accessory in the air fryer.
3) Rub the halibut with salt and pepper. Brush the fish with oil.
4) Place on the grill.
5) Surround the fish fillet with the mixed vegetables and cook for 15 minutes.
6) Assemble the salad by serving the fish fillet with grilled mixed vegetables, lettuce, cherry tomatoes, and hard-boiled eggs.

Nutrition information:
Calories per serving: 312; Carbs:16.8 g; Protein: 19.8g; Fat: 18.3g

Salmon Topped with Creamy Avocado-Cashew Sauce

Serves: 2, Cooking Time: 20 minutes

Ingredients

- ½ clove of garlic
- ½ pound salmon fillet
- 1 avocado, pitted and chopped
- 1 tsp. olive oil
- 2 tbsps. cashew nuts, soaked in water for 10 minutes
- Salt and pepper to taste

Instructions

1) Preheat the air fryer for 5 minutes
2) Season the salmon fillets with salt, pepper, and olive oil.
3) Place in the air fryer and cook for 15 minutes at 400°F.
4) Meanwhile, place the rest of the ingredients in a food processor. Season with salt and pulse until smooth.
5) Serve the salmon fillet with the creamy avocado sauce.

Nutrition information:
Calories per serving: 417; Carbohydrates: 13.7g; Protein: 23.4g; Fat: 29.8g

Salted Tequila 'n Lime Shrimp

Serves: 3, Prep Time: 1 hour, Cooking Time: 16 minutes

Ingredients

- 1-pound large shrimp, peeled and deveined
- 1 pinch ground cumin
- 1 pinch garlic salt
- 1/4 cup olive oil
- 2 tbsps. tequila
- 2 tbsps. lime juice
- 1 large lime, quartered
- ground black pepper to taste

Instructions

1) In a bowl mix well pepper, cumin, garlic salt, olive oil, tequila and lime juice. Stir in shrimp and marinate for at least an hour. Tossing every now and then.
2) Thread shrimps in skewers. Place on skewer rack and cook for 8 minutes at 360°F. If needed cook in batches.
3) Halfway through cooking time, turn over the skewers and baste with lime.
4) Serve and enjoy.

Nutrition information:
Calories per Serving: 222; Carbs: 3.8g; Protein: 18.8g; Fat: 14.6g

Savory Bacalao Tapas Recipe from Portugal

Serves: 4, Cooking Time: 26 minutes

Ingredients

- 1-pound cod fish filet, chopped
- 2 tbsp. butter
- 1 yellow onions, thinly sliced
- 3/4 tsp. red pepper flakes
- freshly ground pepper to taste
- 1/4 cup chopped fresh parsley, divided
- 1 clove garlic, chopped, divided
- 1/4 cup olive oil
- 2 hard cooked eggs, chopped

- 2 Yukon Gold potatoes, peeled and diced
- 5 pitted black olives
- 5 pitted green olives

Instructions
1) Lightly grease baking pan of air fryer with cooking spray. Add and melt butter at 360°F. Stir in onions and cook for 6 minutes until caramelized.
2) Stir in black pepper, red pepper flakes, half of parsley, garlic, olive oil, diced potatoes and chopped fish and cook for 10 minutes at 360°F. Halfway through cooking time, stir well to mix.
3) Cook for 10 minutes at 390°F until tops are lightly browned.
4) Garnish with remaining parsley, eggs, black and green olives.
5) Serve and enjoy with chips.

Nutrition information:
Calories per Serving: 691; Carbs: 25.2g; Protein: 77.1g; Fat: 31.3g

Shrimp, Mushroom 'n Rice Casserole

Serves: 2, Cooking Time: 35 minutes

Ingredients
- 1 tbsp. butter
- 3/4 cup uncooked instant rice
- 3/4 cup water
- 1/2 (4 ounce) can sliced mushrooms, drained
- 1/2 (10.75 ounce) can condensed cream of shrimp soup
- 1/2 tsp. vegetable oil
- 1/2-pound small shrimp, peeled and deveined
- 1/2 (8 ounce) container sour cream
- 1/3 cup shredded Cheddar cheese

Instructions
1) Lightly grease baking pan of air fryer with cooking spray.
2) Add rice, water, mushrooms, butter, vegetable oil and shrimp soup,
3) Cover with foil and cook for 20 minutes at 360°F.
4) Open foil cover, stir in shrimps, return foil and let it rest for 5 minutes.
5) Remove foil completely and stir in sour cream. Mix well and evenly spread rice.
6) Top with cheese. Cook for 7 minutes at 390°F until tops are lightly browned.
7) Serve and enjoy.

Nutrition information:
Calories per Serving: 569; Carbs: 38.5g; Protein: 31.8g; Fat: 31.9g

Soy-Orange Flavored Squid

Serves: 4, Prep Time: 2 hours, Cooking Time: 10 minutes

Ingredients
- ½ cup mirin
- 1 cup soy sauce
- 1/3 cup yuzu or orange juice, freshly squeezed
- 2 cups water
- 2 pounds squid body, cut into rings

Instructions
1) Place all ingredients in a Ziploc bag and allow the squid rings to marinate in the fridge for at least 2 hours.
2) Preheat the air fryer to 390°F.
3) Place the grill pan in the air fryer.
4) Grill the squid rings for 10 minutes.
5) Meanwhile, pour the marinade over a sauce pan and allow to simmer for 10 minutes or until the sauce has reduced.
6) Baste the squid rings with the sauce before serving.

Nutrition information:
Calories per serving: 412; Carbs: 4.1g; Protein: 44.2g; Fat: 24.3g

Spiced Coco-Lime Skewered Shrimp

Serves: 6, Cooking Time: 12 minutes

Ingredients
- 1-pound uncooked medium shrimp, peeled and deveined
- 1/4 cup olive oil
- 1/4 cup soy sauce
- 1/3 cup coconut oil
- 1 lime, zested and juiced
- 1/3 cup chopped fresh cilantro
- 2 garlic cloves
- 2 jalapeno peppers, seeded

Instructions
1) In food processor, process until smooth the soy sauce, olive oil, coconut oil, cilantro, garlic, lime juice, lime zest, and jalapeno.
2) In a shallow dish, mix well shrimp and processed marinade. Toss well to coat and marinate in the fridge for 3 hours.
3) Thread shrimps in skewers. Place on skewer rack in air fryer.
4) Cook for 6 minutes at 360°F. If needed, cook in batches.
5) Serve and enjoy.

Nutrition information:
Calories per Serving: 172; Carbs: 4.8g; Protein: 13.4g; Fat: 10.9g

Sweet Honey-Hoisin Glazed Salmon

Serves: 2, Cooking Time: 12 minutes

Ingredients

- 1 tbsp. honey
- 1 tbsp. olive oil
- 1 tbsp. rice wine
- 1 tbsp. soy sauce
- 1-lb salmon filet, cut into 2-inch rectangles
- 3 tbsps. hoisin sauce

Instructions

1) In a shallow dish, mix well all Ingredients. Marinate in the fridge for 3 hours.
2) Thread salmon pieces in skewers and reserve marinade for basting. Place on skewer rack in air fryer.
3) Cook for 12 minutes at 360°F. Halfway through cooking time, turnover skewers and baste with marinade. If needed, cook in batches.
4) Serve and enjoy.

Nutrition information:

Calories per Serving: 971; Carbs: 23.0g; Protein: 139.4g; Fat: 35.7g

Sweet-Chili Sauce Dip 'n Shrimp Rolls

Serves: 8, Cooking Time: 9 minutes

Ingredients

- 4 ounces raw shrimps, deveined and chopped
- 2 ½ tbsps. sesame oil, divided
- 2 cups cabbage, shredded
- 1 cup carrots, julienned
- 1 cup red bell pepper, seeded and julienned
- ¾ cup snow peas, julienned
- 2 tsps. fish sauce
- ¼ tsp. crushed red pepper
- 8 spring roll wrappers
- ½ cup sweet chili sauce

Instructions

1) Heat sesame oil in a skillet over medium flame and stir in the cabbage, carrots, and bell pepper for 2 minutes. Set aside and allow to cool.
2) Once cooled, Add shrimps and snow peas. Season with fish sauce and red pepper.
3) Lay spring roll wrapper on a flat surface and place 1 tbsp. or two of the vegetable mixtures in the middle of the spring roll wrapper. Fold the wrapper and seal the edges with water.
4) Preheat the air fryer to 390°F.
5) Place the spring rolls in the double layer rack accessory. Spray with cooking oil.
6) Cook for 7 minutes.
7) Serve with chili sauce.

Nutrition information:

Calories per serving: 185; Carbs: 19g; Protein: 7g; Fat: 9g

Tartar Sauce 'n Crispy Cod Nuggets

Serves: 3, Cooking Time: 10 minutes

Ingredients

- 1 ½ pounds cod fillet
- ½ cup flour
- 1 egg, beaten
- 1 tbsp. vegetable oil
- ½ cup non-fat mayonnaise
- ½ tsp. Worcestershire sauce
- 1 cup cracker crumbs
- 1 tbsp. sweet pickle relish
- 1 tsp. honey
- Juice from half a lemon
- Salt and pepper to taste
- Zest from half of a lemon

Instructions

1) Preheat the air fryer to 390°F.
2) Season the cods with salt and pepper.
3) Dredge the fish on flour and dip in the beaten egg before dredging on the cracker crumbs. Brush with oil.
4) Place the fish on the double layer rack and cook for 10 minutes.
5) Meanwhile, prepare the sauce by mixing the remaining ingredients in a bowl.
6) Serve the fish with the sauce.

Nutrition information:
Calories per serving: 470; Carbs: 25.4g; Protein: 42.9g; Fat: 21.8g

Tomato 'n Onion Stuffed Grilled Squid

Serves: 4, Cooking Time: 15 minutes

Ingredients

- 2 pounds squid, gutted and cleaned
- 1 tbsp. fresh lemon juice
- 5 cloves of garlic
- ½ cup green onions, chopped
- ½ cup tomatoes, chopped
- 2 tbsps. olive oil
- Salt and pepper to taste

Instructions

1) Preheat the air fryer to 390°F.
2) Place the grill pan in the air fryer.
3) Season the squid with salt, pepper, and lemon juice.
4) Stuff the cavity with garlic, tomatoes, and onions.
5) Brush the squid with olive oil.
6) Place on the grill pan and cook for 15 minutes.
7) Halfway through the cooking time, flip the squid.

Nutrition information:
Calories per serving: 277; Carbs: 10.7g; Protein: 36g; Fat: 10g

Tortilla-Crusted with Lemon Filets

Serves: 4, Cooking Time: 15 minutes

Ingredients

- 4 fillets of white fish fillet
- 1 cup tortilla chips, pulverized
- 1 egg, beaten
- 1 tbsp. lemon juice
- Salt and pepper to taste

Instructions

1) Preheat the air fryer to 390°F.
2) Place a grill pan in the air fryer.

3) Season the fish fillet with salt, pepper, and lemon juice.
4) Soak in beaten eggs and dredge in tortilla chips.
5) Place on the grill pan.
6) Cook for 15 minutes.
7) Make sure to flip the fish halfway through the cooking time.

Nutrition information:
Calories per serving: 300; Carbs: 8.4g; Protein: 24.8g; Fat:18.6 g

Turmeric Spiced Salmon with Soy Sauce

Serves: 4, Cooking Time: 12 minutes

Ingredients
- 1 slab of salmon fillets, sliced into cubes
- ½ tbsp. turmeric powder
- ½ tbsp. sugar
- 1 tbsp. soy sauce
- A dash of black pepper
- 1 cup cherry tomatoes
- Chopped coriander for garnish

Instructions
1) Season the salmon fillets with turmeric powder, sugar, soy sauce, and black pepper. Allow to marinate for 30 minutes in the fridge.
2) Preheat the air fryer to 330°F.
3) Skewer the salmon cubes alternating with tomatoes
4) Place on the double layer rack.
5) Cook for 10 to 12 minutes. Garnish with coriander and serve.

Nutrition information:
Calories per serving: 302.3; Carbs: 4.2g; Protein: 47.3g; Fat: 10.7g

Very Easy Lime-Garlic Shrimps

Servings: 1, Cooking Time: 6 minutes

Ingredients
- 1 cup raw shrimps
- 1 clove of garlic, minced
- 1 lime, juiced and zested
- Salt and pepper to taste

Instructions
1) In a mixing bowl, combine all Ingredients and give a good stir.
2) Preheat the air fryer to 390°F.
3) Skewer the shrimps onto the metal skewers that come with the double layer rack accessory.
4) Place on the rack and cook for 6 minutes.

Nutrition information:
Calories per serving: 280; Carbs: 8g; Protein: 26g; Fat: 16g

Chapter 3 Air Fryer Vegetarian Recipes

Almond Flour Battered 'n Crisped Onion Rings

Serves: 3, Cooking Time: 15 minutes

Ingredients
- ½ cup almond flour
- 1 tbsp. baking powder
- 1 tbsp. smoked paprika
- 1 egg, beaten
- ¾ cup coconut milk
- 1 big white onion, sliced into rings
- Salt and pepper to taste

Instructions
1) Preheat the air fryer for 5 minutes.
2) In a mixing bowl, mix the almond flour, baking powder, smoked paprika, salt and pepper.
3) In another bowl, combine the eggs and coconut milk.
4) Soak the onion slices into the egg mixture.
5) Dredge the onion slices in the almond flour mixture.
6) Place in the air fryer basket.
7) Close and cook for 15 minutes at 325°F.
8) Halfway through the cooking time, shake the fryer basket for even cooking. Serve with hot.

Nutrition information:
Calories per serving: 217; Carbohydrates: 8.6g; Protein:5.3g; Fat: 17.9g

Almond Flour Battered Wings

Serves: 4, Cooking Time: 25 minutes

Ingredients
- 16 pieces chicken wings
- ¾ cup almond flour
- 2 tbsps. stevia powder
- 4 tbsps. minced garlic
- ¼ cup butter, melted
- Salt and pepper to taste

Instructions
1) Preheat the air fryer for 5 minutes.
2) In a mixing bowl, combine the chicken wings, almond flour, stevia powder, and garlic Season with salt and pepper to taste.
3) Place in the air fryer basket and cook for 25 minutes at 400°F.
4) Halfway through the cooking time, make sure that you give the fryer basket a shake.
5) Once cooked, place in a bowl and drizzle with melted butter. Toss to coat.

Nutrition information:
Calories per serving: 365; Carbohydrates: 7.8g; Protein: 23.7g; Fat: 26.9g

Baby Corn in Chili-Turmeric Spice

Serves: 5, Cooking Time: 8 minutes

Ingredients

- 10 pieces baby corn, blanched
- ¼ cup water
- ¼ tsp. baking soda
- ¼ tsp. salt
- ¼ tsp. turmeric powder
- ½ tsp. curry powder
- ½ tsp. red chili powder
- 1 cup chickpea flour

Instructions

1) Preheat the air fryer to 400°F.
2) Line the air fryer basket with aluminum foil and brush with oil.
3) In a mixing bowl, mix all ingredients except for the corn.
4) Whisk until well combined.
5) Dip the corn in the batter and place inside the air fryer. Cook for 8 minutes until golden brown.

Nutrition information:
Calories per serving: 89; Carbohydrates: 14.35g; Protein: 4.75g; Fat: 1.54g

Baked Cheesy Eggplant with Marinara

Serves: 3, Cooking Time: 45 minutes

Ingredients

- 1 large eggplants
- 1 clove garlic, sliced
- 3 tsps. olive oil
- 1/2 pinch salt, or as needed
- 1/4 tsp. red pepper flakes
- 1/4 cup water, plus more as needed
- 1-1/2 cups prepared marinara sauce
- 1/4 cup and 2 tbsps. ricotta cheese
- 1/4 cup grated Parmesan cheese
- 1-1/2 tsps. olive oil
- 1/4 cup and 2 tbsps. dry bread crumbs
- 2 tbsps. shredded pepper jack cheese
- salt and freshly black pepper to taste

Instructions

1) Cut eggplant crosswise in 5 pieces. Peel and chop two pieces into ½-inch cubes.
2) Lightly grease baking pan of air fryer with 1 ½ olive oil. Heat oil at 390°F for 5 minutes. Add half eggplant strips and cook for 2 minutes per side. Transfer to a plate.
3) Add 1 ½ tsp olive oil and add garlic. Cook for 1 minute. Add chopped eggplants. Season with pepper flakes and salt. Lower heat to 330°F cook for 4 minutes. and continue cooking eggplants until soft, around 8 minutes more.
4) Stir in water and marinara sauce. Cook for 7 minutes until heated through. Stirring every now and then. Transfer to a bowl.

5) In a bowl, whisk well pepper, salt, pepper jack cheese, Parmesan cheese, and ricotta. Evenly spread cheeses over eggplant strips and then fold in half.
6) Lay folded eggplant in baking pan. Pour marinara sauce on top.
7) In a small bowl whisk well olive oil, and bread crumbs. Sprinkle all over sauce.
8) Cook for 15 minutes at 390°F until tops are lightly browned.
9) Serve and enjoy.

Nutrition information:
Calories per Serving: 405; Carbs: 41.1g; Protein: 12.7g; Fat: 21.4g

Baked Polenta with Chili-Cheese

Serves: 3, Cooking Time: 10 minutes

Ingredients
- 1 commercial polenta roll, sliced
- 1 cup cheddar cheese sauce
- 1 tbsp. chili powder

Instructions
1) Place the baking dish in the air fryer.
2) Arrange the polenta slices in the baking dish.
3) Add the chili powder and cheddar cheese sauce.
4) Close the air fryer and cook for 10 minutes at 390°F.

Nutrition information:
Calories per serving: 206; Carbs: 25.3g; Protein: 3.2g; Fat: 4.2g

Baked Portobello, Pasta 'n Cheese

Serves: 4, Cooking Time: 30 minutes

Ingredients
- 1 tbsp. vegetable oil
- 1/4-pound Portobello mushrooms, thinly sliced
- 1/4 tsp. dried basil
- 1 large clove garlic, minced
- 2 tbsps. all-purpose flour
- 1 cup milk
- 1 cup shredded mozzarella cheese
- 1/4 cup margarine
- 2 tbsps. soy sauce
- 4-ounce penne pasta, cooked according to manufacturer's Directions for Cooking
- 5-ounce frozen chopped spinach, thawed

Instructions
1) Lightly grease baking pan of air fryer with oil. For 2 minutes, heat

on 360°F. Add mushrooms and cook for a minute. Transfer to a plate.
2) In same pan, melt margarine for a minute. Stir in basil, garlic, and flour, cook for another 2 minutes. Stir in half of milk slowly while whisking continuously. Mix well. Cook for another 2 minutes. Stir in remaining milk and cook for another 3 minutes.
3) Add cheese and mix well.
4) Stir in soy sauce, spinach, mushrooms, and pasta. Mix well. Top with remaining cheese.
5) Cook for 15 minutes at 390°F until tops are lightly browned.
6) Serve and enjoy.

Nutrition information:
Calories per Serving: 482; Carbs: 32.1g; Protein: 16.0g; Fat: 32.1g

Baked Potato Topped with Cream Cheese

Serves: 1, Cooking Time: 40 minutes

Ingredients

- 1 medium russet potato, scrubbed and peeled
- 2 cup water
- ¼ tsp. onion powder
- 1 tsp. olive oil
- 1/8 tsp. salt
- a dollop of vegan butter
- a dollop of vegan cream cheese
- 1 tbsp. Kalamata olives
- 1 tbsp. chives, chopped

Instructions

1) Place inside the air fryer basket, add water and the potato and cook for 40 minutes. Be sure to turn the potatoes once halfway.
2) Place the potatoes in a mixing bowl and mixed with olive oil, onion powder, salt, and vegan butter.
3) Cook for 5 minutes at 400°F.
4) Serve the potatoes with vegan cream cheese, Kalamata olives, chives, and other vegan toppings that you want.

Nutrition information:
Calories per serving: 504; Carbohydrates: 68.34g; Protein: 9.31g; Fat: 21.53g

Baked Zucchini Recipe from Mexico

Servings: 4, Cooking Time: 30 minutes

Ingredients

- 1 tbsp. olive oil
- 1/2 cup chopped onion
- 1-1/2 pounds zucchini, cubed
- 1/2 tsp. garlic salt
- 1/2 tsp. cayenne pepper, or to taste
- 1/2 tsp. dried oregano
- 1/2 tsp. paprika
- 1/2 cup cooked pinto beans
- 1-1/4 cups salsa
- 1/2 cup cooked long-grain rice
- 3/4 cup shredded Cheddar cheese

Instructions

1) Lightly grease baking pan of air fryer with olive oil. Add onions and zucchini and for 10 minutes, cook at 360°F. Halfway through cooking time, stir.
2) Season with cayenne, oregano, paprika, and garlic salt. Mix well.
3) Stir in salsa, beans, and rice. Cook for 5 minutes.
4) Stir in cheddar cheese and mix well.
5) Cover pan with foil. Cook for 15 minutes at 390°F until bubbly.
6) Serve and enjoy.

Nutrition information:
Calories per Serving: 263; Carbs: 24.6g; Protein: 12.5g; Fat: 12.7g

Banana Pepper Stuffed with Tofu

Serves: 8, Cooking Time: 10 minutes

Ingredients

- 1 package firm tofu, crumbled
- 1 onion, finely chopped
- 3 tbsps. coconut oil
- ½ tsp. turmeric powder
- ½ tsp. red chili powder
- 1 tsp. coriander powder
- 8 banana peppers, top end sliced and seeded
- Salt to taste

Instructions

1) Preheat the air fryer for 5 minutes.
2) In a mixing bowl, combine the tofu, onion, coconut oil, turmeric powder, red chili powder, coriander power, and salt. Mix until well-combined.
3) Scoop the tofu mixture into the hollows of the banana peppers.
4) Place the stuffed peppers in the air fryer.
5) Close and cook for 10 minutes at 325°F.

Nutrition information:
Calories per serving: 72; Carbohydrates: 4.1g; Protein: 1.2g; Fat: 5.6g

Bell Pepper Wrapped in Tortilla

Serves: 4, Cooking Time: 15 minutes

Ingredients
- 4 pieces commercial vegan nuggets, chopped
- 1 tbsp. water
- 1 small yellow onion, diced
- 1 small red bell pepper, chopped
- 2 cobs grilled corn kernels
- 4 large tortillas
- mixed greens for garnish

Instructions
1) Preheat the air fryer to 400°F.
2) In a skillet heated over medium heat, add water and sauté the vegan nuggets together with the onions, bell peppers, and corn kernels. Set aside.
3) Place filling inside the tortillas.
4) Fold the tortillas and place inside the air fryer and cook for 15 minutes until the tortilla wraps are crispy.
5) Serve with mix greens on top.

Nutrition information:
Calories per serving: 548; Carbohydrates: 43.54g; Protein: 46.73g; Fat: 20.76g

Black Bean Burger with Garlic-Chipotle

Servings: 3, Cooking Time: 20 minutes

Ingredients
- ½ cup corn kernels
- ½ tsp. chipotle powder
- ½ tsp. garlic powder
- ¾ cup salsa
- 1 ¼ tsp. chili powder
- 1 ½ cup rolled oats
- 1 can black beans, rinsed and drained
- 1 tbsp. soy sauce

Instructions
1) In a mixing bowl, combine all ingredients by your hands.
2) Form small patties using your hands and set aside.
3) Brush patties with oil if desired.
4) Place the grill pan in the air fryer and place the patties on the grill pan accessory.
5) Close the lid and cook for 20 minutes on each side at 330°F.
6) Halfway through the cooking time, flip the patties to brown the other side evenly

Nutrition information:
Calories per serving: 395; Carbs: 52.2g; Protein: 24.3g; Fat: 5.8g

Brown Rice, Spinach Frittata

Serves: 4, Cooking Time: 55 minutes

Ingredients

- 1 ¾ cups brown rice, cooked
- 1 flax egg (1 tbsp. flaxseed meal + 3 tbsp. cold water)
- 1 tbsp. olive oil
- 4 cloves garlic, crushed
- 4 spring onions, chopped
- 3 big mushrooms, chopped
- 1 yellow pepper, chopped
- ½ cup kale, chopped
- ½ cup baby spinach, chopped
- ½ onion, chopped
- a handful of basil leaves, chopped
- 1 package firm tofu
- 2 tsps. Dijon mustard
- ½ tsp. turmeric
- 2 tbsps. soy sauce
- 3 tbsps. nutritional yeast
- 2 tsps. arrowroot powder
- 2/3 cup almond milk
- 2 vegan frittata

Instructions

1) Preheat the air fryer to 375°F. Grease a pan and put inside the air fryer.
2) Prepare the frittata crust by mixing the brown rice and flax egg. Press the rice onto the baking dish until you form a crust. Brush with a little oil and cook for 10 minutes.
3) Meanwhile, heat olive oil in a skillet over medium flame and sauté the garlic and onions for 2 minutes.
4) Add the pepper and mushroom and continue stirring for 3 minutes.
5) Stir in the kale, spinach, spring onions, and basil. Remove from the pan and set aside.
6) In a food processor, pulse together the tofu, mustard, turmeric, soy sauce, nutritional yeast, vegan milk and arrowroot powder. Pour in a mixing bowl and stir in the sautéed vegetables.
7) Pour the vegan frittata mixture over the rice crust and cook in the air fryer for 40 minutes.

Nutrition information:
Calories per serving: 226; Carbohydrates: 30.44g; Protein: 10.69g; Fat: 8.05g

Brussels Sprouts with Balsamic Oil

Serves: 4, Cooking Time: 15 minutes

Ingredients

- ¼ tsp. salt
- ½ lb. fresh zucchini, cubed
- 1 tbsp. balsamic vinegar
- 2 cups Brussels sprouts, halved
- 2 tbsps. olive oil

Instructions

1) Preheat the air fryer for 5 minutes.
2) Mix all ingredients in a bowl until the zucchini fries are well coated.
3) Place in the air fryer basket.
4) Close and cook for 15 minutes for 350°F.
5) Serve and enjoy.

Nutrition information:
Calories per serving: 82; Carbohydrates: 4.6g; Protein: 1.5g; Fat: 6.8g

Buttered Carrot-Zucchini with Mayo

Servings: 4, Cooking Time: 25 minutes

Ingredients
- 1/2-pound carrots, sliced
- 1-1/2 zucchinis, sliced
- 1 tbsp. grated onion
- 1/4 cup water
- 1/4 tsp. salt
- 1/4 tsp. ground black pepper
- 1/4 tsp. prepared horseradish
- 1/4 cup mayonnaise
- 2 tbsps. butter, melted
- 1/4 cup Italian bread crumbs

Instructions
1) Lightly grease baking pan of air fryer with cooking spray. Add carrots and cook for 8 minutes at 360°F. Add zucchini and continue cooking for another 5 minutes.
2) Meanwhile, in a bowl whisk well pepper, salt, horseradish, onion, mayonnaise, and water. Pour into pan of veggies. Toss well to coat.
3) In a small bowl mix melted butter and bread crumbs. Sprinkle over veggies.
4) Cook for 10 minutes at 390°F until tops are lightly browned.
5) Serve and enjoy.

Nutrition information:
Calories per Serving: 223; Carbs: 13.8g; Protein: 2.7g; Fat: 17.4g

Cauliflower Steak with Thick Sauce

Serves: 2, Cooking Time: 15 minutes

Ingredients
- 1 cauliflower, sliced into two
- 1 tbsp. olive oil
- 2 tbsps. onion, chopped
- ¼ tsp. vegetable stock powder
- ¼ cup almond milk
- salt and pepper to taste

Instructions
1) Soak the cauliflower in salted water or brine for at least 2 hours.
2) Preheat the air fryer to 400°F.
3) Rinse the cauliflower and place inside the air fryer and cook for 15 minutes.
4) Meanwhile, heat oil in a skillet over medium flame. Sauté the onions and stir until translucent. Add the vegetable stock powder and milk.
5) Bring to boil and adjust the heat to low.
6) Allow the sauce to reduce and season with salt and pepper.
7) Place cauliflower steak on a plate and pour over sauce.

Nutrition information:
Calories per serving: 91; Carbohydrates:6.58 g; Protein: 1.02g; Fat: 7.22g

Cheddar 'n Zucchini Casserole

Serves: 4, Cooking Time: 30 minutes

Ingredients

- 1/4 onion, diced
- 1/2-pound zucchini, sliced
- 1/2-pound yellow squash, sliced
- 1 egg
- 1/4 cup butter
- 1-1/2 tsps. white sugar
- 1/2 tsp. salt
- 1/4 cup biscuit baking mix
- 1/2 cup shredded Cheddar cheese
- 5 saltine crackers, crushed
- 2 tbsps. bread crumbs

Instructions

1) Lightly grease baking pan of air fryer with cooking spray. Add onion, zucchini, and yellow squash. Cover pan with foil and for 15 minutes, cook on 360°F or until tender.
2) Stir in salt, sugar, egg, butter, baking mix, and cheddar cheese. Mix well. Fold in crushed crackers. Top with bread crumbs.
3) Cook for 15 minutes at 390°F until tops are lightly browned.
4) Serve and enjoy.

Nutrition information:
Calories per Serving: 285; Carbs: 16.4g; Protein: 8.6g; Fat: 20.5g

Cheesy BBQ Tater Tot

Serves: 6, Cooking Time: 20 minutes

Ingredients

- 1-lb frozen tater tots, defrosted
- 12 slices bacon
- ½ cup shredded Cheddar cheese
- 2 tbsp chives
- Ranch dressing, for serving

Instructions

1) Thread one end of bacon in a skewer, followed by one tater, snuggly thread the bacon around tater like a snake, and then another tater, and then snake the bacon again until you reach the end. Repeat with the rest of the Ingredients.
2) Cook for 10 minutes at 360°F. Halfway through cooking time, turnover skewers. If needed cook in batches.
3) Place skewers on a serving platter and sprinkle cheese and chives on top.
4) Serve and enjoy with ranch dressing on the side.

Nutrition information:
Calories per Serving: 337; Carbs: 17.2g; Protein: 11.5g; Fat: 29.1g

Chives 'n Thyme Spiced Veggie Burger

Serves: 8, Cooking Time: 15 minutes

Ingredients
- ½ pound cauliflower, steamed and diced
- 1 cup bread crumbs
- ¼ cup desiccated coconut
- ½ cup oats
- 1 flax egg (1 flaxseed egg + 3 tbsp. water)
- 1 tsp. mustard powder
- 2 tsps. chives
- 2 tsps. coconut oil melted
- 2 tsps. garlic, minced
- 2 tsps. parsley
- 2 tsps. thyme
- 3 tbsp. plain flour
- salt and pepper to taste

Instructions
1) Preheat the air fryer to 390°F.
2) Place the cauliflower in a tea towel and ring out excess water. Place in a mixing bowl and add all ingredients except the bread crumbs. Mix well until well combined.
3) Form 8 burger patties with the mixture using your hands.
4) Roll the patties in bread crumbs and place in the air fryer basket. Make sure that they do not overlap.
5) Cook for 10 to 15 minutes or until the patties are crisp.

Nutrition information:
Calories per serving: 70; Carbohydrates: 10.85g; Protein: 2.51g; Fat: 1.85g

Coconut Battered Cauliflower Bites

Serves: 4, Cooking Time: 20 minutes

Ingredients
- 1/3 cup oats flour
- 1/3 cup plain flour
- 1/3 cup desiccated coconut
- salt and pepper to taste
- 1 flax egg (1 tbsp. flaxseed meal + 3 tbsp. water)
- 1 small cauliflower, cut into florets
- 1 tsp. mixed spice
- ½ tsp. mustard powder
- 2 tbsps. maple syrup
- 1 clove of garlic, minced
- 2 tbsps. soy sauce

Instructions
1) Preheat the air fryer to 400°F.
2) In a mixing bowl, mix together oats, plain flour, and desiccated coconut. Season with salt and pepper to taste. Set aside.
3) In another bowl, place the flax egg and add a pinch of salt to taste. Set aside.
4) Season the cauliflower with mixed spice and mustard powder.

5) Dredge the florets in the flax egg first then in the flour mixture.
6) Place inside the air fryer and cook for 15 minutes.
7) Meanwhile, place the maple syrup, garlic, and soy sauce in a sauce pan and heat over medium flame. Bring to a boil and adjust the heat to low until the sauce thickens.
8) After 15 minutes, take out the florets from the air fryer and place them in the saucepan. Toss to coat the florets and place inside the air fryer and cook for another 5 minutes.

Nutrition information:
Calories per serving: 154; Carbohydrates: 27.88g; Protein: 4.69g; Fat:2.68 g

Creamy 'n Cheese Broccoli Bake

Serves: 2, Cooking Time: 30 minutes

Ingredients
- 2 tbsps. all-purpose flour
- 1/2 (14 ounce) can evaporated milk, divided
- 1-pound fresh broccoli, coarsely chopped
- 1/2 cup cubed sharp Cheddar cheese
- salt to taste
- 1-1/2 tsps. butter
- 1 tbsp. dry bread crumbs
- 1/4 cup water

Instructions
1) Lightly grease baking pan of air fryer with cooking spray. Mix in half of the milk and flour in pan and cook for 5 minutes at 360°F. Halfway through cooking time, mix well. Add broccoli and remaining milk. Mix well and cook for another 5 minutes.
2) Stir in cheese and mix well until melted.
3) In a small bowl, mix butter and bread crumbs well. Sprinkle on top of broccoli.
4) Cook for 20 minutes at 360°F until tops are lightly browned.
5) Serve and enjoy.

Nutrition information:
Calories per Serving: 444; Carbs: 37.3g; Protein: 23.1g; Fat: 22.4g

Creole Seasoned Vegetables

Serves: 5, Cooking Time: 15 minutes

Ingredients
- 2 medium zucchinis, cut into ½ inch thick slices
- 2 large yellow squash, cut into ½ inch thick slices
- 1 large red bell pepper, sliced
- 3 tbsps. olive oil
- 1 tsp. black pepper
- 1 tsp. salt
- ¼ cup honey
- ¼ cup yellow mustard
- 2 tsps. creole seasoning
- 2 tsps. smoked paprika

Instructions
1) Preheat the air fryer to 330°F.
2) Place the grill pan in the air fryer.
3) In a Ziploc bag, put the zucchini, squash, red bell pepper, olive oil, salt and pepper. Give a shake to season all vegetables.
4) Place on the grill pan and cook for 15 minutes.
5) Meanwhile, prepare the sauce by combining the mustard, honey, paprika, and creole seasoning. Season with salt to taste.
6) Serve the vegetables with the sauce.

Nutrition information:
Calories per serving: 164; Carbs: 21.5g; Protein: 2.6g; Fat: 8.9g

Crisped Baked Cheese Stuffed Chile Pepper

Serves: 3, Cooking Time: 30 minutes

Ingredients
- 1 (7 ounce) can whole green Chile peppers, drained
- 1/4-pound Cheddar cheese, shredded
- 1/4-pound Monterey Jack cheese, shredded
- 1 egg, beaten
- 1 tbsp. all-purpose flour
- 1/2 (5 ounce) can evaporated milk
- 1/2 (8 ounce) can tomato sauce
- 1/4 cup milk

Instructions
1) Lightly grease baking pan of air fryer with cooking spray. Evenly spread chilies and sprinkle cheddar and Jack cheese on top.
2) In a bowl whisk well flour, milk, and eggs. Pour over chilies.
3) Cook for 20 minutes at 360°F.
4) Add tomato sauce on top.
5) Cook for 10 minutes at 390°F until tops are lightly browned.
6) Serve and enjoy.

Nutrition information:
Calories per Serving: 392; Carbs: 12.0g; Protein: 23.9g; Fat: 27.6g

Crisped Noodle Salad Chinese Style

Serves: 2, Cooking Time: 20 minutes

Ingredients
- 1 package wheat noodles
- 1 tbsp. cooking oil
- 1 tbsp. tamari
- 1 tbsp. red chili sauce
- 1 tbsp. lime juice
- 1 carrot, sliced thinly
- 1 cup cabbage, sliced thinly
- 1 green bell pepper, sliced thinly
- 1 onion, sliced thinly
- 1 sprig coriander, chopped
- 1 tomato, chopped
- salt to taste

Instructions
1) In a big pot, boil water and add a tsp. of salt. Bring the water to a boil and add the noodles. Boil the noodles until it is half-cooked. Drain.
2) In a mixing bowl, pour oil over the noodles and mix until the noodles are coated evenly.
3) Place a tin foil on the base of the air fryer basket and place the noodles inside.
4) Cook in a preheated air fryer at 395°F for 15 to 20 minutes or until crisp. Transfer to 2 bowl.
5) Add the green bell pepper, onion, sprig coriander, tomato to the air fryer, cook for 2 minutes at 395 °F.
6) Meanwhile, mix together the tamari, red chili sauce, and lime juice. Season with salt and pepper to taste.
7) Add the cooked vegetables and sauce to the crisp noodle, serve!

Nutrition information:
Calories per serving: 165; Carbohydrates: 20.41g; Protein:4.12 g; Fat:7.39 g

Crisped Tofu with Paprika

Serves: 4, cooking Time: 12 minutes

Ingredients
- ¼ cup cornstarch
- 1 block extra firm tofu, pressed to remove excess water and cut into cubes
- 1 tbsp. smoked paprika
- salt and pepper to taste

Instructions
1) Line the air fryer basket with aluminum foil and brush with oil.
2) Preheat the air fryer to 370°F.
3) Mix all ingredients in a bowl. Toss to combine.
4) Place in the air fryer basket and cook for 12 minutes. Serve!

Nutrition information:
Calories per serving: 155; Carbohydrates:11.56 g; Protein:11.74 g; Fat:6.88 g

Crispy Avocado Fingers

Serves: 4, Cooking Time: 10 minutes

Ingredients
- ½ cup panko bread crumbs
- ½ tsp. salt
- 1 pitted Haas avocado, peeled and sliced
- liquid from 1 can white beans or aquafaba

Instructions
1) Preheat the air fryer at 350°F.
2) In a shallow bowl, toss the bread crumbs and salt until well combined.
3) Dredge the avocado slices first with the aquafaba then in the breadcrumb mixture.
4) Place the avocado slices in a single layer inside the air fryer basket.
5) Cook for 10 minutes and shake halfway through the cooking time.

Nutrition information:
Calories per serving: 51; Carbohydrates: 6.45g; Protein: 1.39g; Fat: 7.51g

Crispy Savory Spring Rolls

Serves: 4, Cooking Time: 15 minutes

Ingredients
- 1 celery stalk, chopped
- 1 medium carrot, shredded
- ½ tsp. ginger, finely chopped
- 1 tsp. coconut sugar
- 1 tbsp. soy sauce
- 1 tsp. nutritional yeast
- 1 cup shiitake mushroom, sliced thinly
- 1 tsp. corn starch + 2 tbsp. water
- 8 spring roll wrappers

Instructions
1) In a mixing bowl, mix together the celery stalk, carrots, ginger, coconut sugar, soy sauce and nutritional yeast.
2) Get shiitake mushroom mixture and place at the center of the spring roll wrappers.
3) Roll and seal the edges of the wrapper with the cornstarch mixture.
4) Cook in a preheated air fryer to 400°F for 15 minutes or until the spring roll wrapper is crisp.

Nutrition information:
Calories per serving: 118; Carbohydrates: 15g; Protein: 10g; Fat: 2g

Crispy Asparagus Dipped in Paprika

Serves: 5, Cooking Time: 15 minutes

Ingredients
- 2 tbsps. parsley, chopped
- ½ tsp. garlic powder
- ¼ cup almond flour
- ½ tsp. smoked paprika
- 10 medium asparagus, trimmed
- 2 large eggs, beaten
- Salt and pepper to taste

Instructions
1) Preheat the air fryer for 5 minutes.
2) In a mixing bowl, combine the parsley, garlic powder, almond flour, and smoked paprika. Season with salt and pepper to taste.
3) Soak the asparagus in the beaten eggs and dredge in the almond flour mixture.
4) Place in the air fryer basket. Close.
5) Cook for 15 minutes at 350°F.

Nutrition information:
Calories per serving: 114; Carbohydrates: 4.9g; Protein: 5.2g; Fat: 8.2g

Crispy Fry Green Tomatoes

Serves: 1, Cooking Time: 7 minutes

Ingredients
- ½ cup panko bread crumbs
- 3 tbsps. cornstarch
- ½ tsp. dried basil, ground
- ½ tsp. cooking oil
- ½ tsp. dried oregano, ground
- ½ tsp. granulated onion
- 1 medium-sized green tomato, sliced
- Salt and pepper to taste

Instructions
1) In a mixing bowl, combine the panko bread crumbs, cornstarch, basil, oregano, onion, salt and pepper.
2) Dredge the tomato slices in the bread crumb mixture.
3) Brush with oil and arrange on the double layer rack.
4) Place the rack with the dredged tomato slices in the air fryer.
5) Close the lid and cook for 7 minutes at 330°F.

Nutrition information:
Calories per serving: 260; Carbs: 54.1g; Protein: 5.4g; Fat: 3.4g

Crispy Onion Seasoned with Paprika 'n Cajun

Serves: 4, Cooking Time: 20 minutes

Ingredients
- 1 large white onion
- ¼ cup coconut milk
- 2 large eggs, beaten
- 1 ½ tsp. paprika
- 1 tsp. garlic powder
- ½ tsp. Cajun seasoning
- ¾ cup almond flour
- Salt and pepper to taste

Instructions
1) Peel the onion and cut off the top and make random slices.
2) In a mixing bowl, combine the coconut milk and the eggs.
3) Soak the onion in the egg mixture.
4) In another bowl, combine the almond flour, paprika, garlic powder, Cajun seasoning, salt and pepper.
5) Dredge the onion in the almond flour mixture.
6) Grease with cooking spray.
7) Place in the air fryer.
8) Cook for 20 minutes at 350°F.

Nutrition information:
Calories per serving: 93; Carbohydrates: 6.7g; Protein: 2.6g; Fat: 6.2g

Crispy Vegetarian Ravioli

Serves: 4, Cooking Time: 6 minutes

Ingredients
- ½ cup panko bread crumbs
- 2 tsps. nutritional yeast
- 1 tsp. dried basil
- 1 tsp. dried oregano
- 1 tsp. garlic powder
- ¼ cup aquafaba
- 8-ounces vegan ravioli
- cooking spray
- salt and pepper to taste

Instructions
1) Line the air fryer basket with aluminum foil and brush with oil.
2) Preheat the air fryer to 400°F.
3) Mix together the panko bread crumbs, nutritional yeast, basil, oregano, and garlic powder. Season with salt and pepper to taste.
4) In another bowl, place the aquafaba.
5) Dip the ravioli in the aquafaba the dredge in the panko mixture.
6) Spray with cooking oil and place in the air fryer.
7) Cook for 6 minutes making sure that you shake the air fryer basket halfway.

Nutrition information:
Calories per serving: 82; Carbohydrates: 12.18g; Protein:3.36 g; Fat: 2.15g

Crispy Vegie Tempura Style

Serves: 3, Cooking Time: 15 minutes

Ingredients

- 1 cup broccoli florets
- 1 red bell pepper, stripped
- 1 small sweet potato, peeled and thick sliced
- 1 small zucchini, thick sliced
- 2/3 cup cornstarch
- 1/3 cup all-purpose flour
- 1 egg, beaten
- ¼ tsp. salt
- ¾ cup club soda
- 1 ½ cups panko break crumbs
- Non-stick cooking spray

Instructions

1) Dredge the vegetables in a cornstarch and all-purpose flour mixture.
2) Once all vegetables are dusted with flour, dip each vegetable in a mixture of egg and club soda before dredging in bread crumbs.
3) Place the vegetables on the double layer rack accessory and spray with cooking oil.
4) Place inside the air fryer.
5) Close and cook for 20 minutes at 330°F.

Nutrition information:

Calories per serving: 277 ; Carbs: 51.6g; Protein: 7.2g; Fat: 4.2g

Crispy Wings with Lemony Old Bay Spice

Serves: 4, Cooking Time: 25 minutes

Ingredients

- ¾ cup almond flour
- 1 tbsp. old bay spices
- 1 tsp. lemon juice, freshly squeezed
- 3 pounds chicken wings
- Salt and pepper to taste
- ½ cup butter

Instructions

1) Preheat the air fryer for 5 minutes.
2) In a mixing bowl, combine all ingredients except for the butter.
3) Place in the air fryer basket.
4) Cook for 25 minutes at 350°F.
5) Halfway through the cooking time, shake the fryer basket for even cooking.
6) Once cooked, drizzle with melted butter.

Nutrition information:

Calories per serving: 750; Carbohydrates: 1.6g; Protein: 52.5g; Fat: 59.2g

Curry 'n Coriander Spiced Bread Rolls

Serves: 5, Cooking Time: 15 minutes

Ingredients

- 5 large potatoes, boiled
- ½ tsp. mustard seeds
- 2 small onions, chopped
- ½ tsp. turmeric powder
- 2 sprigs, curry leaves
- 2 green chilies, seeded and chopped
- 1 bunch coriander, chopped
- 1 tbsp. olive oil
- 8 slices of vegan wheat bread, brown sides discarded
- salt and pepper to taste

Instructions

1) In a bowl, mash the potatoes and season with salt and pepper to taste. Set aside.
2) Heat olive oil in a skillet over medium low flame and add the mustard seeds. Stir until the seeds sputter. Then add the onions and fry until translucent. Stir in the turmeric powder and curry leaves. Continue to cook for 2 more minutes until fragrant. Remove from heat and add to the potatoes. Stir in the green chilies and coriander. This will be the filling.
3) Wet the bread and remove the excess water.
4) Place a tbsp. of the potato mixture in the middle of the bread and gently roll the bread in so that the potato filling is completely sealed inside the bread.
5) Brush with oil and place inside the air fryer.
6) Cook at 400°F for 15 minutes. Make sure to shake the air fryer basket gently halfway through the cooking time for even cooking.

Nutrition information:
Calories per serving: 462; Carbohydrates: 96.65g; Protein: 11.3g; Fat: 3.88g

Easy Baked Root Veggies

Serves: 4, Cooking Time: 45 minutes

Ingredients

- ¼ cup olive oil
- 1 head broccoli, cut into florets
- 1 tbsp. dry onion powder
- 2 sweet potatoes, peeled and cubed
- 4 carrots, cut into chunks
- 4 zucchinis, sliced thickly
- salt and pepper to taste

Instructions

1) Preheat the air fryer to 400°F.
2) In a baking dish that can fit inside the air fryer, mix all the ingredients and bake for 45 minutes or until the vegetables are tender and the sides have browned.

Nutrition information:
Calories per serving: 310; Carbohydrates: 41.05g; Protein: 5.22g; Fat: 13.93g

Easy Fry Portobello Mushroom

Serves: 2, Cooking Time: 10 minutes

Ingredients
- 1 tbsp. cooking oil
- 1-pound Portobello mushroom, sliced
- Salt and pepper to taste

Instructions
1) Place the grill pan accessory in the air fryer.
2) In a bowl, place all Ingredients: and toss to coat and season the mushrooms.
3) Place in the grill pan.
4) Close the air fryer and cook for 10 minutes at 330°F.

Nutrition information:
Calories per serving: 135; Carbs: 12.2g; Protein: 7.8g; Fat: 8.5g

Egg-Less Spinach Quiche

Serves: 4, Cooking Time: 30 minutes

Ingredients
- ¾ cup whole meal flour
- ½ cup cold coconut oil
- cold water
- 2 tbsp. olive oil
- 1 onion, chopped
- 4 ounces mushrooms, sliced
- 1 package firm tofu, pressed to remove excess water then crumbled
- 1-pound spinach, washed and chopped
- ½ tbsp. dried dill
- 2 tbsp. nutritional yeast
- a sprig of fresh parsley, chopped
- salt and pepper

Instructions
1) Preheat the air fryer to 375°F.
2) Create the pastry by sifting the flour and salt together. Add the coconut oil until the flour crumbles. Gradually add water to bind the dough or until you form a stiff dough. Wrap with a cling film and leave inside the fridge to rest for 30 minutes.
3) Heat olive oil in a skillet over medium heat and sauté the onion for 1 minute. Add the mushroom and tofu. Add the spinach, dried dill, and nutritional yeast. Season with salt and pepper to taste. Throw in the parsley last. Set aside.
4) Roll the dough on a floured surface until you form a thin dough. Place the dough in a greased baking dish that fits inside the air fryer. Pour the tofu mixture and cook for 30 minutes or until the pastry is crisp.

Nutrition information:
Calories per serving: 531; Carbohydrates: 49.37g; Protein: 11.4g; Fat: 35.22g

Fried Broccoli Recipe from India

Serves: 6, Cooking Time: 15 minutes

Ingredients
- ¼ tsp. turmeric powder
- ½ pounds broccoli, cut into florets
- 1 tbsp. almond flour
- 1 tsp. garam masala
- 2 tbsps. coconut milk
- Salt and pepper to taste

Instructions
1) Preheat the air fryer for 5 minutes.
2) In a bowl, combine all ingredients until the broccoli florets are coated with the other ingredients.
3) Place in a fryer basket and cook for 15 minutes until crispy.

Nutrition information:
Calories per serving: 96; Carbohydrates: 8.9g; Protein: 3.1g; Fat: 6.9g

Fried Chickpea-Fig on Arugula

Serves: 4, Cooking Time: 20 minutes

Ingredients
- 8 fresh figs, halved
- 2 tbsps. extra-virgin olive oil
- 1 ½ cups chickpeas, cooked
- 1 tsp. cumin seeds, roasted then crushed
- 4 tbsps. balsamic vinegar
- 3 cups arugula rocket, washed and dried
- salt and pepper to taste

Instructions
1) Preheat the air fryer to 375°F.
2) Line the air fryer basket with aluminum foil and brush with oil.
3) Place the figs inside the air fryer and cook for 10 minutes.
4) In a mixing bowl, mix the chickpeas and cumin seeds.
5) Once the figs are cooked, take them out and place the chickpeas. Cook the chickpeas for 10 minutes. Allow to cool
6) Meanwhile, mix the dressing by combining the balsamic vinegar, olive oil, salt and pepper.
7) Place the arugula rocket in a salad bowl and place the cooled figs and chickpeas.
8) Pour over the sauce and toss to coat.
9) Serve immediately.

Nutrition information:
Calories per serving: 388; Carbohydrates: 62.51g; Protein:16.72 g; Fat:7.92 g

Fried Falafel Recipe from the Middle East

Serves: 8, Cooking Time: 15 minutes

Ingredients
- ¼ cup coriander, chopped
- ¼ cup parsley, chopped
- ½ onion, diced
- ½ tsp. coriander seeds
- ½ tsp. red pepper flakes
- ½ tsp. salt
- 1 tbsp. juice from freshly squeezed lemon
- 1 tsp. cumin seeds
- 2 cups chickpeas from can, drained and rinsed
- 3 cloves garlic
- 3 tbsps. all-purpose flour
- cooking spray

Instructions
1) In a skillet over medium heat, toast the cumin and coriander seeds until fragrant.
2) Place the toasted seeds in a mortar and grind the seeds.
3) In a food processor, place all ingredients except for the cooking spray. Add the toasted cumin and coriander seeds.
4) Pulse until fine.
5) Shape the mixture into falafels and spray cooking oil.
6) Place inside a preheated air fryer and make sure that they do not overlap.
7) Cook at 400°F for 15 minutes or until the surface becomes golden brown.

Nutrition information:
Calories per serving: 110; Carbohydrates: 18.48g; Protein: 5.11g; Fat: 1.72g

Fried Tofu Recipe from Malaysia

Serves: 4, Cooking Time: 30 minutes

Ingredients
- 1 block tofu, cut into strips
- 2 cloves of garlic
- 1 tsp. sriracha sauce
- 1 tbsp. maple syrup
- 2 tbsps. soy sauce
- 2 tsps. fresh ginger, coarsely chopped
- juice of 1 fresh lime

Peanut Butter Sauce Ingredients
- 1 tbsp. soy sauce
- 1/2 cup creamy peanut butter
- 1-2 tsps. Sriracha sauce to taste
- 2 cloves of garlic
- 2-inch piece of fresh ginger coarsely chopped
- 6 tbsps. of water
- juice of 1/2 a fresh lemon

Instructions
1) In a blender, blend all peanut butter sauce ingredients until smooth and creamy. Transfer to a

medium bowl and set aside for dipping sauce.
2) In same blender, blend garlic, sriracha, ginger, maple syrup, lime juice, and soy sauce until smooth. Pour into a bowl and add strips of tofu, Marinate for 30 minutes.
3) With the steel skewer, skewer tofu strips.
4) Place on skewer rack and air fry for 15 minutes at 370°F.
5) Serve and enjoy.

Nutrition information:
Calories per Serving: 347; Carbs: 16.6g; Protein: 16.6g; Fat: 23.8g

Garlic 'n Basil Crackers
Serves: 6, Cooking Time: 15 minutes
Ingredients
- ¼ tsp. dried basil powder
- ½ tsp. baking powder
- 1 ¼ cups almond flour
- 1 clove of garlic, minced
- 3 tbsps. coconut oil
- A pinch of cayenne pepper powder
- Salt and pepper to taste

Instructions
1) Preheat the air fryer for 5 minutes.
2) Mix everything in a mixing bowl to create a dough.
3) Transfer the dough on a clean and flat working surface and spread out until 2mm thick. Cut into squares.
4) Place gently in the air fryer basket. Do this in batches if possible.
5) Cook for 15 minutes at 325°F.

Nutrition information:
Calories per serving: 206; Carbohydrates: 2.9g; Protein: 5.3g; Fat: 19.3g

Garlic-Wine Flavored Vegetables
Serves: 4, Cooking Time: 15 minutes
Ingredients
- 1 cup baby Portobello mushrooms, chopped
- 1 package frozen chopped vegetables
- 1 red onion, sliced
- 1 ½ tbsps. honey1 tsp. Dijon mustard
- ¼ cup chopped fresh basil
- 1/3 cup olive oil
- 3 tbsp. red wine vinegar
- 4 cloves of garlic, minced
- Salt and pepper to taste

Instructions
1) Preheat the air fryer to 330°F.
2) Place the grill pan in the air fryer.
3) In a Ziploc bag, combine the vegetables and season with salt, pepper, and garlic. Give a good shake to combine everything.
4) Dump on to the grill pan and cook for 15 minutes.
5) Meanwhile, combine the rest of the Ingredients: on bowl and season with more salt and pepper.

6) Drizzle the grilled vegetables with the sauce.

Nutrition information:
Calories per serving: 200; Carbs: 8.3g; Protein: 2.1g; Fat: 18.2g

Grilled 'n Glazed Strawberries

Serves: 2, Cooking Time: 20 minutes

Ingredients
- 1-lb large strawberries
- 1 tbsp honey
- 1 tsp lemon zest
- 3 tbsp melted butter
- Lemon wedges
- Pinch kosher salt

Instructions
1) Thread strawberries in 4 skewers.
2) In a small bowl, mix well remaining Ingredients: except for lemon wedges. Brush all over strawberries.
3) Place skewer on air fryer skewer rack.
4) For 10 minutes, cook on 360°F. Halfway through cooking time, brush with honey mixture and turnover skewer.
5) Serve and enjoy with a squeeze of lemon.

Nutrition information:
Calories per Serving: 281; Carbs: 27.9g; Protein: 1.8g; Fat: 18.0g

Grilled Tomatoes on Garden Salad

Serves: 4, Cooking Time: 20 minutes

Ingredients
- 3 large green tomatoes
- 1 clove of garlic, minced
- ¼ cup golden raisings
- ¼ cup hazelnuts, toasted and chopped
- ¼ cup pistachios, toasted and chopped
- ½ cup chopped chives
- ¾ cup cilantro leaves, chopped
- ¾ cup fresh parsley, chopped
- 2 tbsps. white balsamic vinegar
- 4 leaves iceberg lettuce
- 5 tbsps. olive oil
- Salt and pepper to taste

Instructions
1) Preheat the air fryer to 330°F.
2) Place the grill pan in the air fryer.
3) In a mixing bowl, season the tomatoes with garlic, oil, salt and pepper to taste.
4) Place on the grill pan and grill for 20 minutes.
5) Once the tomatoes are done, toss in a salad bowl together with the rest of the Ingredients.

Nutrition information:
Calories per serving: 287; Carbs: 12.2g; Protein: 4.8g; Fat: 25.9g

Grilled Drunken Mushrooms

Serves: 4, Cooking Time: 20 minutes

Ingredients

- 2 garlic cloves, finely chopped
- 3 tbsps. chopped fresh thyme and/or rosemary leaves
- Large pinch of crushed red pepper flakes
- 1 tsp. kosher salt, plus more to taste
- 6 scallions, cut crosswise into 2-inch pieces
- 1-pint cherry tomatoes
- 1-pint cremini, button, or other small mushrooms
- 1/2 cup extra-virgin olive oil
- 1/2 tsp. freshly ground black pepper, plus more to taste
- 1/4 cup red wine or Sherry vinegar

Instructions

1) In Ziploc bag, mix well black pepper, salt, red pepper flakes, thyme, vinegar, oil, and garlic. Add mushrooms, tomatoes, and scallions. Mix well and let it marinate for half an hour.
2) Thread mushrooms, tomatoes, and scallions. Reserve sauce for basting. Place on skewer rack in air fryer. If needed, cook in batches.
3) For 10 minutes, cook on 360°F. Halfway through cooking time, turnover skewers and baste with reserved sauce.
4) Serve and enjoy.

Nutrition information:

Calories per Serving: 126; Carbs: 4.1g; Protein: 1.0g; Fat: 11.7g

Grilled Eggplant with Cumin-Paprika Spice

Serves: 2, Cooking Time: 20 minutes

Ingredients

- 1 Chinese eggplant, sliced into 1-inch thick circles
- 1 zucchini, sliced into 1-inch thick circles
- 1 medium bell pepper, cut into chunks
- 1 tbsp. coriander seeds
- 1 tbsp. olive oil
- 1 tsp. cumin
- 1 tsp. paprika
- 1 tsp. salt
- 3 garlic cloves

Instructions

1) In a food processor, process garlic, coriander, olive oil, cumin, paprika, and salt until creamy.
2) Thread bell pepper, eggplant, and zucchini in skewers. Brush with garlic creamy paste. Place on skewer rack in air fryer.
3) Cook for 10 minutes at 360°F. Halfway through cooking time, turnover skewers. If needed, cook in batches.
4) Serve and enjoy.

Nutrition information:

Calories per Serving: 181; Carbs: 22.4g; Protein: 4.2g; Fat: 8.2g

Grilled Olive-Tomato with Dill-Parsley Oil

Serves: 6, Cooking Time: 16 minutes

Ingredients

- 1 big block of feta (about 12-oz.), cut into cubes
- 1 tbsp lemon juice
- 1 clove garlic, smashed
- 1 tbsp Chopped fresh dill
- 1 tbsp chopped fresh parsley
- Flaky sea salt
- Freshly ground black pepper
- 12 pitted Kalamata olives
- 12 cherry tomatoes
- 1 cucumber, cut into 12 large cubes
- 1/4 cup extra-virgin olive oil

Instructions

1) In a medium bowl, whisk well parsley, dill, garlic, lemon juice, and olive oil. Season with pepper and salt. Add feta cheese and marinate for at least 15 minutes.
2) Thread feta, olives, cherry tomatoes, and cucumber in skewers. Place on skewer rack in air fryer. If needed, cook in batches.
3) Cook for 8 minutes at 390°F.
4) Serve and enjoy.

Nutrition information:
Calories per Serving: 217; Carbs: 7.1g; Protein: 8.8g; Fat: 17.0g

Healthy Apple-licious Chips

Serves: 1, Cooking Time: 6 minutes

Ingredients

- ½ tsp. ground cumin
- 1 apple, cored and sliced thinly
- 1 tbsp. sugar
- A pinch of salt

Instructions

1) Place all ingredients in a bowl and toss to coat everything.
2) Put the grill pan in the air fryer and place the sliced apples on the grill pan.
3) Close the air fryer and cook for 6 minutes at 390°F.

Nutrition information:
Calories per serving:130 ; Carbs: 33.6g; Protein: 0.6g; Fat: 0.5g

Healthy Breakfast Casserole

Serves: 2, Cooking Time: 30 minutes

Ingredients

- ½ cup cooked quinoa
- ½ cup diced bell pepper
- 1 large carrot, peeled and chopped
- 2 small celery stalks, chopped
- ½ cup shiitake mushrooms, diced
- ½ tsp black pepper
- ½ tsp ground cumin
- ½ tsp red pepper flakes
- ½ tsp dill
- ½ tsp salt
- 1 tbsp lemon juice
- 1 tsp dried oregano
- 1 small onion, diced
- 1 tsp garlic, minced
- 1 tsp olive oil
- 2 tbsp soy yogurt, plain
- 2 tbsp water
- 2 tbsp yeast
- 7-oz extra firm tofu, drained

Instructions

1) Lightly grease baking pan of air fryer with olive oil. Add garlic and onion.
2) Cook for 2 minutes at 390°F.
3) Remove basket, stir in bell pepper, celery, and carrots. Cook for 3 minutes.
4) Remove basket, give a quick stir. Then add cumin, red pepper flakes, dill, pepper, salt, oregano, and mushrooms. Mix well. Cook for 5 minutes. Mixing halfway through cooking time.
5) Meanwhile, in a food processor pulse lemon juice, water, yogurt, yeast, and tofu. Process until creamy.
6) Transfer creamy tofu mixture into air fryer basket. Add quinoa and give a good stir.
7) Cook for another 15 minutes at 330°F or until golden brown.
8) Let it rest for 5 minutes.
9) Serve and enjoy.

Nutrition information:

Calories per Serving: 280; Carbs: 28.6g; Protein: 18.5g; Fat: 10.1g

Herby Veggie Cornish Pasties

Serves: 4, Cooking Time: 30 minutes

Ingredients

- 1 ½ cups plain flour
- cold water for mixing the dough
- ¾ cup cold coconut oil
- 1 onion, sliced
- 1 stick celery, chopped
- 1 medium carrot, chopped
- 1 medium potato, diced
- ¼ cup mushrooms, chopped
- 1 tsp. oregano
- 1 tbsp. nutritional yeast
- 1 tbsp. olive oil
- salt and pepper to taste

Instructions

1) Preheat the air fryer to 400°F.
2) Prepare the dough by mixing the flour, coconut oil, and salt in a bowl. Use a fork and press the flour to combine everything.
3) Gradually add a drop of water to the dough until you achieve a stiff consistency of the dough. Cover the dough with a cling film and let it rest for 30 minutes inside the fridge.
4) Roll the dough out and cut into squares. Set aside.
5) Heat olive oil over medium heat and sauté the onions for 2 minutes. Add the celery, carrots and potatoes. Continue stirring for 3 to 5 minutes before adding the mushrooms and oregano.
6) Season with salt and pepper to taste. Add nutritional yeast last. Let it cool and set aside.
7) Drop a tbsp. of vegetable mixture on to the dough and seal the edges of the dough with water.
8) Place inside the air fryer basket and cook for 20 minutes or until the dough is crispy.

Nutrition information:
Calories per serving: 659; Carbohydrates: 56.66g; Protein: 8.55g; Fat: 44.97g

Herby Zucchini 'n Eggplant Bake

Serves: 4, Cooking Time: 25 minutes

Ingredients

- 1 fennel bulb, sliced crosswise
- 1 sprig of basil
- 1 sprig flat-leaf parsley
- 1 sprig mint
- 1 tbsp. coriander powder
- 1 tsp. capers
- ½ lemon, juiced
- 2 eggplants, sliced crosswise
- 2 red onions, chopped
- 2 red peppers, sliced crosswise
- 2 tsps. herb de Provence
- 3 large zucchinis, sliced crosswise
- 4 cloves of garlic, minced
- 4 large tomatoes, chopped

- 5 tbsps. olive oil
- salt and pepper to taste

Instructions
1) In a blender, combine basil, parsley, mint, coriander, capers and lemon juice. Season with salt and pepper to taste. Pulse until well combined.
2) Preheat the air fryer to 400°F.
3) Toss the eggplant, onions, garlic, peppers, fennel, and zucchini with olive oil.
4) In a baking dish that can fit in the air fryer, arrange the vegetables and pour over the tomatoes and the herb puree. Season with more salt and pepper and sprinkle with herbs de Provence.
5) Place inside the air fryer and cook for 25 minutes.

Nutrition information:
Calories per serving: 375; Carbohydrates: 47.83g; Protein: 8.99g; Fat: 20.03g

Hollandaise Topped Grilled Asparagus

Serves: 6, Cooking Time: 15 minutes

Ingredients
- 3 pounds asparagus spears, trimmed
- ¼ tsp. black pepper
- ½ cup butter, melted
- ½ lemon juice
- ½ tsp. salt
- ½ tsp. salt
- 1 tsp. chopped tarragon leaves
- 2 tbsps. olive oil
- 3 egg yolks
- A pinch of mustard powder
- A punch of ground white pepper

Instructions
1) Preheat the air fryer to 330°F.
2) Place the grill pan in the air fryer.
3) In a Ziploc bag, combine the asparagus, olive oil, salt and pepper. Give a good shake to combine everything.
4) Dump on to the grill pan and cook for 15 minutes.
5) Meanwhile, on a double boiler over medium flame, whisk the egg yolks, lemon juice, and salt until silky. Add the mustard powder, white pepper and melted butter. Keep whisking until the sauce is smooth. Garnish with tarragon leaves.
6) Drizzle the sauce over asparagus spears.

Nutrition information:
Calories per serving: 253; Carbs: 10.2g; Protein: 6.7g; Fat: 22.4g

Italian Seasoned Easy Pasta Chips

Serves: 2, Cooking Time: 10 minutes

Ingredients
- ½ tsp. salt
- 1 ½ tsp. Italian seasoning blend
- 1 tbsp. nutritional yeast
- 1 tbsp. olive oil
- 2 cups whole wheat bowtie pasta

Instructions
1) Place the baking dish in the air fryer.
2) Give a good stir.
3) Close the air fryer and cook for 10 minutes at 390°F.

Nutrition information:
Calories per serving: 407; Carbs: 47g; Protein: 17.9g; Fat: 17.4g

Jackfruit-Cream Cheese Rangoon

Serves: 2, Cooking Time: 10 minutes

Ingredients
- ¾ Thai curry paste
- 1 can green jackfruit in brine
- 1 cup vegan cream cheese
- 1 scallion, chopped
- 2 cups vegetable broth
- 2 tsp. sesame oil
- Salt and pepper to taste

Instructions
1) Place the baking pan accessory in the air fryer.
2) Add the rest of the ingredients and give a good stir.
3) Close the air fryer and cook for 10 minutes at 390°F.

Nutrition information:
Calories per serving: 457; Carbs: 107.3g; Protein: 0.8g; Fat: 6.8g

Jalapeno Stuffed with Bacon 'n Cheeses

Serves: 8, Cooking Time: 15 minutes

Ingredients
- ¼ cup cheddar cheese, shredded
- 1 tsp. paprika
- 16 fresh jalapenos, sliced lengthwise and seeded
- 16 strips of uncured bacon, cut into half
- 4-ounce cream cheese
- Salt to taste

Instructions
1) In a mixing bowl, mix together the cream cheese, cheddar cheese, salt, and paprika until well-combined.
2) Scoop half a tsp. onto each half of jalapeno peppers.

3) Use a thin strip of bacon and wrap it around the cheese-filled jalapeno half. Wear gloves when doing this step because jalapeno is very spicy.
4) Place in the air fryer basket and cook for 15 minutes in a 350°F preheated air fryer.

Nutrition information:
Calories per serving: 225; Carbohydrates: 3.2g; Protein: 10.6g; Fat: 18.9g

Layered Tortilla Bake

Serves: 6, Cooking Time: 30 minutes

Ingredients
- 1 (15 ounce) can black beans, rinsed and drained
- 1 cup salsa, divided
- 1/2 cup chopped tomatoes
- 1/2 cup sour cream
- 2 (15 ounce) cans pinto beans, drained and rinsed
- 2 cloves garlic, minced
- 2 cups shredded reduced-fat Cheddar cheese
- 2 tbsps. chopped fresh cilantro
- 7 (8 inch) flour tortillas

Instructions
1) Mash pinto beans in a large bowl and mix in garlic and salsa.
2) In another bowl whisk together tomatoes, black beans, cilantro, and salsa.
3) Lightly grease baking pan of air fryer with cooking spray. Spread 1 tortilla, spread pinto bean mixture evenly up to ½-inch away from the edge of tortilla, spread cheese on top. Cover with another tortilla, spread black bean mixture, and then cheese. Repeat twice the layering process. Cover with the last tortilla, top with pinto bean mixture and then cheese.
4) Cover pan with foil.
5) Cook for 25 minutes at 390°F, remove foil and cook for 5 minutes or until tops are lightly browned.
6) Serve and enjoy.

Nutrition information:
Calories per Serving: 409; Carbs: 54.8g; Protein: 21.1g; Fat: 11.7g

Loaded Brekky Hash Browns

Serves: 4, Cooking Time: 20 minutes

Ingredients
- 3 russet potatoes, peeled and grated
- 2 garlic cloves chopped
- 1 tsp. paprika
- salt and pepper to taste
- 1 tsp. canola oil
- 1 tsp. olive oil
- 1/4 cup chopped green peppers
- 1/4 cup chopped red peppers
- 1/4 cup chopped onions

Instructions
1) For 20 minutes, soak the grated potatoes in a bowl of cold water to make it crunchy and remove the starch. Then drain well and completely dry with paper towels.
2) Lightly grease baking pan of air fryer with cooking spray.

3) Add grated potatoes in air fryer. Season with garlic, paprika, salt, and pepper. Add canola and olive oil. Toss well to coat.
4) For 10 minutes, cook on 390ºF.
5) Remove basket and toss the mixture a bit. Stir in green and red peppers, and onions.
6) Cook for another 10 minutes.
7) Serve and enjoy.

Nutrition information:
Calories per Serving: 263; Carbs: 53.2g; Protein: 6.5g; Fat: 2.6g

Melted Cheese 'n Almonds on Tomato

Serves: 3, Cooking Time: 20 minutes

Ingredients
- ¼ cup toasted almonds
- 1 yellow red bell pepper, chopped
- 3 large tomatoes
- 4 ounces Monterey Jack cheese
- Salt and pepper to taste

Instructions
1) Preheat the air fryer to 330ºF.
2) Place the grill pan accessory in the air fryer.
3) Slice the tops of the tomatoes and remove the seeds to create hollow "cups."
4) In a mixing bowl, combine the cheese, bell pepper, and almonds. Season with salt and pepper to taste.
5) Stuff the tomatoes with the cheese filling.
6) Place the stuffed tomatoes on the grill pan and cook for 15 to 20 minutes.

Nutrition information:
Calories per serving: 125; Carbs: 13g; Protein: 10g; Fat: 14g

Minty Green Beans with Shallots

Serves: 6, Cooking Time: 25 minutes

Ingredients
- 1 tbsp. fresh mint, chopped
- 1 tbsp. sesame seeds, toasted
- 1 tbsp. vegetable oil
- 1 tsp. soy sauce
- 1-pound fresh green beans, trimmed
- 2 large shallots, sliced
- 2 tbsps. fresh basil, chopped
- 2 tbsps. pine nuts

Instructions
1) Preheat the air fryer to 330ºF.
2) Place the grill pan accessory in the air fryer.
3) In a mixing bowl, combine the green beans, shallots, vegetable oil, and soy sauce.
4) Dump in the air fryer and cook for 25 minutes.
5) Once cooked, garnish with basil, mints, sesame seeds, and pine nuts.

Nutrition information:
Calories per serving:307 ; Carbs: 11.2g; Protein: 23.7g; Fat: 19.7g

Mushroom 'n Bell Pepper Pizza

Serves: 10, Cooking Time: 10 minutes

Ingredients
- ¼ red bell pepper, chopped
- 1 cup oyster mushrooms, chopped
- 1 shallot, chopped
- 1 vegan pizza dough
- 2 tbsps. parsley
- salt and pepper

Instructions
1) Preheat the air fryer to 400ºF.
2) Slice the pizza dough into squares. Set aside.
3) In a mixing bowl, mix together the oyster mushroom, shallot, bell pepper and parsley.
4) Season with salt and pepper to taste.
5) Place the topping on top of the pizza squares.
6) Place inside the air fryer and cook for 10 minutes.

Nutrition information:
Calories per serving: 100; Carbohydrates: 15.67g; Protein: 2.9g; Fat:2.89 g

Mushrooms Marinated in Garlic Coco-Aminos

Serves: 8, Cooking Time: 20 minutes

Ingredients
- ¼ cup coconut aminos
- 2 cloves of garlic, minced
- 2 pounds mushrooms, sliced
- 3 tbsps. olive oil

Instructions
1) Place all ingredients in a dish and mix until well-combined.
2) Allow to marinate for 2 hours in the fridge.
3) Preheat the air fryer for 5 minutes.
4) Place the mushrooms in a heat-proof dish that will fit in the air fryer.
5) Cook for 20 minutes at 350ºF.

Nutrition information:
Calories per serving: 467; Carbohydrates: 86g; Protein: 6.2g; Fat: 10.9g

Mushrooms Stuffed with Cream Cheese-Pesto

Serves: 5, Cooking Time: 15 minutes

Ingredients
- ¼ cup olive oil
- ½ cup cream cheese
- ½ cup pine nuts
- 1 cup basil leaves
- 1 tbsp. lemon juice, freshly squeezed
- 1-pound cremini mushrooms, stalks removed
- Salt to taste

Instructions
1) Place all ingredients except the mushrooms in a food processor.
2) Pulse until fine.
3) Scoop the mixture and place on the side where the stalks were removed.
4) Place the mushrooms in the fryer basket.
5) Close and cook for 15 minutes in a 350°F preheated air fryer.

Nutrition information:
Calories per serving: 585; Carbohydrates: 71.2g; Protein: 12.6g; Fat: 27.8g

Open-Faced Vegan Flatbread

Serves: 4, Cooking Time: 25 minutes

Ingredients
- 1 can chickpeas, drained and rinsed
- 1 medium-sized head of cauliflower, cut into florets
- 1 tbsp. extra-virgin olive oil
- 2 ripe avocados, mashed
- 2 tbsps. lemon juice
- 4 flatbreads, toasted
- salt and pepper to taste

Instructions
1) Preheat the air fryer to 425°F.
2) In a mixing bowl, combine the cauliflower, chickpeas, olive oil, and lemon juice. Season with salt and pepper to taste.
3) Place inside the air fryer basket and cook for 25 minutes.
4) Once cooked, place on half of the flatbread and add avocado mash.
5) Season with more salt and pepper to taste.
6) Serve with hot sauce.

Nutrition information:
Calories per serving: 529; Carbohydrates: 65g; Protein:11 g; Fat: 25g

Orange Glazed Fried Tofu

Serves: 4, Cooking Time: 25 minutes

Ingredients

- 1 Tbsp. cornstarch (or arrowroot powder)
- 1 Tbsp. tamari
- 1-pound extra-firm tofu drained and pressed (or use super-firm tofu), cut in cubes

Sauce Ingredients

- 1 tsp. orange zest
- 1 tsps. cornstarch (or arrowroot powder)
- 1 tsp. fresh ginger minced
- 1 tsp. fresh garlic minced
- 1 Tbsp. pure maple syrup
- 1/2 cup water
- 1/3 cup orange juice
- 1/4 tsp. crushed red pepper flakes

Instructions

1) In a bowl, mix tofu with tamari and a tbsp. of cornstarch. Marinate for at least 15 minutes. Tossing well to coat every now and then.
2) In a small bowl mix all sauce Ingredients: and set aside.
3) Lightly grease baking pan of air fryer with cooking spray. Add tofu for 10 minutes, cook on 390ºF. Halfway through cooking time, stir. Cook for 10 minutes more.
4) Stir in sauce, toss well to coat. Cook for another 5 minutes.
5) Serve and enjoy.

Nutrition information:

Calories per Serving: 63; Carbs: 11.0g; Protein: 8.0g; Fat: 3.0g

Pineapple with Butter Glaze

Serves: 2, Cooking Time: 10 minutes

Ingredients

- 1 medium-sized pineapple, peeled and sliced
- 1 red bell pepper, seeded and julienned
- 1 tsp. brown sugar
- 2 tsps. melted butter
- Salt to taste

Instructions

1) Preheat the air fryer to 390ºF.
2) Place the grill pan accessory in the air fryer.
3) Mix all ingredients in a Ziploc bag and give a good shake.
4) Dump onto the grill pan and cook for 10 minutes making sure that you flip the pineapples every 5 minutes.

Nutrition information:

Calories per serving: 295; Carbs: 57g; Protein: 1g; Fat: 8g

Pita 'n Tomato Pesto Casserole

Serves: 3, Cooking Time: 5 minutes

Ingredients
- 1 roma (plum) tomatoes, chopped
- 1 tbsp. and 1-1/2 tsps. olive oil
- 1 tbsp. grated Parmesan cheese
- 1/2 bunch spinach, rinsed and chopped
- 1/4 cup crumbled feta cheese
- 2 fresh mushrooms, sliced
- 3 (6 inch) whole wheat pita breads
- 3-ounce sun-dried tomato pesto
- ground black pepper to taste

Instructions
1) Lightly grease baking pan of air fryer with cooking spray.
2) Evenly spread tomato pesto on one side of pita bread. Place one pita bread on bottom of pan, add 1/3 each of Parmesan, feta, mushrooms, spinach, and tomatoes. Season with pepper and drizzle with olive oil.
3) Cook for 5 minutes at 390°F until tops crisped.
4) Repeat process for remaining pita bread.
5) Serve and enjoy.

Nutrition information:
Calories per Serving: 367; Carbs: 41.6g; Protein: 11.6g; Fat: 17.1g

Pull-Apart Bread With Garlicky Oil

Serves: 2, Cooking Time: 10 minutes

Ingredients
- 1 large vegan bread loaf
- 2 tbsps. garlic puree
- 2 tbsps. nutritional yeast
- 2 tbsps. olive oil
- 2 tsps. chives
- salt and pepper to taste

Instructions
1) Preheat the air fryer to 357°F.
2) Slice the bread loaf making sure that you don't slice through the bread.
3) In a mixing bowl, combine the olive oil, garlic puree, and nutritional yeast.
4) Pour over the mixture on top of the slices you made on the bread.
5) Sprinkle with chopped chives and season with salt and pepper.
6) Place inside the air fryer and cook for 10 minutes or until the garlic is thoroughly cooked.

Nutrition information:
Calories per serving: 219; Carbohydrates: 16.07g; Protein: 6.65g; Fat: 14.26g

Quinoa Bowl with Lime-Sriracha

Serves: 4, Cooking Time: 10 minutes

Ingredients
- ¼ cup soy sauce
- 1 block extra firm tofu
- 1 red bell pepper, sliced
- 1 tbsp. sriracha
- 1-pound fresh broccoli florets, blanched
- 2 cups quinoa, cooked according to package instruction
- 2 tbsps. lime juice
- 2 tbsps. sesame oil
- 3 medium carrots, peeled and thinly sliced
- 3 tbsps. molasses
- 8 ounces spinach, blanched
- Salt and pepper to taste

Instructions
1) Season tofu with sesame oil, salt and pepper.
2) Place the grill pan accessory in the air fryer.
3) Place the seasoned tofu on the grill pan accessory.
4) Close the air fryer and cook for 10 minutes at 330°F.
5) Stir the tofu to brown all sides evenly.
6) Set aside and arrange the Buddha bowl.
7) In a mixing bowl, combine the soy sauce, molasses, lime juice and sriracha. Set aside.
8) Place quinoa in bowls and top with broccoli, carrots, red bell pepper, and spinach.
9) Top in tofu and drizzle with the sauce last.

Nutrition information:
Calories per serving: 157; Carbs: 17g; Protein: 9g; Fat: 6g

Roasted Bell Peppers 'n Onions in a Salad

Serves: 4, Cooking Time: 10 minutes

Ingredients
- ½ lemon, juiced
- 1 tbsp. baby capers
- 1 tbsp. extra-virgin olive oil
- 1 tsp. paprika
- 2 large red onions sliced
- 2 yellow pepper, sliced
- 4 long red pepper, sliced
- 6 cloves of garlic, crushed
- 6 plum tomatoes, halved
- salt and pepper to taste

Instructions
1) Preheat the air fryer to 420°F.
2) Place the tomatoes, onions, peppers, and garlic in a mixing bowl.

3) Add in the extra virgin olive oil, paprika, and lemon juice. Season with salt and pepper to taste.
4) Transfer into the air fryer lined with aluminum foil and cook for 10 minutes or until the edges of the vegetables have browned.
5) Place in a salad bowl and add the baby capers. Toss to combine all ingredients.

Nutrition information:
Calories per serving: 163; Carbohydrates: 36.56g; Protein: 3.58g; Fat:2.08 g

Roasted Broccoli with Salted Garlic

Serves: 6
Ingredients
- ½ tsp. black pepper
- ½ tsp. lemon juice.
- 1 clove of garlic, minced
- 1 tsp. salt
- 2 heads broccoli, cut into florets
- 2 tsps. extra virgin olive oil

Instructions
1) Line the air fryer basket with aluminum foil and brush with oil.
2) Preheat the air fryer to 375°F.
3) Combine all ingredients except the lemon juice in a mixing bowl and place inside the air fryer basket.
4) Cook for 15 minutes.
5) Serve with lemon juice.

Nutrition information:
Calories per serving: 51; Carbohydrates: 4.66g; Protein: 4.86g; Fat:1.4 g

Roasted Chat-Masala Spiced Broccoli

Serves: 2, Cooking Time:15 minutes
Ingredients
- ¼ tsp. chat masala
- ¼ tsps. turmeric powder
- ½ tsp. salt
- 1 tbsp. chickpea flour
- 2 cups broccoli florets
- 2 tbsps. yogurt

Instructions
1) Place all ingredients in a bowl and toss the broccoli florets to combine.
2) Place the baking dish accessory in the air fryer and place the broccoli florets.
3) Close the air fryer and cook for 15 minutes at 330°F.
4) Halfway through the cooking time, give the baking dish a shake.

Nutrition information:
Calories per serving:96 ; Carbs: 16.8g; Protein: 7.1g; Fat:1.3 g

Roasted Mushrooms in Herb-Garlic Oil

Serves: 4, Cooking Time: 25 minutes

Ingredients

- ½ tsp. minced garlic
- 2 pounds mushrooms
- 2 tsps. herbs de Provence
- 3 tbsps. coconut oil
- Salt and pepper to taste

Instructions

1) Preheat the air fryer for 5 minutes.
2) Place all ingredients in a baking dish that will fit in the air fryer.
3) Mix to combine.
4) Place the baking dish in the air fryer.
5) Cook for 25 minutes at 350°F.

Nutrition information:
Calories per serving: 746; Carbohydrates: 172.2g; Protein: 12.4g; Fat: 21.9g

Rosemary Olive-Oil Over Shrooms n Asparagus

Serves: 6, Cooking Time: 15 minutes

Ingredients

- ½ pound fresh mushroom, quartered
- 1 bunch fresh asparagus, trimmed and cleaned
- 2 sprigs of fresh rosemary, minced
- 2 tsp. olive oil
- salt and pepper to taste

Instructions

1) Preheat the air fryer to 400°F.
2) Place the asparagus and mushrooms in a bowl and pour the rest of the ingredients.
3) Toss to coat the asparagus and mushrooms.
4) Place inside the air fryer and cook for 15 minutes.

Nutrition information:
Calories per serving: 149; Carbohydrates: 29.2g; Protein: 3.77g; Fat:1.89 g

Salted 'n Herbed Potato Packets

Serves: 3, Cooking Time: 40 minutes

Ingredients

- 1 ½ tsps. seasoning blend
- 1 onion, sliced
- 2 large russet potatoes, peeled and sliced
- 2 medium red sweet potatoes, sliced
- 2 tbsps. olive oil
- Salt and pepper to taste

Instructions

1) Preheat the air fryer to 330°F.
2) Place the grill pan accessory in the air fryer.
3) Take a large foil and place all ingredients in the middle. Give a good stir. Fold the foil and crimp the edges.
4) Place the foil on the grill pan.
5) Cook for 40 minutes.

Nutrition information:
Calories per serving: 362; Carbs: 68.4g; Protein: 6.3g; Fat: 9.4g

Salted Beet Chips

Serves: 2, Cooking Time: 6 minutes

Ingredients
- 1 tbsp. cooking oil
- 1-pound beets, peeled and sliced
- Salt and pepper to taste

Instructions
1) Place all Ingredients: in a bowl and toss to coat everything.
2) Place the sliced beets in the double layer rack.
3) Place the rack with the beets in the air fryer.
4) Close the air fryer and cook for 6 minutes at 390°F.

Nutrition information:
Calories per serving: 167; Carbs: 23.8g; Protein: 4.1g; Fat: 7.2g

Salted Garlic Zucchini Fries

Serves: 6, Cooking Time: 15 minutes

Ingredients
- ¼ tsp. garlic powder
- ½ cup almond flour
- 2 large egg whites, beaten
- 3 medium zucchinis, sliced into fry sticks
- Salt and pepper to taste

Instructions
1) Preheat the air fryer for 5 minutes.
2) Mix all ingredients in a bowl until the zucchini fries are well coated.
3) Place in the air fryer basket.
4) Close and cook for 15 minutes for 425°F.

Nutrition information:
Calories per serving:11; Carbohydrates: 1g; Protein: 0.1g; Fat: 1.5g

Salted Potato-Kale Nuggets

Serves: 4, Cooking Time: 20 minutes

Ingredients
- ¼ tsp. salt
- 1 clove of garlic, minced
- 1 tsp. extra-virgin olive oil
- 1/8 cup almond milk
- 1/8 tsp. black pepper
- 2 cups boiled potatoes, finely chopped
- 4 cups kale, rinsed and chopped
- cooking spray

Instructions
1) Preheat the air fryer to 400°F.
2) Place a foil at the base of the air fryer basket and poke holes to allow air circulation.
3) Heat oil in a large skillet and sauté the garlic for 2 minutes. Add the kale until it wilts. Transfer to a large bowl.

4) Add the potatoes and almond milk. Season with salt and pepper to taste.
5) Form balls and spray with cooking oil.
6) Place inside the air fryer and cook for 20 minutes or until golden brown.

Nutrition information:
Calories per serving: 88; Carbohydrates: 18.05g; Protein:2.13 g; Fat: 0.81g

Savory Zucchini-Bell Pepper Medley

Serves: 4, Cooking Time: 15 minutes

Ingredients
- 1 green pepper, seeded and julienned
- 1 large zucchini
- 1 red pepper, seeded and julienned
- 1 tsp. mixed herbs
- 1 tsp. prepared mustard
- 2 tsp. minced garlic
- 6 tbsps. olive oil
- Salt and pepper to taste

Instructions

1) Preheat the air fryer for 5 minutes.
2) Place all ingredients in a baking dish that will fit in the air fryer.
3) Place in the air fryer.
4) Cook for 15 minutes at 350°F.

Nutrition information:
Calories per serving: 218; Carbohydrates: 6.2g; Protein: 1.7g; Fat: 20.7g

Scrumptiously Healthy Chips

Serves: 2, Cooking Time: 10 minutes

Ingredients
- 1 bunch kale
- 1 tsp. garlic powder
- 2 tbsps. almond flour
- 2 tbsps. olive oil
- Salt and pepper to taste

Instructions

1) Preheat the air fryer for 5 minutes.
2) In a bowl, combine all ingredients until the kale leaves are coated with the other ingredients.
3) Place in a fryer basket and cook for 10 minutes until crispy.

Nutrition information:
Calories per serving: 183; Carbohydrates: 3.1g; Protein: 4.5g; Fat: 16.9g

Shallots 'n Almonds on French Green Beans

Serves: 4, Cooking Time: 10 minutes

Ingredients
- ¼ cup slivered almonds, toasted
- ½ pounds shallots, peeled and cut into quarters
- ½ tsp. ground white pepper
- 1 ½ pound French green beans, stems removed and blanched
- 1 tbsp. salt
- 2 tbsp. olive oil

Instructions
1) Preheat the air fryer to 400°F.
2) Mix all ingredients in a mixing bowl. Toss until well combined.
3) Place inside the air fryer basket and cook for 10 minutes or until lightly browned.

Nutrition information:
Calories per serving: 171; Carbohydrates: 22.51g; Protein: 3.93g; Fat: 7.2g

Shepherd's Pie Vegetarian Approved

Serves: 3, Cooking Time: 35 minutes

Top Layer Ingredients
- 2 tbsps. olive oil
- 1 tsp. salt
- 2-1/2 russet potatoes, peeled and cut into 1-inch cubes
- 1 tbsp. and 1-1/2 tsps. vegan cream cheese substitute (such as Tofutti ®)
- 1/4 cup vegan mayonnaise
- 1/4 cup soy milk

Bottom Layer Ingredients
- 1 carrot, chopped
- 1-1/2 tsps. vegetable oil
- 1/2 large yellow onion, chopped
- 1-1/2 stalks celery, chopped
- 1/2 tomato, chopped
- 1/2 tsp. Italian seasoning
- 1/2 clove garlic, minced, or more to taste
- 1/2 pinch ground black pepper to taste
- 1/2 (14 ounce) package vegetarian ground beef substitute
- 1/4 cup frozen peas
- 1/4 cup shredded Cheddar-style soy cheese

Instructions
1) Boil potatoes until tender. Drain and transfer to a bowl. Mash potatoes with salt, vegan cream cheese, olive oil, soy milk, and vegan mayonnaise. Mix well until smooth. Set aside.
2) Lightly grease baking pan of air fryer with cooking spray. Add carrot, celery, onions, tomato, and peas. For 10 minutes, cook on 360°F. Stirring halfway through cooking time.
3) Stir in pepper, garlic, and Italian seasoning.
4) Stir in vegetarian ground beef substitute. Cook for 5 minutes while halfway through cooking time crumbling and mixing the beef substitute.
5) Evenly spread the beef and veggie mixture in pan. Top evenly with mashed potato mixture.

6) Cook for another 20 minutes or until mashed potatoes are lightly browned.
7) Serve and enjoy.

Nutrition information:
Calories per Serving: 559; Carbs: 64.5g; Protein: 20.2g; Fat: 24.4g

Skewered Corn in Air Fryer

Serves: 2, Cooking Time: 25 minutes

Ingredients
- 1-pound apricot, halved
- 2 ears of corn
- 2 medium green peppers, cut into large chunks
- 2 tsps. prepared mustard
- Salt and pepper to taste

Instructions
1) Preheat the air fryer to 330ºF.
2) Place the grill pan accessory in the air fryer.
3) On the double layer rack with the skewer accessories, skewer the corn, green peppers, and apricot. Season with salt and pepper to taste.
4) Place skewered corn on the double layer rack and cook for 25 minutes.
5) Once cooked, brush with prepared mustard.

Nutrition information:
Calories per serving: 341; Carbs: 82.5g; Protein: 7.43g; Fat: 2.2g

Spicy Veggie Recipe from Thailand

Serves: 4, Cooking Time: 15 minutes

Ingredients
- 1 ½ cups packed cilantro leaves
- 1 tbsp. black pepper
- 1 tbsp. chili garlic sauce
- 1/3 cup vegetable oil
- 2 pounds vegetable of your choice, sliced into cubes
- 2 tbsps. fish sauce
- 8 cloves of garlic, minced

Instructions
1) Preheat the air fryer to 330ºF.
2) Place the grill pan accessory in the air fryer.
3) Place all Ingredients: in a mixing bowl and toss to coat all Ingredients.
4) Put in the grill pan and cook for 15 minutes.

Nutrition information:
Calories per serving: 340; Carbs: 34.44g; Protein:8.8 g; Fat: 19.5g

Spinach Balls Spiced with Garlic 'n Pepper

Serves: 4, Cooking Time: 10 minutes

Ingredients

- ½ onion, chopped
- ½ tsp. black pepper
- ½ tsp. garlic powder
- 1 carrot, peeled and grated
- 1 egg, beaten
- 1 package fresh spinach, blanched and chopped
- 1 tbsp. corn flour
- 1 tbsp. nutritional yeast
- 1 tsp. garlic, minced
- 1 tsp. salt
- 2 slices bread, toasted and made into bread crumbs

Instructions

1) In a mixing bowl, combine all the ingredients except the bread crumbs.
2) Create small balls and roll over the bread crumbs.
3) Place the spinach balls inside the air fryer and cook at 390°F for 10 minutes.

Nutrition information:

Calories per serving: 115; Carbohydrates: 14.01g; Protein: 7.35g; Fat: 3.33g

Sweet 'n Nutty Marinated Cauliflower-Tofu

Serves: 2, Cooking Time: 20 minutes

Ingredients

- ¼ cup brown sugar
- ¼ cup low sodium soy sauce
- ½ tsp. chili garlic sauce
- 1 package extra firm tofu, pressed to release extra water and cut into cubes
- 1 small head cauliflower, cut into florets
- 1 tbsp. sesame oil
- 2 ½ tbsps. almond butter
- 2 cloves of garlic, minced

Instructions

1) Place the garlic, sesame oil, soy sauce, sugar, chili garlic sauce, and almond butter in a mixing bowl. Whisk until well combined.
2) Place the tofu cubes and cauliflower in the marinade and allow to soak up the sauce for at least 30 minutes.
3) Preheat the air fryer to 400°F. Add tofu and cauliflower. Coo for 20 minutes. Shake basket halfway through cooking time.
4) Meanwhile, place the remaining marinade in a saucepan and bring to a boil over medium heat. Adjust the heat to low once boiling and stir until the sauce thickens.
5) Pour the sauce over the tofu and cauliflower.
6) Serve with rice or noodles.

Nutrition information:

Calories per serving: 365; Carbohydrates: 40.1g; Protein: 9.85g; Fat: 18.38g

Tender Butternut Squash Fry

Serves: 2, Cooking Time: 10 minutes

Ingredients
- 1 tbsp. cooking oil
- 1-pound butternut squash, seeded and sliced
- Salt and pepper to taste

Instructions
1) Place the grill pan accessory in the air fryer.
2) In a bowl, place all Ingredients: and toss to coat and season the squash.
3) Place in the grill pan.
4) Close the air fryer and cook for 10 minutes at 330°F.

Nutrition information:
Calories per serving: 171; Carbs: 28.6g; Protein: 2.7g; Fat: 7.1g

Tofu Bites Soaked in Chili-Ginger Peanut Butter

Serves: 3, Cooking Time: 15 minutes

Ingredients
- ¼ cup liquid aminos
- ¼ cup maple syrup
- 1 block extra firm tofu, pressed to remove excess water and cut into cubes
- 1 sprig cilantro, chopped
- 1 tsp. red pepper flakes
- 1 tsp. sesame seeds
- 1-inch fresh ginger, peeled and grated
- 2 cloves of garlic, minced
- 2 tbsps. rice wine vinegar
- 2 tbsps. sesame oil
- 3 tbsp. chili garlic sauce
- 3 tbsps. peanut butter
- toasted peanuts, chopped

Instructions
1) Place the first 9 ingredients in a mixing bowl and whisk until combined. Pour in a Ziploc bag and add the tofu cubes. Marinate for at least 30 minutes.
2) Preheat the air fryer to 425°F.
3) Save the marinade for the sauce and place the marinated tofu cubes in the air fryer. Cook for 15 minutes.
4) Pour the marinade in a sauce pan and heat over medium flame until reduced in half.
5) Place the cooked tofu on top of steaming rice and pour over the sauce. Garnish with toasted peanuts, sesame seeds and cilantro.

Nutrition information:
Calories per serving: 484; Carbohydrates: 32.42g; Protein: 20.11g; Fat: 30.43g

Twice-Fried Cauliflower Tater Tots

Serves: 12, Cooking Time: 16 minutes

Ingredients

- ½ cup bread crumbs
- ½ cup nutritional yeast
- 1 flax egg (1 tbsp. 3 tbsp. desiccated coconuts
- 1 onion, chopped
- 1 tsp. chives, chopped
- 1 tsp. garlic, minced
- 1 tsp. oregano, chopped
- 1 tsp. parsley, chopped
- 1-pound cauliflower, steamed and chopped
- 3 tbsps. oats
- flaxseed meal + 3 tbsp. water)
- salt and pepper to taste

Instructions

1) Preheat the air fryer to 390°F.
2) Place the steamed cauliflower on a paper towel and ring to remove excess water.
3) Place in a mixing bowl and add the rest of the ingredients except the bread crumbs.
4) Mix until well combined and form balls using your hands.
5) Roll the tater tots on the bread crumbs and place in the air fryer basket.
6) Cook for 6 minutes. Once done, increase the cooking temperature to 400°F and cook for another 10 minutes.

Nutrition information:
Calories per serving: 47; Carbohydrates: 7.54g; Protein: 4.19g; Fat: 0.52g

Vegetarian Sushi Rice Bowl

Serves: 4, Cooking Time: 10 minutes

Ingredients

- ¼ cup cucumber, sliced
- 1 tbsp. coconut sugar
- 1 tbsp. mirin rice wine
- 1 tbsp. sesame seeds, toasted
- 1 tsp. salt
- 3 medium-sized eggplants, sliced
- 3 tbsps. sweet white miso paste
- 4 cups sushi rice, cooked
- 4 spring onions
- 7 tbsps. Japanese rice vinegar

Instructions

1) Prepare the cucumber pickles by mixing the cucumber, salt, sugar, and rice wine vinegar. Place a dish on top of the bowl to weight it down completely.
2) Preheat the air fryer to 400°F.
3) In a mixing bowl, combine the eggplants, miso paste, and mirin rice wine. Marinate for 30 minutes.
4) Place the eggplant slices in the air fryer and cook for 10 minutes.
5) Assemble the rice bowl by placing eggplants and pickled cucumbers on top of the rice.
6) Garnish with spring onions and sesame seeds.

Nutrition information:
Calories per serving: 351; Carbohydrates: 78.8g; Protein: 7.4g; Fat: 2.2g

Veggie Wontons with Chili-Oil Seasoning

Serves: 4, Cooking Time: 10 minutes

Ingredients
- ½ cup chopped mushrooms
- ½ cup grated carrots
- ½ cup grated white onion
- ½ tsp. white pepper
- ¾ cup chopped red pepper
- ¾ cup grated cabbage
- 1 tbsp. chili sauce
- 1 tsp. garlic powder
- 2 tbsps. olive oil
- 30 wonton wrappers
- Salt to taste
- Water for sealing wontons

Instructions
1) In a skillet over medium heat, place all vegetables and cook until all moisture have been released from the vegetables.
2) Remove from the heat and season with chili sauce, garlic powder, white pepper, and salt.
3) Put wanton wrapper on a working surface and add a tbsp. of the vegetable mixture in the middle of the wrapper. Wet the edges of the wonton wrapper with water and fold the wrapper to close.
4) Brush with oil and place in the double layer rack.
5) Place the rack with the wonton in the air fryer.
6) Close the air fryer and cook for 10 minutes at 330°F.

Nutrition information:
Calories per serving: 287; Carbs: 44.3g; Protein: 7.4g; Fat: 8.8g

Vegie Grill Recipe with Tandoori Spice

Serves: 6, Cooking Time: 20 minutes

Ingredients
- ½ head cauliflower, cut into florets
- ½ cup yogurt
- 1 carrot, peeled and shaved to 1/8-inch thick
- 1 cup young ears of corn
- 1 handful sugar snap peas
- 1 small zucchini, cut into thick slices
- 1 yellow sweet pepper, seeded and chopped
- 2 small onions, cut into wedges
- 2 tbsps. canola oil
- 2-inch fresh ginger, minced
- 3 tbsps. Tandoori spice blend
- 6 cloves of garlic, minced

Instructions
1) Preheat the air fryer to 330°F.
2) Place the grill pan accessory in the air fryer.
3) In a Ziploc bag, put all Ingredients: and give a shake to season all vegetables.

4) Dump all Ingredients: on the grill pan and cook for 20 minutes.
5) Make sure to give the vegetables a shake halfway through the cooking time.

Nutrition information:
Calories per serving:126 ; Carbs: 17.9g; Protein: 2.9g; Fat: 6.1g

Your Traditional Mac 'n Cheese

Serves: 3, Cooking Time: 32 minutes

Ingredients
- 1/2 pinch ground nutmeg
- 1/2 tsp. Dijon mustard
- 1/2 tsp. salt
- 1/4 cup panko bread crumbs
- 1/8 tsp. cayenne pepper
- 1/8 tsp. dried thyme
- 1/8 tsp. white pepper
- 1/8 tsp. Worcestershire sauce
- 1-1/2 cups milk
- 1-1/2 cups shredded sharp Cheddar cheese, divided
- 1-1/2 tsps. butter, melted
- 2 tbsps. all-purpose flour
- 2 tbsps. butter
- 8-ounce elbow macaroni, cooked according to package Instructions

Instructions
1) Melt 2 tbsp butter in baking pan of air fryer for 2 minutes at 360°F. Stir in flour and cook for 3 minutes, stirring every now and then. Stir in white pepper, cayenne pepper, and thyme. Cook for 2 minutes. Stir in a cup of milk and whisk well. Cook for 5 minutes while mixing constantly.
2) Mix in salt, Worcestershire sauce, and nutmeg . Mix well. Cook for 5 minutes or until thickened while stirring frequently.
3) Add cheese and mix well. Cook for 3 minutes or until melted and thoroughly mixed.
4) Stir in Dijon mustard and mix well. Add macaroni and toss well to coat. Sprinkle remaining cheese on top.
5) In a small bowl mix well 1 ½ tsp butter and panko. Sprinkle on top of cheese.
6) Cook for 15 minutes at 390°F until tops are lightly browned.
7) Serve and enjoy.

Nutrition information:
Calories per Serving: 700; Carbs: 72.8g; Protein: 29.4g; Fat: 32.3g

Zucchini garlic-Sour Cream Bake

Serves: 5, Cooking Time: 20 minutes

Ingredients
- 1 (8 ounce) package cream cheese, softened
- 1 cup sour cream
- 1 large zucchini, cut lengthwise then in half
- 1 tbsp. minced garlic
- 1/4 cup grated Parmesan cheese

- paprika to taste

Instructions
1) Lightly grease baking pan of air fryer with cooking spray.
2) Place zucchini slices in a single layer in pan.
3) In a bowl whisk well, remaining Ingredients: except for paprika. Spread on top of zucchini slices. Sprinkle paprika.
4) Cover pan with foil.
5) For 10 minutes, cook on 390°F.
6) Remove foil and cook for 10 minutes at 330°F.
7) Serve and enjoy.

Nutrition information:
Calories per Serving: 296; Carbs: 6.5g; Protein: 7.3g; Fat: 26.7g

Zucchini Topped with Coconut Cream 'n Bacon

Serves: 3, Cooking Time: 20 minutes

Ingredients
- 1 tbsp. lemon juice
- 3 slices bacon, fried and crumbled
- 3 tbsps. olive oil
- 3 zucchini squashes
- 4 tbsps. coconut cream
- Salt and pepper to taste

Instructions
1) Preheat the air fryer for 5 minutes.
2) Line up chopsticks on both sides of the zucchini and slice thinly until you hit the stick. Brush the zucchinis with olive oil. Set aside.
3) Place the zucchini in the air fryer. Bake for 20 minutes at 350°F.
4) Meanwhile, combine the coconut cream and lemon juice in a mixing bowl. Season with salt and pepper to taste.
5) Once the zucchini is cooked, scoop the coconut cream mixture and drizzle on top.
6) Sprinkle with bacon bits.

Nutrition information:
Calories per serving: 345; Carbohydrates: 9.4g; Protein: 6.6g; Fat: 31.2g

Chapter 4 Air Fryer Meat Recipes

3-Cheese Meatball and Pasta

Serves: 5, Cooking Time: 40 minutes

Ingredients

- 1 jar (24 ounces) pasta sauce with meat
- 1 large Egg, lightly beaten
- 1 small onion, chopped
- 1 tbsp. brown sugar
- 1 tbsp. Italian seasoning
- 1 tsp. garlic powder
- 1/2 carton (15 ounces) part-skim ricotta cheese
- 1/2 package (12 ounces) frozen fully cooked Italian meatballs, thawed
- 1/2 package (16 ounces) mostaccioli, cooked according to package Instructions and drained
- 1/2-pound ground beef
- 1/4 cup grated Romano cheese
- 1/4 cup shaved Parmesan cheese
- 1/4 tsp. pepper
- Minced fresh parsley or fresh baby arugula, optional

Instructions

1) Lightly grease baking pan of air fryer with cooking spray. Add beef and onions.
2) Cook for 10 minutes at 330°F, stirring and crumbling halfway through cooking time.
3) Drain excess fat. Stir in sugar and seasoning.
4) Mix in pasta and sauce. Mix well.
5) Remove half of mixture and transfer to a plate. Evenly spread half of ricotta mixture and half of Romano cheese. Return half of pasta. Evenly spread remaining ricotta and Romano. Top with meatballs and Parmesan.
6) Cover with foil.
7) For 20 minutes, cook on 390°F.
8) Remove foil cook for 10 minutes more until tops are lightly browned.
9) Serve and enjoy.

Nutrition information:

Calories per Serving: 563; Carbs: 55.0g; Protein: 34.0g; Fat: 23.0g

Air Fried Grilled Steak

Serves: 2, Cooking Time: 45 minutes

Ingredients
- 2 top sirloin steaks
- 3 tbsps. butter, melted
- 3 tbsps. olive oil
- Salt and pepper to taste

Instructions
1) Preheat the air fryer for 5 minutes.
2) Season the sirloin steaks with olive oil, salt and pepper.
3) Place the beef in the air fryer basket.
4) Cook for 45 minutes at 350°F.
5) Once cooked, serve with butter.

Nutrition information:
Calories per serving: 1536; Carbohydrates: 2.1g; Protein: 103.4g; Fat: 123.7g

Air Fried Roast Beef

Serves: 8, Cooking Time: 2 hours

Ingredients
- 1 large onion, quartered
- 1 tbsp. fresh rosemary
- 1 tbsp. fresh thyme
- 2 tbsps. Worcestershire sauce
- 3 cups beef broth
- 3 pounds bone-in beef roast
- 4 tbsps. olive oil
- Salt and pepper to taste

Instructions
1) Preheat the air fryer for 5 minutes.
2) Place all ingredients in a baking dish that will fit in the air fryer.
3) Place the dish in the air fryer and cook for 2 hours at 325°F.

Nutrition information:
Calories per serving: 574; Carbohydrates: 2.1g; Protein: 38.1g; Fat: 45.9g

Air Fried Steak

Serves: 4, Cooking Time: 15 minutes

Ingredients
- 2 pounds rib eye steak
- 3 tbsps. olive oil
- A dash of rosemary
- Salt and pepper to taste

Instructions
1) Place all ingredients in a Ziploc bag and allow to marinate in the fridge for at least 2 hours.
2) Preheat the air fryer.
3) Place the steak in the air fryer and cook for 15 minutes at 400°F.

Nutrition information:
Calories per serving: 687; Carbohydrates: 1.1g; Protein: 40.7g; Fat: 57.8g

Air Fryer Beef Casserole

Serves: 4, Cooking Time: 30 minutes

Ingredients

- 1 green bell pepper, seeded and chopped
- 1 onion, chopped
- 1-pound ground beef
- 3 cloves of garlic, minced
- 3 tbsps. olive oil
- 6 cups eggs, beaten
- Salt and pepper to taste

Instructions

1) Preheat the air fryer for 5 minutes.
2) In a baking dish that will fit in the air fryer, mix the ground beef, onion, garlic, olive oil, and bell pepper. Season with salt and pepper to taste.
3) Pour in the beaten eggs and give a good stir.
4) Place the dish with the beef and egg mixture in the air fryer.
5) Bake for 30 minutes at 325°F.

Nutrition information:

Calories per serving: 1520; Carbohydrates: 10.4g; Protein: 87.9g; Fat: 125.11g

Almond Flour 'n Egg Crusted Beef

Serves: 1, Cooking Time: 15 minutes

Ingredients

- ½ cup almond flour
- 1 egg, beaten
- 1 slice of lemon, to serve
- 1/2-pound beef schnitzel
- 2 tbsps. vegetable oil

Instructions

1) Preheat the air fryer for 5 minutes.
2) Mix the oil and almond flour together.
3) Dip the schnitzel into the egg and dredge in the almond flour mixture.
4) Press the almond flour so that it sticks on to the beef.
5) Place in the air fryer and cook for 15 minutes at 350°F.
6) Serve with a slice of lemon.

Nutrition information:

Calories per serving: 732; Carbohydrates: 1.1g; Protein: 55.6g; Fat: 56.1g

Another Easy Teriyaki BBQ Recipe

Serves: 2, Cooking Time: 15 minutes

Ingredients

- 1 tbsp honey
- 1 tbsp mirin
- 1 tbsp soy sauce
- 1 thumb-sized piece of fresh ginger, grated

- 14 oz lean diced steak, with fat trimmed

Instructions
1) Mix all Ingredients in a bowl and marinate for at least an hour. Turning over halfway through marinating time.
2) Thread mead into skewers. Place on skewer rack.
3) Cook for 5 minutes at 390°F or to desired doneness.
4) Serve and enjoy.

Nutrition information:
Calories per Serving: 460; Carbs: 10.6g; Protein: 55.8g; Fat: 21.6g

Apricot Glazed Pork Tenderloins

Serves: 3, Cooking Time: 30 minutes

Ingredients
- 1 tsp. salt
- 1/2 tsp. pepper
- 1-lb pork tenderloin
- 2 tbsps. minced fresh rosemary or 1 tbsp. dried rosemary, crushed
- 2 tbsps. olive oil, divided
- 4 garlic cloves, minced

Apricot Glaze Ingredients
- 1 cup apricot preserves
- 2 garlic cloves, minced
- 3 tbsps. lemon juice

Instructions
1) Mix well pepper, salt, garlic, oil, and rosemary. Brush all over pork. If needed cut pork crosswise in half to fit in air fryer.
2) Lightly grease baking pan of air fryer with cooking spray. Add pork.
3) For 3 minutes per side, brown pork in a preheated 390°F air fryer.
4) Meanwhile, mix well all glaze Ingredients in a small bowl. Baste pork every 5 minutes.
5) Cook for 20 minutes at 330°F.
6) Serve and enjoy.

Nutrition information:
Calories per Serving: 281; Carbs: 27.0g; Protein: 23.0g; Fat: 9.0g

Baby Back Rib Recipe from Kansas City

Serves: 2, Cooking Time: 50 minutes

Ingredients
- ¼ cup apple cider vinegar
- ¼ cup molasses
- ¼ tsp. cayenne pepper
- 1 cup ketchup
- 1 tbsp. brown sugar
- 1 tbsp. liquid smoke seasoning, hickory
- 1 tbsp. Worcestershire sauce
- 1 tsp. dry mustard
- 1-pound pork ribs, small

- 2 cloves of garlic
- Salt and pepper to taste

Instructions
1) Place all ingredients in a Ziploc bag and allow to marinate in the fridge for at least 2 hours.
2) Preheat the air fryer to 390°F.
3) Place the grill pan accessory in the air fryer.
4) Grill meat for 25 minutes per batch.
5) Flip the meat halfway through the cooking time.
6) Pour the marinade in a saucepan and allow to simmer until the sauce thickens.
7) Pour glaze over the meat before serving.

Nutrition information:
Calories per serving: 634; Carbs: 32g; Protein: 32g; Fat: 42g

Bacon, Spinach & Feta Quiche

Serves: 3, Cooking Time: 30 minutes

Ingredients
- 6 eggs
- salt and freshly ground black pepper to taste
- 3 slices bacon, chopped
- 1 1/2 tsps. butter
- 1/2-pound fresh spinach
- 1/2 pinch cayenne pepper
- 1/2 pinch salt
- 1-1/2 ounces crumbled feta cheese
- 1/4 onion, diced

Instructions
1) Lightly grease baking pan of air fryer with butter. Add spinach and for 2 minutes, cook on 360°F.
2) Drain well the spinach and squeeze dry. Chop and set aside.
3) Add bacon in air fryer pan and cook for 6 minutes or until crisped. Discard excess fat.
4) Stir in onion and season with salt. Cook for another 5 minutes. Stir in chopped spinach and cook for another 5 minutes to heat through.
5) Meanwhile, in a bowl whisk well eggs, cayenne pepper, black pepper, and salt.
6) Remove basket, evenly spread mixture in pan, and pour in eggs. Sprinkle feta cheese on top.
7) Cook for another 15 minutes, until eggs are cooked to desired doneness.
8) Serve and enjoy.

Nutrition information:
Calories per Serving: 273; Carbs: 5.1g; Protein: 20.3g; Fat: 19.0g

Bacon-Cheeseburger Casserole

Serves: 6, Cooking Time: 35 minutes

Ingredients
- 1 small onion, chopped
- 1 tbsp. ground mustard
- 1 tbsp. Worcestershire sauce
- 1/2 can (15 ounces) tomato sauce
- 1/2 cup grape tomatoes, chopped
- 1/2 cup shredded cheddar cheese
- 1/4 cup sliced dill pickles
- 1-pound ground beef
- 4-ounces process cheese (Velveeta)
- 6 bacon strips, cooked and crumbled
- 8-ounces frozen Tater Tots

Instructions
1) Lightly grease baking pan of air fryer with cooking spray. Add beef and half of onions.
2) For 10 minutes, cook on 390°F. Halfway through cooking time, stir and crumble beef.
3) Stir in Worcestershire, mustard, Velveeta, and tomato sauce. Mix well. Cook for 4 minutes until melted.
4) Mix well and evenly spread in pan. Top with cheddar cheese and then bacon strips.
5) Evenly top with tater tots. Cover pan with foil.
6) Cook for 15 minutes at 390°F. Uncover and bake for 10 minutes more until tops are lightly browned.
7) Serve and enjoy topped with pickles and tomatoes and remaining onion.

Nutrition information:
Calories per Serving: 483; Carbs: 24.0g; Protein: 27.0g; Fat: 31.0g

Baked Cheese 'n Pepperoni Calzone

Serves: 4, Cooking Time: 25 minutes

Ingredients
- 1 cup chopped pepperoni
- 1 loaf (1 pound) frozen bread dough, thawed
- 1 to 2 tbsps. 2% milk
- 1 tbsp. grated Parmesan cheese
- 1/2 cup pasta sauce with meat
- 1/2 tsp. Italian seasoning, optional
- 1/4 cup shredded part-skim mozzarella cheese

Instructions
1) In a bowl mix well mozzarella cheese, pizza sauce, and pepperoni.
2) On a lightly floured surface, divide dough into four portions. Roll each into a 6-in. circle; top each with a scant 1/3 cup pepperoni mixture. Fold dough over filling; pinch edges to seal.

3) Lightly grease baking pan of air fryer with cooking spray. Place dough in a single layer and if needed, cook in batches.
4) For 25 minutes, cook on 330°F preheated air fryer or until dough is lightly browned.
5) Serve and enjoy.

Nutrition information:
Calories per Serving: 527; Carbs: 59.0g; Protein: 21.0g; Fat: 23.0g

Balsamic Glazed Pork Chops

Serves: 4, Cooking Time: 50 minutes

Ingredients
- ¾ cup balsamic vinegar
- 1 ½ tbsps. sugar
- 1 tbsp. butter
- 3 tbsps. olive oil
- 3 tbsps. salt
- 4 pork rib chops

Instructions
1) Place all ingredients in bowl and allow the meat to marinate in the fridge for at least 2 hours.
2) Preheat the air fryer to 390°F.
3) Place the grill pan accessory in the air fryer.
4) Grill the pork chops for 20 minutes making sure to flip the meat every 10 minutes for even grilling.
5) Meanwhile, pour the balsamic vinegar on a saucepan and allow to simmer for at least 10 minutes until the sauce thickens.
6) Brush the meat with the glaze before serving.

Nutrition information:
Calories per serving: 274; Carbs: 11g; Protein: 17g; Fat: 18g

Beef Brisket Recipe from Texas

Serves: 8, Cooking Time: 1 hour and 30 minutes

Ingredients
- 1 ½ cup beef stock
- 1 bay leaf
- 1 tbsp. garlic powder
- 1 tbsp. onion powder
- 2 pounds beef brisket, trimmed
- 2 tbsps. chili powder
- 2 tsps. dry mustard
- 4 tbsps. olive oil
- Salt and pepper to taste

Instructions
1) Preheat the air fryer for 5 minutes.
2) Place all ingredients in a deep baking dish that will fit in the air fryer.

3) Bake for 1 hour and 30 minutes at 400°F.
4) Stir the beef every after 30 minutes to soak in the sauce.

Nutrition information:
Calories per serving: 306; Carbohydrates: 3.8g; Protein: 18.3g; Fat: 24.1g

Beef Recipe Texas-Rodeo Style

Serves: 6, Cooking Time: 1 hour

Ingredients
- ½ cup honey
- ½ cup ketchup
- ½ tsp. dry mustard
- 1 clove of garlic, minced
- 1 tbsp. chili powder
- 2 onion, chopped
- 3 pounds beef steak sliced
- Salt and pepper to taste

Instructions
1) Place all ingredients in a Ziploc bag and allow to marinate in the fridge for at least 2 hours.
2) Preheat the air fryer to 390°F.
3) Place the grill pan accessory in the air fryer.
4) Grill the beef for 15 minutes per batch making sure that you flip it every 8 minutes for even grilling.
5) Meanwhile, pour the marinade on a saucepan and allow to simmer over medium heat until the sauce thickens.
6) Baste the beef with the sauce before serving.

Nutrition information:
Calories per serving: 542; Carbs: 49g; Protein: 37g; Fat: 22g

Beef Roast in Worcestershire-Rosemary

Serves: 6, Cooking Time: 2 hours

Ingredients
- 1 onion, chopped
- 1 tbsp. butter
- 1 tbsp. Worcestershire sauce
- 1 tsp. rosemary
- 1 tsp. thyme
- 1-pound beef chuck roast
- 2 cloves of garlic, minced
- 2 tbsps. olive oil
- 3 cups water
- 3 stalks of celery, sliced

Instructions

1) Preheat the air fryer for 5 minutes.
2) Place all ingredients in a deep baking dish that will fit in the air fryer.
3) Bake for 2 hours at 350°F.
4) Braise the meat with its sauce every 30 minutes until cooked.

Nutrition information:
Calories per serving: 260; Carbohydrates: 2.9g; Protein: 17.5g; Fat: 19.8

Beefy 'n Cheesy Spanish Rice Casserole

Serves: 3, Cooking Time: 50 minutes

Ingredients

- 2 tbsps. chopped green bell pepper
- 1 tbsp. chopped fresh cilantro
- 1/2-pound lean ground beef
- 1/2 cup water
- 1/2 tsp. salt
- 1/2 tsp. brown sugar
- 1/2 pinch ground black pepper
- 1/3 cup uncooked long grain rice
- 1/4 cup finely chopped onion
- 1/4 cup chile sauce
- 1/4 tsp. ground cumin
- 1/4 tsp. Worcestershire sauce
- 1/4 cup shredded Cheddar cheese
- 1/2 (14.5 ounce) can canned tomatoes

Instructions

1) Lightly grease baking pan of air fryer with cooking spray. Add ground beef. For 10 minutes, cook on 360°F. Halfway through cooking time, stir and crumble beef. Discard excess fat,
2) Stir in pepper, Worcestershire sauce, cumin, brown sugar, salt, chile sauce, rice, water, tomatoes, green bell pepper, and onion. Mix well. Cover pan with foil and cook for 25 minutes. Stirring occasionally.
3) Give it one last good stir, press down firmly and sprinkle cheese on top.
4) Cook uncovered for 15 minutes at 390°F until tops are lightly browned.
5) Serve and enjoy with chopped cilantro.

Nutrition information:
Calories per Serving: 346; Carbs: 24.9g; Protein: 18.5g; Fat: 19.1g

Beefy Bell Pepper 'n Egg Scramble

Serves: 4, Cooking Time: 30 minutes

Ingredients

- 1 green bell pepper, seeded and chopped
- 1 onion, chopped
- 1-pound ground beef
- 3 cloves of garlic, minced
- 3 tbsps. olive oil
- 6 cups eggs, beaten
- Salt and pepper to taste

Instructions

1) Preheat the air fryer for 5 minutes with baking pan insert.
2) In a baking dish mix the ground beef, onion, garlic, olive oil, and bell pepper. Season with salt and pepper to taste.
3) Pour in the beaten eggs and give a good stir.
4) Place the dish with the beef and egg mixture in the air fryer.
5) Bake for 30 minutes at 330°F.

Nutrition information:
Calories per serving: 579; Carbs: 14.5g; Protein: 65.8g; Fat: 28.6g

Beefy Steak Topped with Chimichurri Sauce

Serves: 6, Cooking Time: 60 minutes

Ingredients

- 1 cup commercial chimichurri
- 3 pounds steak
- Salt and pepper to taste

Instructions

1) Place all ingredients in a Ziploc bag and marinate in the fridge for 2 hours.
2) Preheat the air fryer to 390°F.
3) Place the grill pan accessory in the air fryer.
4) Grill the skirt steak for 20 minutes per batch.
5) Flip the steak every 10 minutes for even grilling.

Nutrition information:

Calories per serving: 507; Carbs: 2.8g; Protein: 63g; Fat: 27g

Bourbon-BBQ Sauce Marinated Beef BBQ

Serves: 4, Cooking Time: 60 minutes

Ingredients

- ¼ cup bourbon
- ¼ cup barbecue sauce
- 1 tbsp. Worcestershire sauce
- 2 pounds beef steak, pounded
- Salt and pepper to taste

Instructions

1) Place all ingredients in a Ziploc bag and allow to marinate in the fridge for at least 2 hours.
2) Preheat the air fryer to 390°F.
3) Place the grill pan accessory in the air fryer.
4) Place on the grill pan and cook for 20 minutes per batch.
5) Halfway through the cooking time, give a stir to cook evenly.
6) Meanwhile, pour the marinade on a saucepan and allow to simmer until the sauce thickens.
7) Serve beef with the bourbon sauce.

Nutrition information:

Calories per serving: 346; Carbs: 9.8g; Protein: 48.2g; Fat: 12.6g

Buttered Garlic-Thyme Roast Beef

Serves: 12, Cooking Time: 2 hours

Ingredients
- 1 ½ tbsp. garlic
- 1 cup beef stock
- 1 tsp. black pepper
- 1 tsp. salt
- 1 tsp. thyme leaves, chopped
- 3 tbsps. butter
- 3-pound eye of round roast
- 6 tbsps. olive oil

Instructions
1) Place in a Ziploc bag all the ingredients and allow to marinate in the fridge for 2 hours.
2) Preheat the air fryer for 5 minutes.
3) Transfer all ingredients in a baking dish that will fit in the air fryer.
4) Place in the air fryer and cook for 2 hours for 400°F.
5) Baste the beef with the sauce every 30 minutes.

Nutrition information:
Calories per serving: 273; Carbohydrates: 0.8g; Protein: 34.2g; Fat: 14.7g

Cajun 'n Coriander Seasoned Ribs

Serves: 4, Cooking Time: 1 hour

Ingredients
- ¼ cup brown sugar
- ½ tsp. lemon
- 1 tbsp. paprika
- 1 tbsp. salt
- 1 tsp. coriander seed powder
- 2 slabs spareribs
- 2 tbsps. onion powder
- 2 tsp. Cajun seasoning

Instructions
1) Preheat the air fryer to 390°F.
2) Place the grill pan accessory in the air fryer.
3) In a small bowl, combine the spaces.
4) Rub the spice mixture on to the spareribs.
5) Place the spareribs on the grill pan and cook for 20 minutes per batch.
6) Serve with your favorite barbecue sauce.

Nutrition information:
Calories per serving: 490; Carbs: 18.2g; Protein: 24.4g; Fat: 35.5g

Cajun Sweet-Sour Grilled Pork

Serves: 3, Cooking Time: 12 minutes

Ingredients
- ¼ cup brown sugar
- 1/4 cup cider vinegar
- 1-lb pork loin, sliced into 1-inch cubes
- 2 tbsps. Cajun seasoning
- 3 tbsps. brown sugar

Instructions
1) In a shallow dish, mix well pork loin, 3 tbsps. brown sugar, and Cajun seasoning. Toss well to coat. Marinate in the ref for 3 hours.
2) In a medium bowl mix well, brown sugar and vinegar for basting.
3) Thread pork pieces in skewers. Baste with sauce and place on skewer rack in air fryer.
4) For 12 minutes, cook on 360ºF. Halfway through cooking time, turnover skewers and baste with sauce. If needed, cook in batches.
5) Serve and enjoy.

Nutrition information:
Calories per Serving: 428; Carbs: 30.3g; Protein: 39.0g; Fat: 16.7g

Capers 'n Olives Topped Flank Steak

Serves: 4, Cooking Time: 45 minutes

Ingredients
- 1 anchovy fillet, minced
- 1 clove of garlic, minced
- 1 cup pitted olives
- 1 tbsp. capers, minced
- 1/3 cup olive oil
- 2 pounds flank steak, pounded
- 2 tbsps. fresh oregano
- 2 tbsps. garlic powder
- 2 tbsps. onion powder
- 2 tbsps. smoked paprika
- Salt and pepper to taste

Instructions
1) Preheat the air fryer to 390ºF.
2) Place the grill pan accessory in the air fryer.
3) Season the steak with salt and pepper. Rub the oregano, paprika, onion powder, and garlic powder all over the steak.
4) Place on the grill pan and cook for 45 minutes. Make sure to flip the meat every 10 minutes for even cooking.
5) Meanwhile, mix together the olive oil, olives, capers, garlic, and anchovy fillets.
6) Serve the steak with the tapenade.

Nutrition information:
Calories per serving: 553; Carbs: 11.6g; Protein: 51.5g; Fat: 33.4g

Caraway, Sichuan 'n Cumin Lamb Kebabs

Serves: 3, Cooking Time: 1 hour

Ingredients

- 1 ½ pounds lamb shoulder, bones removed and cut into pieces
- 1 tbsp. Sichuan peppercorns
- 1 tsp. sugar
- 2 tbsps. cumin seeds, toasted
- 2 tsps. caraway seeds, toasted
- 2 tsps. crushed red pepper flakes
- Salt and pepper to taste

Instructions

1) Place all ingredients in bowl and allow the meat to marinate in the fridge for at least 2 hours.
2) Preheat the air fryer to 390°F.
3) Place the grill pan accessory in the air fryer.
4) Grill the meat for 15 minutes per batch.
5) Flip the meat every 8 minutes for even grilling.

Nutrition information:
Calories per serving: 465; Carbs: 7.7g; Protein: 22.8g; Fat: 46.9g

Champagne-Vinegar Marinated Skirt Steak

Serves: 2, Cooking Time: 40 minutes

Ingredients

- ¼ cup Dijon mustard
- 1 tbsp. rosemary leaves
- 1-pound skirt steak, trimmed
- 2 tbsps. champagne vinegar
- Salt and pepper to taste

Instructions

1) Place all ingredients in a Ziploc bag and marinate in the fridge for 2 hours.
2) Preheat the air fryer to 390°F.
3) Place the grill pan accessory in the air fryer.
4) Grill the skirt steak for 20 minutes per batch.
5) Flip the beef halfway through the cooking time.

Nutrition information:
Calories per serving: 516; Carbs: 4.2g; Protein: 60.9g; Fat: 28.4g

Char-Grilled Skirt Steak with Fresh Herbs

Serves: 3, Cooking Time: 30 minutes

Ingredients

- 1 ½ pounds skirt steak, trimmed
- 1 tbsp. lemon zest
- 1 tbsp. olive oil
- 2 cups fresh herbs like tarragon, sage, and mint, chopped
- 4 cloves of garlic, minced
- Salt and pepper to taste

Instructions

1) Preheat the air fryer to 390°F.
2) Place the grill pan accessory in the air fryer.
3) Season the steak with salt, pepper, lemon zest, herbs, and garlic.

4) Brush with oil.
5) Grill for 15 minutes and if needed cook in batches.

Nutrition information:
Calories per serving: 478; Carbs: 18g; Protein: 25g; Fat: 34g

Charred Onions 'n Steak Cube BBQ

Serves: 3, Cooking Time: 40 minutes

Ingredients
- 1 cup red onions, cut into wedges
- 1 tbsp. dry mustard
- 1 tbsp. olive oil
- 1-pound boneless beef sirloin, cut into cubes
- Salt and pepper to taste

Instructions
1) Preheat the air fryer to 390°F.
2) Place the grill pan accessory in the air fryer.
3) Toss all ingredients in a bowl and mix until everything is coated with the seasonings.
4) Place on the grill pan and cook for 40 minutes.
5) Halfway through the cooking time, give a stir to cook evenly.

Nutrition information:
Calories per serving: 260; Carbs: 5.2g; Protein: 35.7g; Fat: 10.7g

Cheddar Cheese 'n Bacon Stuffed Pastry Pie

Serves: 3, Cooking Time: 18 minutes

Ingredients
- 1/2 cup bacon, cooked
- 1/2 cup cheddar cheese, shredded
- 1/2 cup sausage crumbles, cooked
- 5 eggs
- one box puff pastry sheets

Instructions
1) Scramble the eggs and cook.
2) Lightly grease baking pan of air fryer with cooking spray.
3) Evenly spread half of the puff sheets on bottom of pan.
4) Spread eggs, cooked sausage, crumbled bacon, and cheddar cheese.
5) Top with remaining puff pastry and gently push down with a fork.
6) Cover top of baking pan with foil.
7) For 8 minutes, cook on 330°F. Remove foil and continue cooking for another 5 minutes or until tops of puff pastry is golden brown.
8) Serve and enjoy.

Nutrition information:
Calories per Serving: 355; Carbs: 9.4g; Protein: 18.6g; Fat: 26.9g

Cheesy Ground Beef 'n Mac Taco Casserole

Serves: 5, Cooking Time: 25 minutes

Ingredients

- 1-ounce shredded Cheddar cheese
- 1-ounce shredded Monterey Jack cheese
- 2 tbsps. chopped green onions
- 1/2 (10.75 ounce) can condensed tomato soup
- 1/2-pound lean ground beef
- 1/2 cup crushed tortilla chips
- 1/4-pound macaroni, cooked according to manufacturer's Instructions
- 1/4 cup chopped onion
- 1/4 cup sour cream (optional)
- 1/2 (1.25 ounce) package taco seasoning mix
- 1/2 (14.5 ounce) can diced tomatoes

Instructions

1) Lightly grease baking pan of air fryer with cooking spray. Add onion and ground beef. For 10 minutes, cook on 360°F. Halfway through cooking time, stir and crumble ground beef.
2) Add taco seasoning, diced tomatoes, and tomato soup. Mix well. Mix in pasta.
3) Sprinkle crushed tortilla chips. Sprinkle cheese.
4) Cook for 15 minutes at 390°F until tops are lightly browned and cheese is melted.
5) Serve and enjoy.

Nutrition information:
Calories per Serving: 329; Carbs: 28.2g; Protein: 15.6g; Fat: 17.0g

Cheesy Herbs Burger Patties

Serves: 2, Cooking Time: 25 minutes

Ingredients

- ¼ cup cheddar cheese
- ½ tsp. dried rosemary, crushed
- 1-pound lean ground beef
- 2 green onions, sliced thinly
- 2 tbsps. chopped parsley
- 2 tbsps. ketchup
- 3 tbsps. Dijon mustard
- 3 tbsps. dry breadcrumbs
- Salt and pepper to taste

Instructions

1) In a mixing bowl, combine all ingredients except for the cheddar cheese.
2) Mix using your hands. Use your hands to make burger patties.
3) At the center of each patty, place a tbsp. of cheese and cover with the meat mixture.
4) Preheat the air fryer to 390°F.
5) Place the grill pan accessory and cook the patties for 25 minutes. Flip the patties halfway through the cooking time.

Nutrition information:
Calories per serving: 358; Carbs: 29g; Protein: 29g; Fat: 14g

Cheesy Potato Casserole the Amish Way

Serves: 6, Cooking Time: 45 minutes

Ingredients

- 2 cups frozen shredded hash brown potatoes, thawed
- 5 medium eggs, lightly beaten
- 1 cup shredded Cheddar cheese
- 1/2-pound sliced bacon, diced
- 1/2 sweet onion, chopped
- 1/2 cup and 2 tbsps. shredded Swiss cheese
- 3/4 cup small curd cottage cheese

Instructions

1) Lightly grease baking pan of air fryer with cooking spray.
2) For 10 minutes, cook on 330°F the onion and bacon. Discard excess fat.
3) Meanwhile, in a bowl, whisk well Swiss cheese, cottage cheese, cheddar cheese, eggs, and potatoes. Pour into pan of cooked bacon and mix well.
4) Cook for another 25 minutes.
5) Let it stand in air fryer for another 10 minutes.
6) Serve and enjoy.

Nutrition information:
Calories per Serving: 341; Carbs: 12.1g; Protein: 21.7g; Fat: 22.8g

Cheesy Sausage 'n Grits Bake From Down South

Serves: 4, Cooking Time: 30 minutes

Ingredients

- 1/2 cup uncooked grits
- 1/4-pound ground pork sausage
- 1-1/2 cups water
- 2 tbsps. butter, divided
- 2 tbsps. milk
- 3 eggs
- 3/4 cup shredded Cheddar cheese, divided
- salt and pepper to taste

Instructions

1) In a large saucepan bring water to a boil. Stir in grits and simmer until liquid is absorbed, around 5 minutes. Stir in ¼ cup cheese and 1 tbsp butter. Mix well until thoroughly incorporated.
2) Lightly grease baking pan of air fryer with cooking spray. Add pork sausage and for 5 minutes, cook on 360°F. Crumble sausage and discard excess fat.
3) Transfer grits into pan of sausage.
4) In a bowl whisk well, milk and eggs and pour into pan. Mix well.
5) Dot the top with butter and sprinkle cheese. Season with pepper and salt.
6) Cook until tops are browned, around 20 minutes.
7) Serve and enjoy.

Nutrition information:
Calories per Serving: 403; Carbs: 16.8g; Protein: 16.5g; Fat: 29.9g

Chili-Espresso Marinated Steak

Serves: 3, Cooking Time: 50 minutes

Ingredients
- ½ tsp. garlic powder
- 1 ½ pounds beef flank steak
- 1 tsp. instant espresso powder
- 2 tbsps. olive oil
- 2 tsps. chili powder
- Salt and pepper to taste

Instructions
1) Preheat the air fryer to 390°F.
2) Place the grill pan accessory in the air fryer.
3) Make the dry rub by mixing the chili powder, salt, pepper, espresso powder, and garlic powder.
4) Rub all over the steak and brush with oil.
5) Place on the grill pan and cook for 40 minutes.
6) Halfway through the cooking time, flip the beef to cook evenly.

Nutrition information:
Calories per serving: 249; Carbs: 4g; Protein: 20g; Fat: 17g

Chives on Bacon & Cheese Bake

Serves: 6, Cooking Time: 50 minutes

Ingredients
- 4 slices bread, crusts removed
- 1 cup egg substitute (such as Egg Beaters®)
- 1 tbsp. chopped fresh chives
- 6 slices cooked bacon, crumbled
- 1 cup Cheddar cheese
- 1 1/2 cups skim milk

Instructions
1) Cook bacon in baking pan of air fryer for 10 minutes at 360°F. Once done, discard excess fat and then crumble bacon.
2) In a bowl, whisk well eggs. Stir in milk and chives.
3) In same air fryer baking pan, evenly spread bread slices. Pour egg mixture over it. Top with bacon. Cover pan with foil and let it rest in the fridge for at least an hour.
4) Preheat air fryer to 330°F.
5) Cook while covered in foil for 20 minutes. Remove foil and sprinkle cheese. Continue cooking uncovered for another 15 minutes.
6) Serve and enjoy.

Nutrition information:
Calories per Serving: 207; Carbs: 12.1g; Protein: 15.3g; Fat: 10.8g

Cilantro-Mint Pork BBQ Thai Style

Serves: 3, Cooking Time: 15 minutes

Ingredients
- 1 minced hot chile
- 1 minced shallot
- 1-pound ground pork
- 2 tbsps. fish sauce
- 2 tbsps. lime juice
- 3 tbsps. basil
- 3 tbsps. chopped mint
- 3 tbsps. cilantro

Instructions

1) In a shallow dish, mix well all Ingredients with hands. Form into 1-inch ovals.
2) Thread ovals in skewers. Place on skewer rack in air fryer.
3) For 15 minutes, cook on 360°F. Halfway through cooking time, turnover skewers. If needed, cook in batches.
4) Serve and enjoy.

Nutrition information:
Calories per Serving: 455; Carbs: 2.5g; Protein: 40.2g; Fat: 31.5g

Coriander Lamb with Pesto 'n Mint Dip

Serves: 4, Cooking Time: 16 minutes

Ingredients
- 1 1/2 tsps. coriander seeds, ground in spice mill or in mortar with pestle
- 1 large red bell pepper, cut into 1-inch squares
- 1 small red onion, cut into 1-inch squares
- 1 tbsp. extra-virgin olive oil plus additional for brushing
- 1 tsp. coarse kosher salt
- 1-pound trimmed lamb meat, cut into 1 1/4-inch cubes
- 4 large garlic cloves, minced

Mint-Pesto Dip Ingredients
- 1 cup (packed) fresh mint leaves
- 2 tbsps. pine nuts
- 2 tbsps. freshly grated Parmesan cheese
- 1 tbsp. fresh lemon juice
- 1 medium garlic clove, peeled
- 1/2 cup (packed) fresh cilantro leaves
- 1/2 tsp. coarse kosher salt
- 1/2 cup (or more) extra-virgin olive oil

Instructions
1) In a blender, puree all dip Ingredients until smooth and creamy. Transfer to a bowl and set aside.
2) In a large bowl, mix well coriander, salt, garlic, and oil. Add lamb, toss well to coat. Marinate for at least an hour in the ref.
3) The thread lamb, bell pepper, and onion alternately in a skewer. Repeat until all Ingredients re used up. Place in skewer rack in air fryer.
4) For 8 minutes, cook on 390°F. Halfway through cooking time, turnover.
5) Serve and enjoy with sauce on the side.

Nutrition information:
Calories per Serving: 307; Carbs: 6.3g; Protein: 21.1g; Fat: 21.9

Coriander, Mustard 'n Cumin Rubbed Flank Steak

Serves: 3, Cooking Time: 45 minutes

Ingredients
- ½ tsp. coriander
- ½ tsp. ground cumin
- 1 ½ pounds flank steak
- 1 tbsp. chili powder

- 1 tbsp. paprika
- 1 tsp. garlic powder
- 1 tsp. mustard powder
- 2 tbsps. sugar
- 2 tsps. black pepper
- 2 tsps. salt

Instructions
1) Preheat the air fryer to 390°F.
2) Place the grill pan accessory in the air fryer.
3) In a small bowl, combine all the spices and rub all over the flank steak.
4) Place on the grill and cook for 15 minutes per batch.
5) Make sure to flip the meat every 8 minutes for even grilling.

Nutrition information:
Calories per serving: 330; Carbs: 10.2g; Protein:50 g; Fat:12.1 g

Cornbread, Ham 'n Eggs Frittata

Serves: 3, Cooking Time: 45 minutes

Ingredients
- 1 stalk celery, diced
- 1/2 (14.5 ounce) can chicken broth
- 1/2 (14-ounce) package seasoned cornbread stuffing mix
- 1/2 cup chopped onion
- 1/4 cup butter
- 1/4 cup water
- 1/4 tsp. paprika, for garnish
- 2 cups diced cooked ham
- 3 eggs
- 3/4 cup shredded Cheddar cheese

Instructions
1) Lightly grease baking pan of air fryer with cooking spray. Add celery and onions.
2) For 5 minutes, cook on 360°F. Open and stir in ham. Cook for another 5 minutes.
3) Open and stir in butter, water, and chicken broth. Mix well and continue cooking for another 5 minutes.
4) Toss in stuffing mix and toss well to coat. Cover pan with foil.
5) Cook for another 15 minutes.
6) Remove foil and make 3 indentation in the stuffing to hold an egg. Break an egg in each hole.
7) Cook uncovered for another 10 minutes or until egg is cooked to desired doneness.
8) Sprinkle with cheese and paprika. Let it stand in air fryer for another 5 minutes.
9) Serve and enjoy.

Nutrition information:
Calories per Serving: 847; Carbs: 54.4g; Protein: 37.5g; Fat: 53.2g

Country Style Sausage & Hash Browns

Serves: 4, Cooking Time: 45 minutes

Ingredients

- 1 cup shredded Cheddar cheese
- 1 stalk green onion, chopped
- 1/2 (2.64-ounce) package country gravy mix
- 1/2 cup milk
- 3 eggs, lightly beaten
- 8-ounce bulk breakfast sausage
- 8-ounce package hash brown potatoes
- A dash of paprika or to taste (optional)

Instructions

1) Lightly grease baking pan of air fryer with cooking spray.
2) For 10 minutes, cook sausage and crumble at 360°F. Halfway through cooking time, open air fryer and continue crumbling sausage.
3) Once done cooking remove excess oil.
4) Stir in green onions and evenly spread crumbled sausage. Spread hash brown on top and sprinkle evenly with cheese.
5) In a bowl, whisk well gravy, milk, and eggs until smooth. Pour over cheese mixture. Sprinkle top with paprika.
6) Cover pan with foil.
7) Cook for 20 minutes, remove foil and cook for another 10 minutes.
8) Let it stand for 5 minutes.
9) Serve and enjoy.

Nutrition information:
Calories per Serving: 406; Carbs: 13.3g; Protein: 21.7g; Fat: 29.5g

Creamy Burger & Potato Bake

Serves: 3, Cooking Time: 55 minutes

Ingredients

- salt to taste
- freshly ground pepper, to taste
- 1/2 (10.75 ounce) can condensed cream of mushroom soup
- 1/2-pound lean ground beef
- 1-1/2 cups peeled and thinly sliced potatoes
- 1/2 cup shredded Cheddar cheese
- 1/4 cup chopped onion
- 1/4 cup and 2 tbsps. milk

Instructions

1) Lightly grease baking pan of air fryer with cooking spray. Add ground beef. For 10 minutes, cook on 360°F. Stir and crumble halfway through cooking time.
2) Meanwhile, in a bowl, whisk well pepper, salt, milk, onion, and mushroom soup. Mix well.
3) Drain fat off ground beef and transfer beef to a plate.
4) In same air fryer baking pan, layer ½ of potatoes on bottom, then ½ of soup mixture, and then ½ of beef. Repeat process.
5) Cover pan with foil.
6) Cook for 30 minutes. Remove foil and cook for another 15 minutes or until potatoes are tender.
7) Serve and enjoy.

Nutrition information:
Calories per Serving: 399; Carbs: 17.1g; Protein: 22.1g; Fat: 26.9g

Crispy Fried Pork Chops the Southern Way

Serves: 4, Cooking Time: 25 minutes

Ingredients
- ½ cup all-purpose flour
- ½ cup low fat buttermilk
- ½ tsp. black pepper
- 1 ½ tsp. Tabasco sauce
- 1 tsp. paprika
- 4 bone-in pork chops

Instructions
1) Place the buttermilk and hot sauce in a Ziploc bag and add the pork chops. Allow to marinate for at least an hour in the fridge.
2) In a bowl, combine the flour, paprika, and black pepper.
3) Remove pork from the Ziploc bag and dredge in the flour mixture.
4) Preheat the air fryer to 390°F.
5) Spray the pork chops with cooking oil.
6) Place in the air fryer basket and cook for 25 minutes.

Nutrition information:
Calories per serving: 427; Carbs:12.6 g; Protein: 46.4g; Fat: 21.2g

Crispy Roast Garlic-Salt Pork

Serves: 4, Cooking Time: 45 minutes

Ingredients
- 1 tsp. Chinese five spice powder
- 1 tsp. white pepper
- 2 pounds pork belly
- 2 tsps. garlic salt

Instructions
1) Preheat the air fryer to 390°F.
2) Mix all the spices in a bowl to create the dry rub.
3) Score the skin of the pork belly with a knife and season the entire pork with the spice rub.
4) Place in the air fryer basket and cook for 40 to 45 minutes until the skin is crispy.
5) Chop before serving.

Nutrition information:
Calories per serving: 785; Carbs: 0.7g; Protein: 14.2g; Fat: 80.7g

Cumin 'n Chili Rubbed Steak Fajitas

Serves: 2, Cooking Time: 25 minutes

Ingredients
- ¼ tsp. chili powder
- ¼ tsp. oregano
- ½ cup cotija cheese
- ½ medium red onion, chopped
- ½ tsp. ground cumin
- 1 small bell pepper

- 1-pound sliced beef, cut into strips
- 2 chopped serrano peppers
- 2 tbsps. olive oil
- Corn tortillas
- Salt and pepper to taste

Instructions
1) Preheat the air fryer to 390°F.
2) Place the grill pan accessory in the air fryer.
3) In a mixing bowl, combine the beef and season with salt, pepper, oregano, ground cumin, chili powder, and olive oil.
4) Place on the grill pan and cook for 25 minutes.
5) Halfway through the cooking time, stir the meat to brown evenly.
6) Once cooked, serve the beef with corn tortillas, cheese, and Serrano peppers.

Nutrition information:
Calories per serving: 599; Carbs: 16.8g; Protein: 54.9g; Fat: 34.7

Cumin-Paprika Rubbed Beef Brisket

Serves: 12, Cooking Time: 2 hours

Ingredients
- ¼ tsp. cayenne pepper
- 1 ½ tbsps. paprika
- 1 tsp. garlic powder
- 1 tsp. ground cumin
- 1 tsp. onion powder
- 2 tsps. dry mustard
- 2 tsps. ground black pepper
- 2 tsps. salt
- 5 pounds brisket roast
- 5 tbsps. olive oil

Instructions
1) Place all ingredients in a Ziploc bag and allow to marinate in the fridge for at least 2 hours.
2) Preheat the air fryer for 5 minutes.
3) Place the meat in a baking dish that will fit in the air fryer.
4) Place in the air fryer and cook for 2 hours at 350°F.

Nutrition information:
Calories per serving: 269; Carbohydrates: 2.8g; Protein: 35.6g; Fat: 12.8g

Cumin-Sichuan Lamb BBQ with Dip

Serves: 4, Cooking Time: 25 minutes

BBQ Ingredients
- 1 1/4 pounds boneless lamb shoulder, cut into 1-inch pieces
- 1 tbsp. Sichuan peppercorns or 1 tsp. black peppercorns
- 1 tsp. sugar
- 2 tbsps. cumin seeds
- 2 tsps. caraway seeds
- 2 tsps. crushed red pepper flakes

- Finely grated lemon zest (for serving)
- Kosher salt, freshly cracked pepper

For the Garlic Yogurt Dip:
- 1 garlic clove, grated
- 1 tbsp. fresh lemon juice
- 1 cup plain Greek yogurt
- Kosher salt, freshly ground pepper
- 1/2 tsp. finely grated lemon zest

Instructions
1) In a food processor, process cumin seeds, peppercorns, caraway seeds, pepper flakes, and sugar until smooth.
2) Thread lamb pieces into skewers. Season with salt. Rub paste all over meat pieces.
3) Place on skewer rack.
4) Cook for 5 minutes at 390°F or to desired doneness.
5) Meanwhile, in a medium bowl whisk well dip Ingredients and set aside.
6) Serve and enjoy with dip.

Nutrition information:
Calories per Serving: 265; Carbs: 7.6g; Protein: 34.3g; Fat: 10.8g

Curry Pork Roast in Coconut Sauce

Serves: 6, Cooking Time: 60 minutes

Ingredients
- ½ tsp. curry powder
- ½ tsp. ground turmeric powder
- 1 can unsweetened coconut milk
- 1 tbsps. sugar
- 2 tbsps. fish sauce
- 2 tbsps. soy sauce
- 3 pounds pork shoulder
- Salt and pepper to taste

Instructions
1) Place all Ingredients in bowl and allow the meat to marinate in the fridge for at least 2 hours.
2) Preheat the air fryer to 390°F.
3) Place the grill pan accessory in the air fryer.
4) Grill the meat for 20 minutes making sure to flip the pork every 10 minutes for even grilling and cook in batches.
5) Meanwhile, pour the marinade in a saucepan and allow to simmer for 10 minutes until the sauce thickens.
6) Baste the pork with the sauce before serving.

Nutrition information:
Calories per serving: 688; Carbs: 38g; Protein: 17g; Fat: 52g

Eastern Chunky Shish Kebabs

Serves: 4, Cooking Time: 20 minutes

Ingredients

- 1 tbsp. prepared mustard
- 1 tbsp. Worcestershire sauce
- 1 clove garlic, minced
- 1 tsp. coarsely cracked black pepper
- 16 mushroom caps
- 2 green bell peppers, cut into chunks
- 1 red bell pepper, cut into chunks
- 1 large onion, cut into large squares
- 1/2 cup soy sauce
- 1 1/2 tsps. salt
- 1 1/2 pounds lean beef, cut into 1-inch cubes
- 1/3 cup vegetable oil
- 1/4 cup lemon juice

Instructions

1) In a resealable bag, mix well salt, pepper, garlic, Worcestershire, mustard, lemon juice, soy sauce, and oil. Add beef and toss well to coat. Remove excess air and seal. Marinate for 8 hours. Add mushroom and marinate for an additional 8 hours.
2) Thread mushrooms, bell peppers, onion, and meat in skewers.
3) Pour marinade in saucepan and thicken for 10 minutes and transfer to a bowl for basting.
4) Place skewers on skewer rack in air fryer. If needed, cook in batches.
5) For 10 minutes, cook on 390°F. Halfway through cooking time, baste and turnover skewers.
6) Serve and enjoy.

Nutrition information:
Calories per Serving: 426; Carbs: 15.8g; Protein: 26.2g; Fat: 28.6g

Easy & The Traditional Beef Roast Recipe

Serves: 12, Cooking Time: 2 hours

Ingredients

- 1 cup organic beef broth
- 3 pounds beef round roast
- 4 tbsps. olive oil
- Salt and pepper to taste

Instructions

1) Place in a Ziploc bag all the ingredients and allow to marinate in the fridge for 2 hours.
2) Preheat the air fryer for 5 minutes.
3) Transfer all ingredients in a baking dish that will fit in the air fryer.
4) Place in the air fryer and cook for 2 hours for 400°F.

Nutrition information:
Calories per serving: 284; Carbohydrates: 0.4 g; Protein: 23.7g; Fat: 20.8g

Easy Corn Dog Bites

Serves: 2, Cooking Time: 10 minutes

Ingredients
- ½ cup all-purpose flour
- 1 ½ cup crushed cornflakes
- 2 large beef hot dogs, cut in half crosswise
- 2 large eggs, beaten
- Salt and pepper to taste

Instructions
1) Preheat the air fryer to 330°F.
2) Skewer the hot dogs using the metal skewers included in the double layer rack accessory.
3) In a mixing bowl, combine the flour and eggs to form a batter. Season with salt and pepper to taste. Add water if too dry.
4) Dip the skewered hot dogs in the batter and dredge in cornflakes.
5) Place on the double layer rack accessory and cook for 10 minutes.

Nutrition information:
Calories per serving: 79; Carbs: 8 g; Protein: 5g; Fat: 3g

Egg Noodles, Ground Beef & Tomato Sauce Bake

Serves: 3, Cooking Time: 45 minutes

Ingredients
- 1 (15 ounce) can tomato sauce
- 4-ounce egg noodles, cooked according to manufacturer's directions
- 1/2-pound ground beef
- 1/2 tsp. white sugar
- 1/2 tsp. salt
- 1/2 tsp. garlic salt
- 1/2 cup sour cream
- 1/2 large white onion, diced
- 1/4 cup shredded sharp Cheddar cheese, or more to taste
- 1.5-ounce cream cheese

Instructions
1) Lightly grease baking pan of air fryer with cooking spray. Add ground beef, for 10 minutes cook on 360°F. Halfway through cooking time crumble beef.
2) When done cooking, discard excess fat.
3) Stir in tomato sauce, garlic salt, salt, and sugar. Mix well and cook for another 15 minutes. Transfer to a bowl.
4) In another bowl, whisk well onion, cream cheese, and sour cream.
5) Place half of the egg noodles on bottom of air fryer baking pan. Top with half of the sour cream mixture, then half the tomato sauce mixture. Repeat layering. And then top off with cheese.
6) Cover pan with foil.
7) Cook for another 15 minutes. Uncover and cook for another 5 minutes.
8) Serve and enjoy.

Nutrition information:
Calories per Serving: 524; Carbs: 39.4g; Protein: 24.5g; Fat: 29.8g

Eggs 'n Bacon on Biscuit Brekky

Serves: 4, Cooking Time: 28 minutes

Ingredients
- ¼ cup milk
- ½ of 16-ounces refrigerated breakfast biscuits
- 1 cup shredded extra sharp cheddar cheese
- 4 scallions, chopped
- 5 eggs
- 8 slices cooked center cut bacon

Instructions
1) In baking pan cook bacon for 8 minutes at 360ºF or until crisped. Remove bacon and discard excess fat.
2) Evenly spread biscuits on bottom. For 5 minutes, cook at same temperature.
3) Meanwhile, whisk eggs, milk, and scallions.
4) Remove basket, evenly layer bacon on top of biscuit, sprinkle cheese on top, and pour eggs.
5) Cook for another 15 minutes or until eggs are set.
6) Serve and enjoy.

Nutrition information:
Calories per Serving: 241; Carbs: 4.3g; Protein: 22.6g; Fat: 23.7g

Fat Burger Bombs

Serves: 6, Cooking Time: 20 minutes

Ingredients
- ½ pound ground beef
- 1 cup almond flour
- 12 slices uncured bacon, chopped
- 2 eggs, beaten
- 3 tbsps. olive oil
- Salt and pepper to taste

Instructions
1) In a mixing bowl, combine all ingredients except for the olive oil.
2) Use your hands to form small balls with the mixture. Place in a baking sheet and allow to set in the fridge for at least 2 hours.
3) Preheat the air fryer for 5 minutes.
4) Brush the meat balls with olive oil on all sides.
5) Place in the air fryer basket.
6) Cook for 20 minutes at 350ºF.
7) Halfway through the cooking time, shake the fryer basket for a more even cooking.

Nutrition information:
Calories per serving: 412; Carbohydrates: 1.5g; Protein: 19.2g; Fat: 36.6g

Flatiron Steak Grill on Parsley Salad

Serves: 4, Cooking Time: 45 minutes

Ingredients

- ½ cup parmesan cheese, grated
- 1 ½ pounds flatiron steak
- 1 tbsp. fresh lemon juice
- 2 cups parsley leaves
- 3 tbsps. olive oil
- Salt and pepper to taste

Instructions

1) Preheat the air fryer to 390°F.
2) Place the grill pan accessory in the air fryer.
3) Mix together the steak, oil, salt and pepper.
4) Grill for 15 minutes per batch and make sure to flip the meat halfway through the cooking time.
5) Meanwhile, prepare the salad by combining in a bowl the parsley leaves, parmesan cheese and lemon juice. Season with salt and pepper.

Nutrition information:
Calories per serving: 595; Carbs: 4.9g; Protein: 47g; Fat: 43g

Fried Pork with Sweet and Sour Glaze

Serves: 4, Cooking Time: 30 minutes

Ingredients

- ¼ cup rice wine vinegar
- ¼ tsp. Chinese five spice powder
- 1 cup potato starch
- 1 green onion, chopped
- 2 large eggs, beaten
- 2 pounds pork chops cut into chunks
- 2 tbsps. cornstarch + 3 tbsps. water
- 5 tbsps. brown sugar
- Salt and pepper to taste

Instructions

1) Preheat the air fryer to 390°F.
2) Season pork chops with salt and pepper to taste.
3) Dip the pork chops in egg. Set aside.
4) In a bowl, combine the potato starch and Chinese five spice powder.
5) Dredge the pork chops in the flour mixture.
6) Place in the double layer rack and cook for 30 minutes.
7) Meanwhile, place the vinegar and brown sugar in a saucepan. Season with salt and pepper to taste. Stir in the cornstarch slurry and allow to simmer until thick.
8) Serve the pork chops with the sauce and garnish with green onions.

Nutrition information:
Calories per serving: 420; Carbs: 9.1g; Protein: 69.2g; Fat: 11.8g

Garlic Lemon-Wine on Lamb Steak

Serves: 4, Cooking Time: 1 hour and 30 minutes

Ingredients
- ¼ cup extra virgin olive oil
- ½ cup dry white wine
- 1 tbsp. brown sugar
- 2 pounds lamb steak, pounded
- 2 tbsps. lemon juice
- 3 tbsps. ancho chili powder
- 8 cloves of garlic, minced
- Salt and pepper to taste

Instructions
1) Place all Ingredients in bowl and allow the meat to marinate in the fridge for at least 2 hours.
2) Preheat the air fryer to 390°F.
3) Place the grill pan accessory in the air fryer.
4) Grill the meat for 20 minutes per batch.
5) Meanwhile, pour the marinade in a saucepan and allow to simmer for 10 minutes until the sauce thickens.

Nutrition information:
Calories per serving: 500; Carbs: 8g; Protein: 38g; Fat: 35g

Garlic-Cumin 'n Orange Juice Marinated Steak

Serves: 4, Cooking Time: 60 minutes

Ingredients
- ¼ cup orange juice
- 1 tsp. ground cumin
- 2 pounds skirt steak, trimmed from excess fat
- 2 tbsps. lime juice
- 2 tbsps. olive oil
- 4 cloves of garlic, minced
- Salt and pepper to taste

Instructions
1) Place all ingredients in a mixing bowl and allow to marinate in the fridge for at least 2 hours
2) Preheat the air fryer to 390°F.
3) Place the grill pan accessory in the air fryer.
4) Grill for 15 minutes per batch and flip the beef every 8 minutes for even grilling.
5) Meanwhile, pour the marinade on a saucepan and allow to simmer for 10 minutes or until the sauce thickens.
6) Slice the beef and pour over the sauce.

Nutrition information:
Calories per serving: 568; Carbs: 4.7g; Protein: 59.1g; Fat: 34.7g

Garlicky Buttered Chops

Serves: 4, Cooking Time: 30 minutes

Ingredients
- 1 tbsps. butter, melted
- 2 tsps. chopped parsley
- 2 tsps. grated garlic
- 4 pork chops
- Salt and pepper to taste

Instructions
1) Preheat the air fryer to 330oF.
2) Place the grill pan accessory in the air fryer.
3) Season the pork chops with the remaining Ingredients.
4) Place on the grill pan and cook for 30 minutes.
5) Flip the pork chops halfway through the cooking time.

Nutrition information:
Calories per serving: 352; Carbs: 1.6g; Protein: 40.7g; Fat: 20.3g

Garlic-Mustard Rubbed Roast Beef

Serves: 12, Cooking Time: 2 hours

Ingredients
- ¼ cup Dijon mustard
- ¼ cup freshly parsley, chopped
- ¼ cup unsalted butter
- 2 cups almond flour
- 2 tbsps. olive oil
- 3 ½ cups beef broth
- 3 pounds boneless beef eye round roast
- 4 cloves of garlic, chopped
- Salt and pepper to taste

Instructions
1) In a mixing bowl, combine the garlic, almond flour, parsley, salt and pepper.
2) Heat a butter and olive oil in a skillet and brown the beef on all sides.
3) Rub the almond flour mixture all over the beef.
4) Brush with Dijon mustard.
5) Place the crusted beef in a baking dish.
6) Pour slowly the beef broth.
7) Place the baking dish with the bee in the air fryer. Close.
8) Cook for 2 hours at 400oF.
9) Baste the beef with the sauce every 30 minutes.

Nutrition information:
Calories per serving: 310; Carbohydrates: 7.2g; Protein: 24.6g; Fat: 20.30g

Garlic-Rosemary Lamb BBQ

Serves: 2, Cooking Time: 12 minutes

Ingredients
- 1-lb cubed lamb leg
- juice of 1 lemon
- fresh rosemary
- 3 smashed garlic cloves
- salt and pepper
- 1/2 cup olive oil

Instructions
1) In a shallow dish, mix well all Ingredients and marinate for 3 hours.
2) Thread lamb pieces in skewers. Place on skewer rack in air fryer.
3) For 12 minutes, cook on 390°F. Halfway through cooking time, turnover skewers. If needed, cook in batches.
4) Serve and enjoy.

Nutrition information:
Calories per Serving: 560; Carbs: 5.4g; Protein: 46.5g; Fat: 39.1g

Garlic-Rosemary Rubbed Beef Rib Roast

Serves: 14, Cooking Time: 2 hours

Ingredients
- 1 cup dried porcini mushrooms
- 1 medium shallot, chopped
- 2 cloves of garlic, minced
- 2 cups water
- 3 tbsps. unsalted pepper
- 3 tbsps. vegetable oil
- 4 sprigs of thyme
- 6 ribs, beef rib roast
- Salt and pepper to taste

Instructions
1) Preheat the air fryer for 5 minutes.
2) Place all ingredients in a baking dish that will fit in the air fryer.
3) Place the dish in the air fryer and cook for 2 hours at 325°F.

Nutrition information: Calories per serving: 320; Carbohydrates: 0.9g; Protein: 32.4g; Fat: 20.7g

Ginger Soy Beef Recipe from the Orient

Serves: 3, Cooking Time: 5 minutes

Ingredients
- 2 tbsps. soy sauce
- 1 green onions, chopped
- 1 clove garlic, minced
- 1 tbsp. and 1-1/2 tsps. hoisin sauce
- 1 tbsp. and 1-1/2 tsps. sherry
- 1/2 tsp. barbeque sauce
- 1-1/2 tsps. minced fresh ginger root

- 3/4-pound flank steak, thinly sliced

Instructions
1) In a resealable bag, mix well ginger, garlic, green onions, barbecue sauce, soy sauce, sherry, and hoisin. Add steak and mix well. Remove excess air, seal, and marinate for at least 2 hours.
2) Thread steak into skewers and discard marinade.
3) For 5 minutes, cook on preheated 390°F air fryer.
4) Serve and enjoy.

Nutrition information:
Calories per Serving: 130; Carbs: 6.7g; Protein: 14.7g; Fat: 4.9g

Ginger, Garlic 'n Pork Dumplings

Serves: 8, Cooking Time: 15 minutes

Ingredients
- ¼ tsp. crushed red pepper
- ½ tsp. sugar
- 1 tbsp. chopped fresh ginger
- 1 tbsp. chopped garlic
- 1 tsp. canola oil
- 1 tsp. toasted sesame oil
- 18 dumpling wrappers
- 2 tbsps. rice vinegar
- 2 tsps. soy sauce
- 4 cups bok choy, chopped
- 4 ounces ground pork

Instructions
1) Heat oil in a skillet and sauté the ginger and garlic until fragrant. Stir in the ground pork and cook for 5 minutes.
2) Stir in the bok choy and crushed red pepper. Season with salt and pepper to taste. Allow to cool.
3) Place the meat mixture in the middle of the dumpling wrappers. Fold the wrappers to seal the meat mixture in.
4) Place the bok choy in the grill pan.
5) Cook the dumplings in the air fryer at 330°F for 15 minutes.
6) Meanwhile, prepare the dipping sauce by combining the remaining Ingredients in a bowl.

Nutrition information:
Calories per serving: 137; Carbs: 16g; Protein: 7g; Fat: 5g

Ginger-Orange Beef Strips

Serves: 3, Cooking Time: 25 minutes

Ingredients
- 1 ½ pounds stir fry steak slices
- 1 ½ tsp. sesame oil
- 1 navel oranges, segmented
- 1 tbsp. olive oil
- 1 tbsp. rice vinegar
- 1 tsp. grated ginger
- 2 scallions, chopped
- 3 cloves of garlic, minced
- 3 tbsps. molasses
- 3 tbsps. soy sauce

- 6 tbsps. cornstarch

Instructions
1) Preheat the air fryer to 330°F.
2) Season the steak slices with soy sauce and dust with cornstarch.
3) Place in the air fryer basket and cook for 25 minutes.
4) Meanwhile, place in the skillet oil and heat over medium flame.
5) Sauté the garlic and ginger until fragrant.
6) Stir in the oranges, molasses, and rice vinegar. Season with salt and pepper to taste.
7) Once the meat is cooked, place in the skillet and stir to coat the sauce.
8) Drizzle with sesame oil and garnish with scallions.

Nutrition information:
Calories per serving: 306; Carbs: 43.6g; Protein: 9.4g; Fat: 10.4g

Gravy Smothered Country Fried Steak

Serves: 2, Cooking Time: 25 minutes

Ingredients
- 1 cup flour
- 1 cup panko bread crumbs
- 1 tsp. garlic powder
- 1 tsp. onion powder
- 2 cups milk
- 2 tbsps. flour
- 3 eggs, beaten
- 6 ounces ground sausage meat
- 6 ounces sirloin steak, pounded thin
- Salt and pepper to taste

Instructions
1) Preheat the air fryer to 330°F.
2) Season the steak with salt and pepper to taste.
3) Dip the steak in egg and dredge in flour mixture (comprised of flour, bread crumbs, onion powder, and garlic powder).
4) Place in the air fryer and cook for 25 minutes.
5) Meanwhile, place the sausage meat in a saucepan and allow the fat to render. Stir in flour to form a roux and add milk. Season with salt and pepper to taste. Keep stirring until the sauce thickens.
6) Serve the steak with the milk gravy

Nutrition information:
Calories per serving: 1048; Carbs: 88.1g; Protein:64.2 g; Fat: 48.7g

Grilled Beef with Grated Daikon Radish

Serves: 2, Cooking Time: 40 minutes

Ingredients
- ¼ cup grated daikon radish
- ½ cup rice wine vinegar
- ½ cup soy sauce
- 1 tbsp. olive oil
- 2 strip steaks
- Salt and pepper to taste

Instructions
1) Preheat the air fryer to 390°F.
2) Place the grill pan accessory in the air fryer.
3) Season the steak with salt and pepper.
4) Brush with oil.
5) Grill for 20 minutes per piece and make sure to flip the beef halfway through the cooking time
6) Prepare the dipping sauce by combining the soy sauce and vinegar.
7) Serve the steak with the sauce and daikon radish.

Nutrition information:
Calories per serving: 510; Carbs:19.3 g; Protein: 54g; Fat: 24g

Grilled Prosciutto Wrapped Fig

Serves: 2, Cooking Time: 8 minutes

Ingredients
- 2 whole figs, sliced in quarters
- 8 prosciutto slices
- Pepper and salt to taste

Instructions
1) Wrap a prosciutto slice around one slice of fid and then thread into skewer. Repeat process for remaining Ingredients. Place on skewer rack in air fryer.
2) For 8 minutes, cook on 390°F. Halfway through cooking time, turnover skewers.
3) Serve and enjoy.

Nutrition information:
Calories per Serving: 277; Carbs: 10.7g; Protein: 36.0g; Fat: 10.0g

Grilled Sausages with BBQ Sauce

Serves: 3, Cooking Time: 30 minutes

Ingredients
- ½ cup prepared BBQ sauce
- 6 sausage links

for Cooking:
1) Preheat the air fryer to 390°F.
2) Place the grill pan accessory in the air fryer.
3) Place the sausage links and grill for 30 minutes.
4) Flip halfway through the cooking time.
5) Before serving brush with prepared BBQ sauce.

Nutrition information:
Calories per serving: 265; Carbs: 6.4g; Protein: 27.7g; Fat: 14.2g

Grilled Spicy Carne Asada

Serves: 2, Cooking Time: 50 minutes

Ingredients
- 1 chipotle pepper, chopped
- 1 dried ancho chilies, chopped
- 1 tbsp. coriander seeds
- 1 tbsp. cumin
- 1 tbsps. soy sauce
- 2 slices skirt steak
- 2 tbsps. Asian fish sauce
- 2 tbsps. brown sugar
- 2 tbsps. of fresh lemon juice
- 2 tbsps. olive oil
- 3 cloves of garlic, minced

Instructions
1) Place all ingredients in a Ziploc bag and marinate in the fridge for 2 hours.
2) Preheat the air fryer to 390°F.
3) Place the grill pan accessory in the air fryer.
4) Grill the skirt steak for 20 minutes.
5) Flip the steak every 10 minutes for even grilling.

Nutrition information:
Calories per serving: 697; Carbs: 10.2g; Protein: 62.7 g; Fat: 45g

Grilled Steak on Tomato-Olive Salad

Serves: 5, Cooking Time: 50 minutes

Ingredients
- ¼ cup extra virgin olive oil
- ¼ tsp. cayenne pepper
- ½ cup green olives, pitted and sliced
- 1 cup red onion, chopped
- 1 tbsp. oil
- 1 tsp. paprika
- 2 ½ pound flank
- 2 pounds cherry tomatoes, halved
- 2 tbsps. Sherry vinegar
- Salt and pepper to taste

Instructions
1) Preheat the air fryer to 390°F.
2) Place the grill pan accessory in the air fryer.
3) Season the steak with salt, pepper, paprika, and cayenne pepper. Brush with oil
4) Place on the grill pan and cook for 45 to 50 minutes.
5) Meanwhile, prepare the salad by mixing the remaining ingredients.
6) Serve the beef with salad.

Nutrition information:
Calories per serving: 351; Carbs: 8g; Protein: 30g; Fat: 22g

Grilled Tri Tip over Beet Salad

Serves: 6, Cooking Time: 45 minutes

Ingredients

- 1 bunch arugula, torn
- 1 bunch scallions, chopped
- 1-pound tri-tip, sliced
- 2 tbsps. olive oil
- 3 beets, peeled and sliced thinly
- 3 tbsps. balsamic vinegar
- Salt and pepper to taste

Instructions

1) Preheat the air fryer to 390°F.
2) Place the grill pan accessory in the air fryer.
3) Season the tri-tip with salt and pepper. Drizzle with oil.
4) Grill for 15 minutes per batch.
5) Meanwhile, prepare the salad by tossing the rest of the ingredients in a salad bowl.
6) Toss in the grilled tri-trip and drizzle with more balsamic vinegar.

Nutrition information:
Calories per serving: 221; Carbs: 20.7g; Protein: 17.2g; Fat: 7.7g

Ground Beef on Deep Dish Pizza

Serves: 4, Cooking Time: 25 minutes

Ingredients

- 1 can (10-3/4 ounces) condensed tomato soup, undiluted
- 1 can (8 ounces) mushroom stems and pieces, drained
- 1 cup shredded part-skim mozzarella cheese
- 1 cup warm water (110°F to 115°F)
- 1 package (1/4 ounce) active dry yeast
- 1 small green pepper, julienned
- 1 tsp. dried rosemary, crushed
- 1 tsp. each dried basil, oregano and thyme
- 1 tsp. salt
- 1 tsp. sugar
- 1/4 tsp. garlic powder
- 1-pound ground beef, cooked and drained
- 2 tbsps. canola oil
- 2-1/2 cups all-purpose flour

Instructions

1) In a large bowl, dissolve yeast in warm water. Add the sugar, salt, oil and 2 cups flour. Beat until smooth. Stir in enough remaining flour to form a soft dough. Cover and let rest for 20 minutes. Divide into two and store half in the freezer for future use.
2) On a floured surface, roll into a square the size of your air fryer. Transfer to a greased air fryer baking pan. Sprinkle with beef.
3) Mix well seasonings and soup in a small bowl and pour over beef.
4) Sprinkle top with mushrooms and green pepper. Top with cheese.
5) Cover pan with foil.
6) For 15 minutes, cook on 390°F.
7) Remove foil, cook for another 10 minutes or until cheese is melted.
8) Serve and enjoy.

Nutrition information:
Calories per Serving: 362; Carbs: 39.0g; Protein: 20.0g; Fat: 14.0g

Ground Beef, Rice 'n Cabbage Casserole

Serves: 6, Cooking Time: 50 minutes

Ingredients

- 1-pound ground beef
- 1 (14 ounce) can beef broth
- 1/2 cup chopped onion
- 1/2 (29 ounce) can tomato sauce
- 1/2 cup uncooked white rice
- 1/2 tsp. salt
- 1-3/4 pounds chopped cabbage

Instructions

1) Lightly grease baking pan of air fryer with cooking spray. Add beef and for 10 minutes, cook on 360°F. Halfway through cooking time, stir and crumble beef.
2) Meanwhile, in a large bowl whisk well salt, rice, cabbage, onion, and tomato sauce. Add to pan of meat and mix well. Pour broth.
3) Cover pan with foil.
4) Cook for 25 minutes at 330°F, uncover, mix and cook for another 15 minutes.
5) Serve and enjoy.

Nutrition information:

Calories per Serving: 356; Carbs: 25.5g; Protein: 17.1g; Fat: 20.6g

Hanger Steak in Mole Rub

Serves: 2, Cooking Time: 60 minutes

Ingredients

- 1 tbsp. ground black pepper
- 2 hanger steaks
- 2 tbsps. coriander seeds
- 2 tbsps. ground coffee
- 2 tbsps. olive oil
- 2 tbsps. salt
- 4 tsps. unsweetened cocoa powder
- 4 tsps. brown sugar

Instructions

1) Preheat the air fryer to 390°F.
2) Place the grill pan accessory in the air fryer.
3) In a bowl, make the spice rub by combining the coriander seeds, ground coffee, salt, brown sugar, cocoa powder, and black pepper.
4) Rub the spice mixture on the steaks and brush with oil.
5) Grill for 30 minutes and make sure to flip the meat every 10 minutes for even grilling and cook in batches.

Nutrition information:

Calories per serving: 680; Carbs: 16g; Protein:48 g; Fat: 47g

Hickory Smoked Beef Jerky

Serves: 2, Cooking Time: 1 hour

Ingredients
- ¼ cup Worcestershire sauce
- ½ cup brown sugar
- ½ cup soy sauce
- ½ tsp. black pepper
- ½ tsp. smoked paprika
- 1 tbsp. chili pepper sauce
- 1 tbsp. liquid smoke, hickory
- 1 tsp. garlic powder
- 1 tsp. onion powder
- 1-pound ground beef, sliced thinly

Instructions

1) Combine all Ingredients in a mixing bowl or Ziploc bag.
2) Marinate in the fridge overnight.
3) Preheat the air fryer to 330°F.
4) Place the beef slices on the double layer rack.
5) Cook for one hour until the beef jerky is very dry.

Nutrition information:
Calories per serving: 723; Carbs: 79.8g; Protein: 55.6g; Fat: 20.2g

Italian Beef Roast

Serves: 10, Cooking Time: 3 hours

Ingredients
- ¼ tsp. black pepper
- ½ cup water
- ½ tsp. thyme
- 1 onion, sliced thinly
- 1 tsp. basil
- 1 tsp. salt
- 2 ½ pounds beef round roast
- 4 tbsps. olive oil

Instructions

1) Place all ingredients in a baking dish and make sure that the entire surface of the beef is coated with the spices.
2) Place the baking dish with the bee in the air fryer. Close.
3) Cook for 3 hours at 400°F.

Nutrition information:
Calories per serving: 282; Carbohydrates: 0.2g; Protein: 23.6g; Fat: 20.7g

Italian Sausage & Tomato Egg Bake

Serves: 1, Cooking Time: 16 minutes

Ingredients

- ½ Italian sausage, sliced into ¼-inch thick
- 1 tbsp. olive oil
- 3 eggs
- 4 cherry tomatoes (in half)
- Chopped parsley
- Grano Padano cheese (or parmesan)
- Salt/Pepper

Instructions

1) Lightly grease baking pan of air fryer with cooking spray.
2) Add Italian sausage and cook for 5 minutes at 360°F.
3) Add olive oil and cherry tomatoes. Cook for another 6 minutes.
4) Meanwhile, whisk well eggs, parsley, cheese, salt, and pepper in a bowl.
5) Remove basket and toss the mixture a bit. Pour eggs over mixture.
6) Cook for another 5 minutes.
7) Serve and enjoy.

Nutrition information:
Calories per Serving: 295; Carbs: 7.8g; Protein: 14.4g; Fat: 22.9g

Keto-Approved Cheeseburger Bake

Serves: 4, Cooking Time: 35 minutes

Ingredients

- 1 clove garlic, minced
- 1/2 cup heavy whipping cream
- 1/2-pound bacon, cut into small pieces
- 1/4 tsp. onion powder
- 1/4 tsp. salt
- 1/8 tsp. ground black pepper
- 1-pound ground beef
- 4 eggs
- 6-ounce shredded Cheddar cheese, divided

Instructions

1) Lightly grease baking pan of air fryer with cooking spray. Add beef, onion powder, and garlic. For 10 minutes, cook on 360°F. stirring and crumbling halfway through cooking time.
2) Discard excess fat and evenly spread ground beef on bottom of pan. Top with evenly spread bacon slices. Sprinkle half of the cheese on top.
3) In a bowl, whisk well pepper, salt, heavy cream, and eggs. Pour over bacon.
4) Sprinkle remaining cheese on top of eggs.
5) Cover pan with foil and cook for 15 minutes.
6) Uncover and cook for another 10 minutes until tops are browned and eggs are set.
7) Serve and enjoy.

Nutrition information:
Calories per Serving: 454; Carbs: 1.6g; Protein: 28.7g; Fat: 36.9g

Maple 'n Soy Marinated Beef

Serves: 4, Cooking Time: 45 minutes

Ingredients
- 2 pounds sirloin flap steaks, pounded
- 3 tbsps. balsamic vinegar
- 3 tbsps. maple syrup
- 3 tbsps. soy sauce
- 4 cloves of garlic, minced

Instructions
1) Preheat the air fryer to 390°F.
2) Place the grill pan accessory in the air fryer.
3) On a deep dish, place the flap steaks and season with soy sauce, balsamic vinegar, and maple syrup, and garlic.
4) Place on the grill pan and cook for 15 minutes in batches.

Nutrition information:
Calories per serving: 331; Carbs: 9g; Protein: 31g; Fat: 19g

Maras Pepper Lamb Kebab Recipe from Turkey

Serves: 2, Cooking Time: 15 minutes

Ingredients
- 1-lb lamb meat, cut into 2-inch cubes
- Kosher salt
- Freshly cracked black pepper
- 2 tbsps. Maras pepper, or 2 tsps. other dried chili powder mixed with 1 tbsp. paprika
- 1 tsp. minced garlic
- 2 tbsps. roughly chopped fresh mint
- 1/2 cup extra-virgin olive oil, divided
- 1/2 cup dried apricots, cut into medium dice

Instructions
1) In a bowl, mix pepper, salt, and half of olive oil. Add lamb and toss well to coat. Thread lamb into 4 skewers.
2) Cook for 5 minutes at 390°F or to desired doneness.
3) In a large bowl, mix well remaining oil, mint, garlic, Maras pepper, and apricots. Add cooked lamb. Season with salt and pepper. Toss well to coat
4) Serve and enjoy.

Nutrition information:
Calories per Serving: 602; Carbs: 25.8g; Protein: 40.3g; Fat: 37.5g

Meat Balls with Mint Yogurt Dip From Morocco

Serves: 2, Cooking Time: 25 minutes

Ingredients

- ¼ cup bread crumbs
- ¼ cup sour cream
- ½ cup Greek yogurt
- 1 clove of garlic, minced
- 1 egg, beaten
- 1 tbsp. mint, chopped
- 1 tsp. cayenne pepper
- 1 tsp. ground coriander
- 1 tsp. ground cumin
- 1 tsp. red chili paste
- 1-pound ground beef
- 2 cloves of garlic, minced
- 2 tbsp. flat leaf parsley, chopped
- 2 tbsps. buttermilk
- 2 tbsps. honey
- 2 tbsps. mint
- Salt and pepper to taste

Instructions

1) In a mixing bowl, combine the ground beef, cumin, coriander, cayenne pepper, red chili paste, minced garlic, parsley, chopped mint, egg, and bread crumbs. Season with salt and pepper to taste. Use your hands and form small balls. Set aside and allow to rest in the fridge for at least 30 minutes.
2) Preheat the air fryer to 330°F.
3) Place the meatballs in the air fryer basket and cook for 25 minutes. Give the air fryer basket a shake to cook evenly.
4) Meanwhile, mix the Greek yogurt, sour cream, buttermilk, mint, garlic, and honey in a bowl. Season with salt and pepper.
5) Serve the meatballs with the yogurt sauce.

Nutrition information:
Calories per serving:779 ; Carbs: 28.5g; Protein: 65g; Fat: 45g

Meatballs 'n Parmesan-Cheddar Pizza

Serves: 4, Cooking Time: 15 minutes

Ingredients

- 1 prebaked 6-inch pizza crust
- 1 tsp. garlic powder
- 1 tsp. Italian seasoning
- 4 tbsp grated Parmesan cheese
- 1 small onion, halved and sliced
- 1/2 can (8 ounces) pizza sauce
- 6 frozen fully cooked Italian meatballs (1/2 ounce each), thawed and halved
- 1/2 cup shredded part-skim mozzarella cheese
- 1/2 cup shredded cheddar cheese

Instructions

1) Lightly grease baking pan of air fryer with cooking spray.
2) Place crust on bottom of pan. Spread sauce on top. Sprinkle with parmesan, Italian seasoning, and garlic powder.
3) Top with meatballs and onion. Sprinkle remaining cheese.
4) For 15 minutes, cook on preheated 390°F air fryer.
5) Serve and enjoy.

Nutrition information:
Calories per Serving: 324; Carbs: 28.0g; Protein: 17.0g; Fat: 16.0g

Meatloaf with Sweet-Sour Glaze

Serves: 3, Cooking Time: 30 minutes

Ingredients

- ½ medium onion, chopped
- ½ Tbsp lightly dried (or fresh chopped) Parsley
- 1 Tbsp Worcestershire sauce
- 1 tsp (or 2 cloves) minced garlic
- 1 tsp dried basil
- 1/3 cup Kellogg's corn flakes crumbs
- 1-2 tsp freshly ground black pepper
- 1-2 tsp salt
- 1-pound lean ground beef (93% fat free), raw
- 3 tsp Splenda (or Truvia) brown sugar blend
- 5 Tbsp Heinz reduced-sugar ketchup
- 8-oz tomato sauce, divided

Instructions

1) Lightly grease baking pan of air fryer with cooking spray.
2) In a large bowl, mix well 6-oz tomato sauce, garlic, pepper, salt, corn flake crumbs, and onion. Stir in ground beef and mix well with hands.
3) Evenly spread ground beef mixture in pan, ensuring that it is lumped altogether.
4) In a medium bowl, whisk all remaining Ingredients together to make a glaze. Pour on top of ground beef.
5) Cover pan with foil.
6) For 15 minutes, cook on 360°F. Remove foil and continue cooking for another 10 minutes.
7) Let it stand for 5 minutes.
8) Serve and enjoy.

Nutrition information:
Calories per Serving: 427; Carbs: 25.7g; Protein: 42.5g; Fat: 17.1

Meaty Pasta Bake from the Southwest

Serves: 6, Cooking Time: 45 minutes

Ingredients

- 1 can (14-1/2 ounces each) diced tomatoes, undrained
- 1 cup shredded Monterey Jack cheese
- 1 cup uncooked elbow macaroni, cooked according to manufacturer's instructions
- 1 jalapeno pepper, seeded and chopped
- 1 large onion, chopped
- 1 tsp. chili powder
- 1 tsps. salt
- 1/2 can (16 ounces) kidney beans, rinsed and drained
- 1/2 can (4 ounces) chopped green chilies, drained
- 1/2 can (6 ounces) tomato paste
- 1/2 tsp. ground cumin
- 1/2 tsp. pepper
- 1-pound ground beef
- 2 garlic cloves, minced

Instructions

1) Lightly grease baking pan of air fryer with cooking spray. Add ground beef, onion, and garlic. For 10 minutes, cook on 360°F. Halfway through cooking time, stir and crumble beef.

2) Mix in diced tomatoes, kidney beans, tomato paste, green chilies, salt, chili powder, cumin, and pepper. Mix well. Cook for another 10 minutes.
3) Stir in macaroni and mix well. Top with jalapenos and cheese.
4) Cover pan with foil.
5) Cook for 15 minutes at 390°F, remove foil and continue cooking for another 10 minutes until tops are lightly browned.
6) Serve and enjoy.

Nutrition information:
Calories per Serving: 323; Carbs: 23.0g; Protein: 24.0g; Fat: 15.0g

Monterey Jack 'n Sausage Brekky Casserole

Serves: 2, Cooking Time: 20 minutes

Ingredients

- ½ cup shredded Cheddar-Monterey Jack cheese blend
- 1 green onion, chopped
- 1 pinch cayenne pepper
- 1/4-lb breakfast sausage
- 2 tbsp red bell pepper, diced
- 4 eggs

Instructions
1) Lightly grease baking pan of air fryer with cooking spray.
2) Add sausage and for 8 minutes, cook on 390°F. Halfway through, crumble sausage and stir well.
3) Meanwhile, whisk eggs in a bowl and stir in bell pepper, green onion, and cayenne.
4) Remove basket and toss the mixture a bit. Evenly spread cheese and pour eggs on top.
5) Cook for another 12 minutes at 330°F or until eggs are set to desired doneness.
6) Serve and enjoy.

Nutrition information:
Calories per Serving: 383; Carbs: 2.9g; Protein: 31.2g; Fat: 27.4g

Mustard 'n Italian Dressing on Flank Steak

Serves: 3, Cooking Time: 45 minutes

Ingredients

- ½ cup yellow mustard
- ½ tsp. black pepper
- 1 ¼ pounds beef flank steak
- 1 cup Italian salad dressing
- Salt to taste

Instructions
1) Place all ingredients in a Ziploc bag and allow to marinate in the fridge for at least 2 hours.
2) Preheat the air fryer to 390°F.
3) Place the grill pan accessory in the air fryer.
4) Grill for 15 minutes per batch making sure to flip the meat halfway through the cooking time.

Nutrition information:
Calories per serving: 576; Carbs: 3.1g; Protein: 35 g; Fat: 47g

Mustard 'n Pepper Roast Beef

Serves: 9, Cooking Time: 1 hour and 30 minutes

Ingredients

- ¼ cup flat-leaf parsley, chopped
- 1 ½ pounds medium shallots, chopped
- 1 boneless rib roast
- 2 tbsps. whole grain mustard
- 3 tbsps. mixed peppercorns
- 4 medium shallots, chopped
- 4 tbsps. olive oil
- Salt to taste

Instructions

1) Preheat the air fryer for 5 minutes.
2) Place all ingredients in a baking dish that will fit in the air fryer.
3) Place the dish in the air fryer and cook for 1 hour and 30 minutes at 325°F.

Nutrition information:
Calories per serving: 451; Carbohydrates: 15.4g; Protein: 30.5g; Fat: 29.7g

New York Steak with Yogurt-Cucumber Sauce

Serves: 2, Cooking Time: 50 minutes

Ingredients

- ½ cup parsley, chopped
- 1 cucumber, seeded and chopped
- 1 cup Greek yogurt
- 2 New York strip steaks
- 3 tbsps. olive oil
- Salt and pepper to taste

Instructions

1) Preheat the air fryer to 390°F.
2) Place the grill pan accessory in the air fryer.
3) Season the strip steaks with salt and pepper. Drizzle with oil.
4) Grill the steak for 20 minutes per batch and make sure to flip the meat every 10 minutes for even grilling.
5) Meanwhile, combine the cucumber, yogurt, and parsley.
6) Serve the beef with the cucumber yogurt.

Nutrition information:
Calories per serving: 460; Carbs: 5.2g; Protein: 50.8g; Fat: 26.3g

Onion 'n Garlic Rubbed Trip Tip

Serves: 4, Cooking Time: 50 minutes

Ingredients

- ½ cup red wine vinegar
- 1 tsp. garlic powder
- 1 tsp. onion powder
- 1-pound beef tri-tip
- 3 avocadoes, seeded and sliced
- 3 tbsps. olive oil

Instructions

1) In a Ziploc bag, place all ingredients except for the avocado slices.

2) Allow to marinate in the fridge for 2 hours.
3) Preheat the air fryer to 330°F.
4) Place the grill pan accessory in the air fryer.
5) Grill the avocado for 2 minutes while the beef is marinating. Set aside.
6) After two hours, grill the beef for 50 minutes. Flip the beef halfway through the cooking time.
7) Serve the beef with grilled avocadoes

Nutrition information:
Calories per serving: 515; Carbs: 8g; Protein: 33g; Fat: 39g

Oregano-Paprika on Breaded Pork

Serves: 4, Cooking Time: 30 minutes

Ingredients
- ¼ cup water
- ¼ tsp. dry mustard
- ½ tsp. black pepper
- ½ tsp. cayenne pepper
- ½ tsp. garlic powder
- ½ tsp. salt
- 1 cup panko breadcrumbs
- 1 egg, beaten
- 2 tsps. oregano
- 4 lean pork chops
- 4 tsps. paprika

Instructions
1) Preheat the air fryer to 390°F.
2) Pat dry the pork chops.
3) In a mixing bowl, combine the egg and water. Then set aside.
4) In another bowl, combine the rest of the Ingredients.
5) Dip the pork chops in the egg mixture and dredge in the flour mixture.
6) Place in the air fryer basket and cook for 25 to 30 minutes until golden.

Nutrition information:
Calories per serving: 364; Carbs: 2.5g; Protein: 42.9g; Fat: 20.2g

Paprika Beef 'n Bell Peppers Stir Fry

Serves: 4, Cooking Time: 40 minutes

Ingredients
- 1 ¼ pounds beef flank steak, sliced thinly
- 1 red bell pepper, julienned
- 1 tbsp. cayenne pepper
- 1 tbsp. garlic powder
- 1 tbsp. onion powder
- 1 yellow bell pepper, julienned
- 3 tbsps. olive oil
- 3 tbsps. paprika powder
- Salt and pepper to taste

Instructions
1) Preheat the air fryer to 390°F.
2) Place the grill pan accessory in the air fryer.
3) In a bowl, toss all ingredients to coat everything with the seasonings.
4) Place on the grill pan and cook for 40 minutes.
5) Make sure to stir every 10 minutes for even cooking.

Nutrition information:
Calories per serving: 334; Carbs: 9.8g; Protein: 32.5g; Fat: 18.2g

Peach Puree on Ribeye
Serves: 2, Cooking Time: 45 minutes

Ingredients
- ¼ cup balsamic vinegar
- 1 cup peach puree
- 1 tbsp. paprika
- 1 tsp. thyme
- 1-pound T-bone steak
- 2 tsps. lemon pepper seasoning
- Salt and pepper to taste

Instructions
1) Place all ingredients in a Ziploc bag and allow to marinate in the fridge for at least 2 hours.
2) Preheat the air fryer to 390°F.
3) Place the grill pan accessory in the air fryer.
4) Grill for 20 minutes and flip the meat halfway through the cooking time.

Nutrition information:
Calories per serving: 570; Carbs: 35.7g; Protein: 47g; Fat: 26.5g

Pickling 'n Jerk Spiced Pork
Serves: 3, Cooking Time: 15 minutes

Ingredients
- ½ cup ready-made jerk sauce
- 1 cup rum
- 1 cup water
- 1-lb pork tenderloin, sliced into 1-inch cubes
- 2 tsps. pickling spices
- 3 tbsps. brown sugar
- 3 tbsps. each salt
- 4 garlic cloves

Instructions
1) In a saucepan, bring to a boil water salt and brown sugar. Stir in garlic and pickling spices and simmer for 3 minutes. Turn off fire and whisk in rum.

2) Transfer sauce to a shallow dish, mix well pork tenderloin and marinate in the ref for 3 hours.
3) Thread pork pieces in skewers. Baste with jerk sauce and place on skewer rack in air fryer.
4) For 12 minutes, cook on 360°F. Halfway through cooking time, turnover skewers and baste with sauce. If needed, cook in batches.
5) Serve and enjoy.

Nutrition information:
Calories per Serving: 295; Carbs: 19.9g; Protein: 41.0g; Fat: 5.7g

Pineapple, Mushrooms & Beef Kebabs

Serves: 4, Cooking Time: 20 minutes

Ingredients
- 2 tbsps. soy sauce
- 1 green bell peppers, cut into 2-inch pieces
- 1 cup cherry tomatoes
- 1 1/2 tbsps. light brown sugar
- 1 1/2 tbsp. distilled white vinegar
- 1-pound beef sirloin steak, cut into 1 1/2-inch cubes
- 1/2 fresh pineapple - peeled, cored and cubed
- 1/4 tsp. garlic powder
- 1/4 tsp. seasoned salt
- 1/4 tsp. garlic pepper seasoning
- 1/4 cup lemon-lime flavored carbonated beverage
- 1/4-pound fresh mushrooms, stems removed

Instructions
1) Whisk well carbonated beverage, garlic pepper seasoning, seasoned salt, garlic powder, white vinegar, light brown sugar, and soy sauce. Transfer ¼ cup to a bowl for basting. Place remaining sauce in a Ziploc bag.
2) Add steak in bag and marinate for at least overnight. Ensuring to turnover at least twice.
3) Thread pineapple, tomatoes, mushrooms, green peppers, and steak in skewers. Place on skewer rack on air fryer. Cook in batches. Baste with reserved sauce.
4) For 10 minutes, cook on 360°F. Halfway through cooking time, baste and turnover skewers.
5) Serve and enjoy.

Nutrition information:
Calories per Serving: 330; Carbs: 19.2g; Protein: 24.0g; Fat: 17.4g

Pineapple-Teriyaki Beef Skewer

Serves: 6, Cooking Time: 12 minutes

Ingredients

- 2 tbsps. pineapple juice (optional)
- 2 tbsps. water
- 1 tbsp. vegetable oil
- 1/4 cup and 2 tbsps. light brown sugar
- 1/4 cup soy sauce
- 1-pound boneless round steak, cut into 1/4-inch slices
- 3/4 large garlic cloves, chopped

Instructions

1) In a resealable bag, mix all Ingredients thoroughly except for beef. Then add beef, remove excess air, and seal. Place in ref and marinate for at least a day.
2) Thread beef into skewers and place on skewer rack in air fryer. If needed, cook in batches.
3) For 6 minutes, cook on 390°F.
4) Serve and enjoy.

Nutrition information:
Calories per Serving: 191; Carbs: 15.2g; Protein: 15.9g; Fat: 7.4g

Pork Belly Marinated in Onion-Coconut Cream

Serves: 3, Cooking Time: 25 minutes

Ingredients

- ½ pork belly, sliced to thin strips
- 1 onion, diced
- 1 tbsp. butter
- 4 tbsps. coconut cream
- Salt and pepper to taste

Instructions

1) Place all ingredients in a mixing bowl and allow to marinate in the fridge for 2 hours.
2) Preheat the air fryer for 5 minutes.
3) Place the pork strips in the air fryer and bake for 25 minutes at 350°F.

Nutrition information:
Calories per serving: 449; Carbohydrates: 1.9g; Protein: 19.1g; Fat: 40.6g

Pork Belly with Sweet-Sour Sauce

Serves: 4, Cooking Time: 60 minutes

Ingredients

- ¼ cup lemon juice
- ½ cup soy sauce
- 1 bay leaf
- 2 pounds pork belly
- 2 tbsps. hoisin sauce
- 3 tbsps. brown sugar
- 3-star anise
- Salt and pepper to taste

Instructions
1) Place all Ingredients in a Ziploc bag and allow to marinate in the fridge for at least 2 hours.
2) Preheat the air fryer to 390°F.
3) Place the grill pan accessory in the air fryer.
4) Grill the pork for at least 20 minutes per batch.
5) Make sure to flip the pork every 10 minutes.
6) Chop the pork before serving and garnish with green onions.

Nutrition information:
Calories per serving: 1301; Carbs: 15.5g; Protein:24 g; Fat: 126.4g

Pork Chops Crusted in Parmesan-Paprika

Serves: 6, Cooking Time: 35 minutes
Ingredients
- ¼ tsp. pepper
- ½ tsp. chili powder
- ½ tsp. onion powder
- ½ tsp. salt
- 1 cup pork rind crumbs
- 1 tsp. smoked paprika
- 2 large eggs, beaten
- 3 tbsps. parmesan cheese
- 6 thick pork chops

Instructions
1) Season the pork chops with salt, pepper, paprika, onion, and chili powder. Allow to marinate in the fridge for at least 3 hours.
2) In a bowl, place the beaten egg.
3) In another bowl, combine the pork rind and parmesan cheese.
4) Preheat the air fryer to 390°F.
5) Dip the pork in beaten egg before dredging in the pork rind crumb mixture.
6) Place in the air fryer basket and cook for 30 to 35 minutes.

Nutrition information:
Calories per serving: 316; Carbs: 1.2g; Protein: 26.9g; Fat: 22.6g

Pork Chops Marinate in Honey-Mustard

Serves: 4, Cooking Time: 25 minutes
Ingredients
- 2 tbsps. honey
- 2 tbsps. minced garlic
- 4 pork chops
- 4 tbsps. mustard
- Salt and pepper to taste

Instructions
1) Preheat the air fryer to 330°F.
2) Place the air fryer basket.
3) Season the pork chops with the rest of the Ingredients.
4) Place inside the basket.
5) Cook for 20 to 25 minutes until golden.

Nutrition information:
Calories per serving: 376; Carbs: 12.3g; Protein: 41.3g; Fat: 17.9g

Pork Chops On the Grill Simple Recipe

Serves: 6, Cooking Time: 50 minutes

Ingredients
- 1 cup salt
- 1 cup sugar
- 6 pork chops
- 8 cups water

Instructions
1) Place all ingredients in a deep bowl and allow to soak the pork chops in the brine solution for at least 2 days in the fridge.
2) Preheat the air fryer to 390°F.
3) Place the grill pan accessory in the air fryer.
4) Place the meat on the grill pan and cook for 50 minutes making sure to flip every 10 minutes for even grilling.

Nutrition information:
Calories per serving: 384; Carbs:16.6 g; Protein: 40.2g; Fat: 17.4g

Pork Stuffed with Gouda 'n Horseradish

Serves: 2, Cooking Time: 15 minutes

Ingredients
- 1/4 tsp. salt
- 1/8 tsp. pepper
- 2 cups fresh baby spinach
- 2 pork sirloin cutlets (3 ounces each)
- 2 slices smoked Gouda cheese (about 2 ounces)
- 2 tbsps. grated Parmesan cheese
- 2 tbsps. horseradish mustard
- 3 tbsps. dry bread crumbs

Instructions
1) Mix well Parmesan and bread crumbs in a small bowl.
2) On a flat surface, season pork with pepper and salt. Add spinach and cheese on each cutlet and fold to enclose filling. With toothpicks secure pork.
3) Brush mustard all over pork and dip in crumb mixture.
4) Lightly grease baking pan of air fryer with cooking spray. Add pork.
5) For 15 minutes, cook on 330°F. Halfway through cooking time, turnover.
6) Serve and enjoy.

Nutrition information:
Calories per Serving: 304; Carbs: 10.0g; Protein: 30.0g; Fat: 16.0g

Pork with Balsamic-Raspberry Jam

Serves: 4, Cooking Time: 30 minutes

Ingredients
- ¼ cup all-purpose flour
- ¼ cup milk
- 1 cup chopped pecans
- 1 cup panko breadcrumbs
- 2 large eggs, beaten
- 2 tbsps. raspberry jam
- 2 tbsps. sugar
- 2/3 cup balsamic vinegar
- 4 smoked pork chops
- Salt and pepper to taste

Instructions
1) Preheat the air fryer to 330°F.
2) Season pork chops with salt and pepper to taste.
3) In a small bowl, whisk together eggs and milk. Set aside.
4) Dip the pork chops in flour then in the egg mixture before dredging in the panko mixed with pecans.
5) Place in the air fryer and cook for 30 minutes.
6) Meanwhile, prepare the sauce by putting in the saucepan the remaining Ingredients. Season with salt and pepper.
7) Drizzle the pork chops with the sauce once cooked.

Nutrition information:
Calories per serving: 624; Carbs: 24.6g; Protein: 45.6g; Fat: 38.1g

Pureed Onion Marinated Beef
Serves: 3, Cooking Time: 45 minutes
Ingredients
- 1 ½ pounds skirt steak
- 1 large red onion, grated or pureed
- 1 tbsp. vinegar
- 2 tbsps. brown sugar
- Salt and pepper to taste

Instructions
1) Place all ingredients in a Ziploc bag and allow to marinate in the fridge for at least 2 hours.
2) Preheat the air fryer to 390°F.
3) Place the grill pan accessory in the air fryer.
4) Grill for 15 minutes per batch.
5) Flip every 8 minutes for even grilling.

Nutrition information:
Calories per serving: 512; Carbs: 6g; Protein: 60.1g; Fat: 27.5g

Rib Eye Steak Recipe from Hawaii
Serves: 6, Cooking Time: 45 minutes
Ingredients
- ½ cup soy sauce
- ½ cup sugar
- 1-inch ginger, grated
- 2 cups pineapple juice
- 2 tsps. sesame oil
- 3 pounds rib eye steaks
- 5 tbsp. apple cider vinegar

Instructions
1) Combine all ingredients in a Ziploc bag and allow to marinate in the fridge for at least 2 hours.
2) Preheat the air fryer to 390°F.
3) Place the grill pan accessory in the air fryer.
4) Grill the meat for 15 minutes while flipping the meat every 8 minutes and cook in batches.

5) Meanwhile, pour the marinade in a saucepan and allow to simmer until the sauce thickens.
6) Brush the grilled meat with the glaze before serving.

Nutrition information:
Calories per serving: 612; Carbs: 28g; Protein: 44g; Fat: 36g

Rib Eye Steak Seasoned with Italian Herb
Serves: 4, Cooking Time: 45 minutes
Ingredients
- 1 packet Italian herb mix
- 1 tbsp. olive oil
- 2 pounds bone-in rib eye steak
- Salt and pepper to taste

Instructions
1) Preheat the air fryer to 390°F.
2) Place the grill pan accessory in the air fryer.
3) Season the steak with salt, pepper, Italian herb mix, and olive oil. Cover top with foil.
4) Grill for 45 minutes and flip the steak halfway through the cooking time.

Nutrition information:
Calories per serving: 481; Carbs:1.1 g; Protein: 50.9g; Fat: 30.3g

Roast Beef with Balsamic-Honey Sauce
Serves: 10, Cooking Time: 2 hours
Ingredients
- ½ cup balsamic vinegar
- ½ tsp. red pepper flakes
- 1 cup beef organic beef broth
- 1 tbsp. coconut aminos
- 1 tbsp. honey
- 1 tbsp. Worcestershire sauce
- 3 pounds boneless roast beef
- 4 cloves of garlic, minced
- 4 tbsps. olive oil

Instructions
1) Place all ingredients in a baking dish and make sure that the entire surface of the beef is coated with the spices.
2) Place the baking dish with the bee in the air fryer. Close.
3) Cook for 2 hours at 400°F.

Nutrition information:
Calories per serving: 325; Carbohydrates: 6.9g; Protein: 36.2g; Fat: 16.9g

Roast Beef with Buttered Garlic-Celery

Serves: 8, Cooking Time: 1 hour

Ingredients

- 1 bulb of garlic, peeled and crushed
- 1 tbsp. butter
- 2 medium onions, chopped
- 2 pounds topside of beef
- 2 sticks of celery, sliced
- 3 tbsps. olive oil
- A bunch of fresh herbs of your choice
- Salt and pepper to taste

Instructions

1) Preheat the air fryer for 5 minutes.
2) In a baking dish that will fit in the air fryer, place all the ingredients and give a good stir.
3) Place the dish in the air fryer and bake for 1 hour at 350°F.

Nutrition information:
Calories per serving: 243; Carbohydrates: 3.1g; Protein: 16.7g; Fat: 18.2g

Roasted Ribeye Steak with Rum

Serves: 4, Cooking Time: 50 minutes

Ingredients

- ½ cup rum
- 2 pounds bone-in ribeye steak
- 2 tbsps. extra virgin olive oil
- Salt and black pepper to taste

Instructions

1) Place all Ingredients in a Ziploc bag and allow to marinate in the fridge for at least 2 hours.
2) Preheat the air fryer to 390°F.
3) Place the grill pan accessory in the air fryer.
4) Grill for 25 minutes per piece.
5) Halfway through the cooking time, flip the meat for even grilling.

Nutrition information:
Calories per serving: 390; Carbs: 0.1g; Protein: 48.9g; Fat: 21.5g

Saffron Spiced Rack of Lamb

Serves: 4, Cooking Time: 1 hour and 10 minutes

Ingredients

- ½ tsp. crumbled saffron threads
- 1 cup plain Greek yogurt
- 1 tsp. lemon zest
- 2 cloves of garlic, minced
- 2 racks of lamb, rib bones frenched
- 2 tbsps. olive oil
- Salt and pepper to taste

Instructions

1) Preheat the air fryer to 390°F.
2) Place the grill pan accessory in the air fryer.
3) Season the lamb meat with salt and pepper to taste. Set aside.
4) In a bowl, combine the rest of ingredients.
5) Brush the mixture onto the lamb.
6) Place on the grill pan and cook for 1 hour and 10 minutes.

Nutrition information:
Calories per serving: 1260; Carbs: 2g; Protein: 70g; Fat: 108g

Sage Sausage 'n Chili-Hot Breakfast
Serves: 4, Cooking Time: 27 minutes
Ingredients
- 1 cup freshly grated sweet potato
- 1 cup Mexican blend shredded cheese
- 1 cup sage sausage
- 1 large Anaheim chili peppers, chopped
- 1 stalk scallions, diced
- 2 cups freshly grated white Yukon gold potatoes
- 4 jumbo eggs, boiled, peeled and mashed
- 6 strips of bacon
- Salt to taste

Instructions
1) Place bacon on baking pan of air fryer.
2) For 5 minutes, cook on 390°F. Remove bacon.
3) Add sausage and cook for 5 minutes at same temperature. Halfway through, remove basket and crumble sausage and stir. Continue cooking.
4) Meanwhile crumble bacon.
5) Remove basket and toss the mixture a bit. Stir in bacon, shredded Yukon potatoes and sweet potatoes. Return to air fryer and cook for 4 minutes.
6) Meanwhile, in a medium bowl, whisk well eggs, chili peppers, and scallions. Season generously with salt.
7) Remove basket, toss well mixture, sprinkle cheese evenly, and pour eggs.
8) Cook for another 13 minutes at 330°F.
9) Serve and enjoy.

Nutrition information:
Calories per Serving: 295; Carbs: 19.1g; Protein: 17.7g; Fat: 17.3g

Salt and Pepper Pork Chinese Style

Serves: 4, Cooking Time: 25 minutes

Ingredients

- ½ tsp. sea salt
- ¾ cup potato starch
- 1 egg white, beaten
- 1 red bell pepper, chopped
- 1 tsp. Chinese five-spice powder
- 1 tsp. sesame oil
- 2 green bell peppers, chopped
- 2 tbsps. toasted sesame seeds
- 4 pork chops

Instructions

1) Preheat the air fryer to 330°F.
2) Season the pork chops with salt and five spice powder.
3) Dip in egg white and dredge in potato starch.
4) Place in the air fryer basket and cook for 25 minutes.
5) Meanwhile, heat oil in a skillet and stir-fry the bell peppers.
6) Serve the bell peppers on top of pork chops and garnish with sesame seeds.

Nutrition information:
Calories per serving: 394; Carbs: 9.3g; Protein: 43.1g; Fat: 20.5g

Salted 'n Peppered Scored Beef Chuck

Serves: 6, Cooking Time: 1 hour and 30 minutes

Ingredients

- 2 ounces black peppercorns
- 2 tbsps. olive oil
- 3 pounds beef chuck roll, scored with knife
- 3 tbsps. salt

Instructions

1) Preheat the air fryer to 390°F.
2) Place the grill pan accessory in the air fryer.
3) Season the beef chuck roll with black peppercorns and salt.
4) Brush with olive oil and cover top with foil.
5) Grill for 1 hour and 30 minutes.
6) Flip the beef every 30 minutes for even grilling on all sides.

Nutrition information:
Calories per serving: 360; Carbs: 1.4g; Protein: 46.7g; Fat: 18g

Salted Corned Beef with Onions

Serves: 12, Cooking Time: 50 minutes

Ingredients

- 1 large onion, chopped
- 2 tbsps. Dijon mustard

- 3 pounds corned beef brisket, cut into chunks
- 4 cups water
- Salt and pepper to taste

Instructions
1) Preheat the air fryer for 5 minutes
2) Place all ingredients in a baking dish that will fit in the air fryer.
3) Cook for 50 minutes at 400°F.

Nutrition information:
Calories per serving: 241; Carbohydrates: 1.5g; Protein: 15.2g; Fat:19.3g

Salted Porterhouse with Sage 'n Thyme Medley

Serves: 2, Cooking Time: 40 minutes

Ingredients
- ¼ cup fish sauce
- 2 porterhouse steaks
- 2 tbsps. marjoram
- 2 tbsps. sage
- 2 tbsps. thyme
- Salt and pepper to taste

Instructions
1) Place all ingredients in a Ziploc bag and allow to marinate in the fridge for at least 2 hours.
2) Preheat the air fryer to 390°F.
3) Place the grill pan accessory in the air fryer.
4) Grill for 20 minutes per batch.
5) Flip every 10 minutes for even grilling.

Nutrition information:
Calories per serving: 1189; Carbs: 6.3g; Protein: 112.5g; Fat: 79.3g

Salted Steak Pan Fried Steak

Serves: 1, Cooking Time: 15 minutes

Ingredients
- 1-pound beef steak, bones removed
- 3 tbsps. coconut oil
- A dash of oregano
- Salt and pepper to taste

Instructions
1) Place all ingredients in a Ziploc bag and allow to marinate in the fridge for at least 2 hours.
2) Preheat the air fryer.
3) Place the steak in the air fryer and cook for 15 minutes at 400°F.

Nutrition information:
Calories per serving: 1151; Carbohydrates: 4.2g; Protein: 65.9g; Fat: 96.7g

Sausage 'n Cauliflower Frittata

Serves: 3, Cooking Time: 27 minutes

Ingredients

- 1-pound hot pork sausage, diced
- ½ cup shredded Cheddar cheese
- 1 tsps. salt
- ½ cup milk
- 1 small cauliflower, riced
- 3 large eggs
- 1/2 (30 ounce) package frozen hash brown potatoes, thawed
- 1/2 tsp. ground black pepper

Instructions

1) Lightly grease baking pan of air fryer with cooking spray. And add diced sausage and cook for 10 minutes on 360°F.
2) Add hash brown and riced cauliflower. Cook for another 5 minutes.
3) Meanwhile, whisk well eggs, salt, pepper, and milk.
4) Remove basket and toss the mixture a bit. Evenly spread cheese and pour eggs.
5) Cook for another 12 minutes or until set
6) Serve and enjoy.

Nutrition information:
Calories per Serving: 612; Carbs: 33.4g; Protein: 49.2g; Fat: 44.6g

Sausage 'n Rice Bake from Mexico

Serves: 4, Cooking Time: 45 minutes

Ingredients

- 1/2-pound ground pork breakfast sausage
- 1/2 (16 ounce) jar picante sauce
- 1/2 (8 ounce) container sour cream
- 1-1/3 cups water
- 1/4-pound Cheddar cheese, shredded
- 2/3 cup uncooked long grain white rice

Instructions

1) Ring water to a boil in a saucepan and stir in rice. Cover and simmer for 20 minutes until all liquid is absorbed. Turn off fire and fluff rice.
2) Lightly grease baking pan of air fryer with cooking spray. Add sausage and cook for 10 minutes at 360°F. Halfway through cooking time, crumble and stir sausage.
3) Stir in cooked rice, sour cream, and picante sauce. Mix well. Sprinkle cheese on top
4) Cook for 15 minutes at 390°F until tops are lightly browned.
5) Serve and enjoy.

Nutrition information:
Calories per Serving: 452; Carbs: 31.0g; Protein: 18.9g; Fat: 28.0g

Scallion Sauce on Lemongrass-Chili Marinated Tri-Tip

Serves: 4, Cooking Time: 20 minutes

Ingredients

- 1 cup canned unsweetened coconut milk
- 2 tbsps. packed light brown sugar
- 1 tbsp. fresh lime juice
- 6 garlic cloves
- 4 red or green Thai chiles, stemmed
- 2 lemongrass stalks, bottom third only, tough outer layers removed
- 1-pound tri-tip fat cap left on, cut into 1-inch cubes
- 1 1 1/2" piece ginger, peeled
- 1/4 cup fish sauce

Scallion Dip Ingredients

- 15 scallions, very thinly sliced
- 3 tbsps. grapeseed oil
- 2 tbsps. black vinegar
- 2 tbsps. toasted sesame seeds
- 1/4 cup fish sauce

Basting Sauce Ingredients

- 1 1/2 tbsps. fresh lime juice
- 1/2 cup canned unsweetened coconut milk
- 2 garlic cloves, crushed
- 3 tbsps. fish sauce

Instructions

1) Except for meat, puree all Ingredients in a blender. Transfer into a bowl and marinate beef at least overnight in the ref.
2) In a medium bowl, mix well all scallion dip Ingredients and set aside.
3) In a separate bowl mix all basting sauce Ingredients.
4) Thread meat into skewers and place on skewer rack in air fryer. Baste with sauce.
5) Cook for 10 minutes at 390°F or to desired doneness. Halfway through cooking time, baste and turnover skewers.
6) Serve and enjoy with the dip on the side.

Nutrition information:
Calories per Serving: 579; Carbs: 15.3g; Protein: 32.0g; Fat: 43.3g

Seasoned Ham 'n Mushroom Egg Bake

Serves: 2, Cooking Time: 8 minutes

Ingredients

- 2 eggs
- Pinch of salt
- ½ cup ham, diced
- 2 mushrooms, sliced
- 1 stalk green onions, chopped
- 1 tsp. McCormick Good Morning Breakfast Seasoning – Garden Herb
- 1/4 cup milk
- 1/4 cup shredded cheese

Instructions

1) Lightly grease baking pan of air fryer with cooking spray. Spread ham on bottom, followed by mushrooms and cheese.
2) In a bowl, whisk eggs well. Season with salt and McCormick. Add milk and whisk well. Pour over mixture in air fryer pan.
3) For 8 minutes, cook on 330°F.
4) Sprinkle green onions and let it rest for a minute or two.
5) Serve and enjoy.

Nutrition information: Calories per Serving: 209; Carbs: 3.5g; Protein: 21.5g; Fat: 12.1g

Shepherd's Pie Made of Ground Lamb

Serves: 4, Cooking Time: 50 minutes

Ingredients

- 1-pound lean ground lamb
- 2 tbsps. and 2 tsps. all-purpose flour
- salt and ground black pepper to taste
- 1 tsp. minced fresh rosemary
- 2 tbsps. cream cheese
- 2 ounces Irish cheese (such as Dubliner®), shredded
- salt and ground black pepper to taste
- 1 tbsp. milk
- 1-1/2 tsps. olive oil
- 1-1/2 tsps. butter
- 1/2 onion, diced
- 1/2 tsp. paprika
- 1-1/2 tsps. ketchup
- 1-1/2 cloves garlic, minced
- 1/2 (12 ounce) package frozen peas and carrots, thawed
- 1-1/2 tsps. butter
- 1/2 pinch ground cayenne pepper
- 1/2 egg yolk
- 1-1/4 cups water, or as needed
- 1-1/4 pounds Yukon Gold potatoes, peeled and halved
- 1/8 tsp. ground cinnamon

Instructions

1) Bring a large pan of salted water to boil and add potatoes. Simmer for 15 minutes until tender.
2) Meanwhile, lightly grease baking pan of air fryer with butter. Melt for 2 minutes at 360°F.
3) Add ground lamb and onion. Cook for 10 minutes, stirring and crumbling halfway through cooking time.
4) Add garlic, ketchup, cinnamon, paprika, rosemary, black pepper, salt, and flour. Mix well and cook for 3 minutes.
5) Add water and deglaze pan. Continue cooking for 6 minutes.
6) Stir in carrots and peas. Evenly spread mixture in pan.
7) Once potatoes are done, drain well and transfer potatoes to a bowl. Mash potatoes and stir in Irish cheese, cream cheese, cayenne pepper, and butter. Mix well. Season with pepper and salt to taste.
8) In a small bowl, whisk well milk and egg yolk. Stir into mashed potatoes.
9) Top the ground lamb mixture with mashed potatoes.
10) Cook for another 15 minutes or until tops of potatoes are lightly browned.
11) Serve and enjoy.

Nutrition information:
Calories per Serving: 485; Carbs: 28.3g; Protein: 29.2g; Fat: 28.3g

Sherry 'n Soy Garlicky Steak

Serves: 3, Cooking Time: 50 minutes

Ingredients

- 1 tbsp. brown sugar
- ½ tsp. dry mustard
- 1 clove of garlic, minced
- 1 ½ pounds beef top round steak
- 2 green onions, chopped
- 1/3 cup soy sauce
- 1/3 cup dry sherry

Instructions

1) Place all ingredients except for the green onions in a Ziploc bag and allow to marinate in the fridge for at least 2 hours.
2) Preheat the air fryer to 390°F.
3) Place the grill pan accessory in the air fryer. Add meat and cover top with foil.
4) Grill for 50 minutes.
5) Halfway through the cooking time, flip the meat for even grilling.
6) Meanwhile, pour the marinade into a saucepan and simmer for 10 minutes until the sauce thickens.
7) Baste the meat with the sauce and garnish with green onions before serving.

Nutrition information:
Calories per serving: 170; Carbs: 3g; Protein: 28g; Fat: 5g

Simple Garlic 'n Herb Meatballs

Serves: 4, Cooking Time: 20 minutes

Ingredients

- 1 clove of garlic, minced
- 1 egg, beaten
- 1 tbsp. breadcrumbs or flour
- 1 tsp. dried mixed herbs
- 1-pound lean ground beef

Instructions

1) Place all Ingredients in a mixing bowl and mix together using your hands.
2) Form small balls using your hands and set aside in the fridge to set.
3) Preheat the air fryer to 390°F.
4) Place the meatballs in the air fryer basket and cook for 20 minutes.
5) Halfway through the cooking time, give the meatballs a shake to cook evenly.

Nutrition information:
Calories per serving: 599; Carbs: 16.7g; Protein: 54.9g; Fat: 34.7g

Simple Herbs de Provence Pork Loin Roast

Serves: 4, Cooking Time: 35 minutes

Ingredients

- 4 pounds pork loin
- A pinch of garlic salt
- A pinch of herbs de Provence

Instructions

1) Preheat the air fryer to 330°F.
2) Season pork with the garlic salt and herbs,
3) Place in the air fryer grill pan.
4) Cook for 30 to 35 minutes.

Nutrition information:
Calories per serving: 922; Carbs: 0.9g; Protein: 116.7g; Fat: 50.2g

Simple Lamb BBQ with Herbed Salt

Serves: 8, Cooking Time: 1 hour 20 minutes

Ingredients
- 2 ½ tbsps. herb salt
- 2 tbsps. olive oil
- 4 pounds boneless leg of lamb, cut into 2-inch chunks

Instructions
1) Preheat the air fryer to 390°F.
2) Place the grill pan accessory in the air fryer.
3) Season the meat with the herb salt and brush with olive oil.
4) Grill the meat for 20 minutes per batch.
5) Make sure to flip the meat every 10 minutes for even cooking.

Nutrition information:
Calories per serving: 347; Carbs: 0g; Protein: 46.6g; Fat: 17.8g

Simple Salt and Pepper Skirt Steak

Serves: 3, Cooking Time: 30 minutes

Ingredients
- 1 ½ pounds skirt steak
- Salt and pepper to taste

Instructions
1) Preheat the air fryer to 390°F.
2) Place the grill pan accessory in the air fryer.
3) Season the skirt steak with salt and pepper.
4) Place on the grill pan and cook for 15 minutes per batch.
5) Flip the meat halfway through the cooking time.

Nutrition information:
Calories per serving: 469; Carbs: 1g; Protein: 60g; Fat: 25g

Sirloin with Yogurt 'n Curry-Paprika

Serves: 3, Cooking Time: 25 minutes

Ingredients
- ¼ cup mint, chopped
- ½ cup low-fat yogurt
- 1 ½ pounds boneless beef top loin steak
- 2 tsps. curry powder
- 2 tsps. paprika
- 3 tbsps. lemon juice
- 6 cloves of garlic, minced
- Salt and pepper to taste

Instructions
1) Place all Ingredients except for the green onions in a Ziploc bag and

allow to marinate in the fridge for at least 2 hours.
2) Preheat the air fryer to 390°F.
3) Place the grill pan accessory in the air fryer.
4) Grill for 25 to 30 minutes.
5) Flip the steaks halfway through the cooking time for even grilling.

Nutrition information:
Calories per serving: 596; Carbs: 8.9g; Protein: 70.5g; Fat: 30.9g

Skirt Steak BBQ Recipe from Korea

Serves: 1, Cooking Time: 30 minutes

Ingredients
- 1 skirt steak, halved
- 3 tbsps. gochujang sauce
- 3 tbsps. olive oil
- 3 tbsps. rice vinegar
- Salt and pepper to taste

Instructions
1) Preheat the air fryer to 390°F.
2) Place the grill pan accessory in the air fryer.
3) Rub all spices and seasonings on the skirt steak.
4) Place on the grill and cook for 15 minutes per batch.
5) Flip the steak halfway through the cooking time.
6) Serve with more gochujang or kimchi.

Nutrition information:
Calories per serving: 467; Carbs: 8.3g; Protein:9.3 g; Fat: 44g

Smoked Brisket with Dill Pickles

Serves: 6, Cooking Time: 1 hour

Ingredients
- ¼ tsp. liquid smoke
- 1 cup dill pickles
- 3 pounds flat-cut brisket
- Salt and pepper to taste

Instructions
1) Preheat the air fryer to 390°F.
2) Place the grill pan accessory in the air fryer.
3) Season the brisket with liquid smoke, salt, and pepper.
4) Place on the grill pan and cook for 30 minutes per batch.
5) Flip the meat halfway through cooking time for even grilling.
6) Serve with dill pickles.

Nutrition information:
Calories per serving: 309; Carbs: 1.2g; Protein: 49g; Fat:12 g

Smoked Sausage 'n Shrimp Jambalaya

Serves: 4, Cooking Time: 40 minutes

Ingredients

- salt to taste
- 1 cup chicken broth
- 1/2 pound peeled and deveined medium shrimp (30-40 per pound)
- 1-1/2 tsps. olive oil
- 1/2 large onion, chopped
- 1/2 cup chopped green bell pepper
- 1/2 cup chopped celery
- 1/2 cup uncooked white rice
- 1-1/2 tsps. minced garlic
- 1-1/2 bay leaves
- 1/4-pound smoked sausage (such as Conecuh©), cut into 1/4-inch thick slices
- 1/4 tsp. Cajun seasoning, or to taste
- 1/8 tsp. dried thyme leaves
- 1/2 (14.5 ounce) can diced tomatoes with juice

Instructions

1) Lightly grease baking pan of air fryer with olive oil. Add sausage and for 5 minutes, cook on 360°F. Stir in Cajun seasoning, salt, celery, bell pepper, and onion. Cook for another 5 minutes.
2) Add the rice and mix well. Stir in thyme leaves, bay leaves, chicken broth, garlic, vegetable mixture, and tomatoes with juice. Cover with foil.
3) Cook for another 15 minutes.
4) Remove foil, stir in shrimp. Cook for 8 minutes.
5) Let it stand for 5 minutes.
6) Serve and enjoy.

Nutrition information:
Calories per Serving: 276; Carbs: 24.6g; Protein: 18.4g; Fat: 11.5g

Sriracha-Hoisin Glazed Grilled Beef

Serves: 5, Cooking Time: 16 minutes

Ingredients

- 1-pound flank steak, sliced at an angle 1" x ¼" thick
- 1 tbsp. lime juice
- 1 chopped green onions
- 1-1/2 tsps. honey
- 1/2 clove garlic, minced
- 1/2 tsp. kosher salt
- 1/2 tsp. peeled and grated fresh ginger root
- 1/2 tsp. sesame oil (optional)
- 1/2 tsp. chile-garlic sauce (such as Sriracha®)
- 1-1/2 tsps. toasted sesame seeds
- 1/4 cup hoisin sauce
- 1/4 tsp. crushed red pepper flakes
- 1/8 tsp. ground black pepper

Instructions

1) In a shallow dish, mix well pepper, red pepper flakes, chile-garlic sauce, sesame oil, ginger, salt, honey, lime juice, and hoisin sauce. Add steak and toss well to coat. Marinate in the ref for 3 hours.
2) Thread steak in skewers. Place on skewer rack in air fryer.
3) For 8 minutes, cook on 360°F. If needed, cook in batches.
4) Serve and enjoy with a drizzle of green onions and sesame seeds.

Nutrition information: Calories per Serving: 123; Carbs: 8.3g; Protein: 11.7g; Fat: 4.7g

Tasty Beef Pot Pie

Serves: 6, Cooking Time: 30 minutes

Ingredients
- 1 cup almond flour
- 1 green bell pepper, julienned
- 1 onion, chopped
- 1 red bell pepper, julienned
- 1 tbsp. butter
- 1 yellow bell pepper, julienned
- 1-pound ground beef
- 2 beaten eggs
- 2 cloves of garlic, minced
- 4 tbsps. coconut oil
- Salt and pepper to taste

Instructions
1) Preheat the air fryer for 5 minutes.
2) In a baking dish that will fit in the air fryer, combine the first 9 ingredients. Mix well then set aside.
3) In a mixing bowl, mix the almond flour and eggs to create a dough.
4) Press the dough over the beef mixture.
5) Place in the air fryer and cook for 30 minutes at 350°F.

Nutrition information:
Calories per serving: 363; Carbohydrates: 5.3g; Protein: 21.3g; Fat: 28.5g

Tasty Stuffed Gyoza

Serves: 4, Cooking Time: 20 minutes

Ingredients
- ¼ cup chopped onion
- ¼ tsp. ground cumin
- ¼ tsp. paprika
- ½ cup chopped tomatoes
- 1 egg, beaten
- 1 tbsp. olive oil
- 1/8 tsp. ground cinnamon
- 2 tsps. chopped garlic
- 3 ounces chopped cremini mushrooms
- 3 ounces lean ground beef
- 6 pitted green olives, chopped
- 8 gyoza wrappers

Instructions
1) Heat oil in a skillet over medium flame and stir in the beef for 3 minutes. Add the onions and garlic until fragrant. Stir in the mushrooms, olives, paprika, cumin, cinnamon, and tomatoes.
2) Close the lid and allow to simmer for 5 minutes. Allow to cool before making the empanada.
3) Place the meat mixture in the middle of the gyoza wrapper. Fold the gyoza wrapper and seal the edges by brushing with the egg mixture.
4) Preheat the air fryer to 390°F.
5) Place the grill pan accessory.

6) Place the prepared empanada on the grill pan accessory.
7) Cook for 10 minutes.
8) Flip the empanadas halfway through the cooking time.

Nutrition information:
Calories per serving: 339; Carbs: 25g; Protein: 17g; Fat: 19g

Tomato Salsa Topped Grilled Flank Steak

Serves: 4, Cooking Time: 40 minutes

Ingredients
- ¼ cup chopped cilantro
- 1 ½ pounds flank steak, pounded
- 1 red onion, chopped
- 1 tsp. coriander powder
- 2 cups chopped tomatoes
- Salt and pepper to taste

Instructions
1) Preheat the air fryer to 390°F.
2) Place the grill pan accessory in the air fryer.
3) Season the flank steak with salt and pepper.
4) Grill for 20 minutes per batch and make sure to flip the beef halfway through the cooking time.
5) Meanwhile, prepare the salsa by mixing in a bowl the tomatoes, cilantro, onions, and coriander. Season with more salt and pepper to taste.

Nutrition information:
Calories per serving: 243; Carbs: 4g; Protein: 37.4g; Fat: 8.6g

Top Loin Beef Strips with Blue Cheese

Serves: 4, Cooking Time: 50 minutes

Ingredients
- 1 tbsp. pine nuts, toasted
- 2 pounds crumbled blue cheese
- 2 tbsps. butter, softened
- 2 tbsps. cream cheese
- 4 boneless beef top loin steaks
- Salt and pepper to taste

Instructions
1) Preheat the air fryer to 390°F.
2) Place the grill pan accessory in the air fryer.
3) Season the beef with salt and pepper. Brush all sides with butter.
4) Grill for 25 minutes per batch making sure to flip halfway through the cooking time.
5) Slice the beef and serve with blue cheese, cream cheese and pine nuts.

Nutrition information:
Calories per serving: 682; Carbs: 1g; Protein: 75g; Fat: 42g

Top Round Roast with Mustard-Rosemary-Thyme Blend

Serves: 10, Cooking Time: 1 hour

Ingredients
- 1 tsp. dry mustard
- 2 tsps. dried rosemary
- 3 tbsps. olive oil
- 4 pounds beef top round roast
- 4 tsps. dried oregano
- 4 tsps. dried thyme
- Salt and pepper to taste

Instructions
1) Preheat the air fryer for 5 minutes.
2) Place all ingredients in a baking dish that will fit in the air fryer.
3) Place the dish in the air fryer and cook for 1 hour at 325°F.

Nutrition information:
Calories per serving: 334; Carbohydrates: 0.8g; Protein: 32.9g; Fat: 22.1g

Traditional Beef 'n Tomato Stew

Serves: 4, Cooking Time: 40 minutes

Ingredients
- 2 tbsps. quick-cooking tapioca
- 1 tsp. sugar
- 1 tsps. salt
- 1-pound beef stew meat, cut into 1-inch cubes
- 2 medium carrots, cut into 1-inch chunks
- 1 large potato, peeled and quartered
- 1 small onion, cut into chunks
- 1 slice bread, cubed
- 1/2 can (14-1/2 ounces) diced tomatoes, undrained
- 1/2 cup water
- 1/2 tsp. pepper
- 1 celery rib, cut into 3/4-inch chunks

Instructions
1) Lightly grease baking pan of air fryer with cooking spray. Add all Ingredients and toss well to coat.
2) Cover pan with foil.
3) For 25 minutes, cook on 390°F. Halfway through cooking time, stir.
4) Remove foil, stir well, and cook for 15 minutes at 330°F.
5) Serve and enjoy.

Nutrition information:
Calories per Serving: 296; Carbs: 31.0g; Protein: 25.0g; Fat: 8.0g

Traditional Beefy Spaghetti

Serves: 4, Cooking Time: 40 minutes

Ingredients

- 8- ounce spaghetti, cooked according to manufacturer's Instructions
- 1 egg
- 3 tbsps. grated Parmesan cheese
- 3 tbsps. butter, melted
- 1 cup small curd cottage cheese, divided
- 2 cups shredded mozzarella cheese, divided
- 1/2-pound ground beef
- 1/2 onion, chopped
- 1/2 (32 ounce) jar meatless spaghetti sauce
- 1/4 tsp. seasoned salt

Instructions

1) Lightly grease baking pan of air fryer with cooking spray. Add ground beef and onion. For 10 minutes, cook on 360°F. Crumble and mix well halfway through cooking time. Discard excess fat.
2) Mix in seasoned salt and spaghetti sauce. Mix well and transfer to a bowl.
3) In a large bowl, whisk well butter, parmesan cheese, and eggs.
4) In same air fryer baking pan, spread evenly half of the pasta, add half the spaghettis sauce, and then half of the mozzarella and cottage cheese. Repeat layering.
5) Cover pan with foil.
6) Cook for another 20 minutes, remove foil and cook for another 10 minutes.
7) Serve and enjoy.

Nutrition information:
Calories per Serving: 720; Carbs: 61.9g; Protein: 42.5g; Fat: 33.6g

Tri-Tip in Agave Nectar & Red Wine Marinade

Serves: 4, Cooking Time: 40 minutes

Ingredients

- ¼ cup red wine
- 1 tbsp. agave nectar
- 1 tbsp. smoked paprika
- 2 cloves of garlic, minced
- 2 cups chopped parsley
- 2 pounds tri-tip steak, pounded
- 2 tbsps. olive oil
- Salt and pepper to taste

Instructions

1) Place all ingredients in a Ziploc bag and allow to marinate for at least an hour.
2) Preheat the air fryer to 390°F.
3) Place the grill pan accessory in the air fryer.
4) Grill the meat for 40 minutes making sure to flip the meat every 10 minutes for even cooking.

Nutrition information:
Calories per serving: 667; Carbs: 4.4g; Protein: 69.3g; Fat: 41.3g

Tri-Tip Skewers Hungarian Style

Serves: 3, Cooking Time: 12 minutes

Ingredients
- 1-lb beef tri-tip, sliced to 2-inch cubes
- 2 smashed garlic cloves
- a pinch of salt
- 2 tsps. crushed caraway seeds
- 1 medium red onion, sliced into quarters
- 1 medium bell pepper seeded and cut into chunks
- 1/2 cup olive oil
- 1/2 tsp. paprika

Instructions
1) In a shallow dish, mix well all Ingredients except for bell pepper and onion. Toss well to coat. Marinate in the ref for 3 hours.
2) Thread beef, onion, and bell pepper pieces in skewers. Place on skewer rack in air fryer.
3) For 12 minutes, cook on 360°F. Halfway through cooking time, turnover skewers. If needed, cook in batches.
4) Serve and enjoy.

Nutrition information:
Calories per Serving: 530; Carbs: 3.3g; Protein: 33.1g; Fat: 42.7g

Very Tasty Herbed Burgers

Serves: 4, Cooking Time: 25 minutes

Ingredients
- ¼ cup grated cheddar cheese
- ½ pound minced pork or beef
- 1 onion, chopped
- 1 tbsp. basil
- 1 tsp. minced garlic
- 1 tsp. mixed herbs
- 1 tsp. mustard
- 1 tsp. tomato puree
- 4 bread buns
- Mixed greens
- Salt and pepper to taste

Instructions
1) Preheat the air fryer to 390°F.
2) Place the grill pan accessory in the air fryer.
3) In a mixing bowl, combine the pork, onion, garlic, tomato puree, mustard, basil, mixed herbs, salt and pepper.
4) Form four patties using your hands.
5) Place on the grill pan accessory.
6) Cook for 25 minutes. Flip the burgers halfway through the cooking time.
7) Serve patties on bread buns and top with cheese and mixed greens.

Nutrition information:
Calories per serving: 548; Carbs: 24.4g; Protein: 16.1g; Fat: 42.8g

Chapter 5 Air Fryer Poultry Recipes

Air Fried Chicken Tenderloin

Serves: 8, Cooking Time: 15 minutes

Ingredients
- ½ cup almond flour
- 1 egg, beaten
- 2 tbsps. coconut oil
- 8 chicken tenderloins
- Salt and pepper to taste

Instructions
1) Preheat the air fryer for 5 minutes.
2) Season the chicken tenderloin with salt and pepper to taste.
3) Soak in beaten eggs then dredge in almond flour.
4) Place in the air fryer and brush with coconut oil.
5) Cook for 15 minutes at 375°F.
6) Halfway through the cooking time, give the fryer basket a shake to cook evenly.

Nutrition information:
Calories per serving: 130.3; Carbohydrates: 0.7g; Protein: 8.7 g; Fat: 10.3 g

Almond Flour Battered Chicken Cordon Bleu

Serves: 1, Cooking Time: 30 minutes

Ingredients
- ¼ cup almond flour
- 1 slice cheddar cheese
- 1 slice of ham
- 1 small egg, beaten
- 1 tsp. parsley
- 2 chicken breasts, butterflied
- Salt and pepper to taste

Instructions
1) Season the chicken with parsley, salt and pepper to taste.
2) Place the cheese and ham in the middle of the chicken and roll. Secure with toothpick.
3) Soak the rolled-up chicken in egg and dredge in almond flour.
4) Place in the air fryer.
5) Cook for 30 minutes at 350°F.

Nutrition information:
Calories per serving: 1142; Carbohydrates: 5.5g; Protein: 79.4g; Fat: 89.1g

Almond Flour Coco-Milk Battered Chicken

Serves: 4, Cooking Time: 30 minutes

Ingredients
- ¼ cup coconut milk
- ½ cup almond flour
- 1 ½ tbsps. old bay Cajun seasoning
- 1 egg, beaten
- 4 small chicken thighs
- Salt and pepper to taste

Instructions
1) Preheat the air fryer for 5 minutes.
2) Mix the egg and coconut milk in a bowl.
3) Soak the chicken thighs in the beaten egg mixture.
4) In a mixing bowl, combine the almond flour, Cajun seasoning, salt and pepper.
5) Dredge the chicken thighs in the almond flour mixture.
6) Place in the air fryer basket.
7) Cook for 30 minutes at 350°F.

Nutrition information:
Calories per serving: 590; Carbohydrates: 3.2g; Protein:32.5 g; Fat: 38.6g

Bacon 'n Egg-Substitute Bake

Serves: 4, Cooking Time: 35 minutes

Ingredients
- 1 (6 ounce) package Canadian bacon, quartered
- 1/2 cup 2% milk
- 1/4 tsp. ground mustard
- 1/4 tsp. salt
- 2 cups shredded Cheddar-Monterey Jack cheese blend
- 3/4 cup and 2 tbsps. egg substitute (such as Egg Beaters® Southwestern Style)
- 4 frozen hash brown patties

Instructions
1) Lightly grease baking pan of air fryer with cooking spray.
2) Evenly spread hash brown patties on bottom of pan. Top evenly with bacon and then followed by cheese.
3) In a bowl, whisk well mustard, salt, milk, and egg substitute. Pour over bacon mixture.
4) Cover air fryer baking pan with foil.
5) Preheat air fryer to 330°F.
6) Cook for another 20 minutes, remove foil and continue cooking for another 15 minutes or until eggs are set.
7) Serve and enjoy.

Nutrition information:
Calories per Serving: 459; Carbs: 21.0g; Protein: 29.4g; Fat: 28.5g

Baked Rice, Black Bean and Cheese

Serves: 4, Cooking Time: 62 minutes

Ingredients

- 1 cooked skinless boneless chicken breast halves, chopped
- 1 cup shredded Swiss cheese
- 1/2 (15 ounce) can black beans, drained
- 1/2 (4 ounce) can diced green chile peppers, drained
- 1/2 cup vegetable broth
- 1/2 medium zucchini, thinly sliced
- 1/4 cup sliced mushrooms
- 1/4 tsp. cumin
- 1-1/2 tsps. olive oil
- 2 tbsps. and 2 tsps. diced onion
- 3 tbsps. brown rice
- 3 tbsps. shredded carrots
- ground cayenne pepper to taste
- salt to taste

Instructions

1) Lightly grease baking pan of air fryer with cooking spray. Add rice and broth. Cover pan with foil cook for 10 minutes at 390°F. Lower heat to 300°F and fluff rice. Cook for another 10 minutes. Let it stand for 10 minutes and transfer to a bowl and set aside.
2) Add oil to same baking pan. Stir in onion and cook for 5 minutes at 330°F.
3) Stir in mushrooms, chicken, and zucchini. Mix well and cook for 5 minutes.
4) Stir in cayenne pepper, salt, and cumin. Mix well and cook for another 2 minutes.
5) Stir in ½ of the Swiss cheese, carrots, chiles, beans, and rice. Toss well to mix. Evenly spread in pan. Top with remaining cheese.
6) Cover pan with foil.
7) Cook for 15 minutes at 390°F and then remove foil and cook for another 5 to 10 minutes or until tops are lightly browned.
8) Serve and enjoy.

Nutrition information:
Calories per Serving: 337; Carbs: 11.5g; Protein: 25.3g; Fat: 21.0g

Basil-Garlic Breaded Chicken Bake

Serves: 2, Cooking Time: 28 minutes

Ingredients

- 2 boneless skinless chicken breast halves (4 ounces each)
- 1 tbsp. butter, melted
- 1 large tomato, seeded and chopped
- 2 garlic cloves, minced
- 1 1/2 tbsps. minced fresh basil
- 1/2 tbsp. olive oil
- 1/2 tsp. salt
- 1/4 cup all-purpose flour
- 1/4 cup egg substitute
- 1/4 cup grated Parmesan cheese
- 1/4 cup dry bread crumbs
- 1/4 tsp. pepper

Instructions

1) In shallow bowl, whisk well egg substitute and place flour in a

separate bowl. Dip chicken in flour, then egg, and then flour. In small bowl whisk well butter, bread crumbs and cheese. Sprinkle over chicken.
2) Lightly grease baking pan of air fryer with cooking spray. Place breaded chicken on bottom of pan. Cover with foil.
3) For 20 minutes, cook on 390°F.
4) Meanwhile, in a bowl whisk well remaining ingredient.
5) Remove foil from pan and then pour over chicken the remaining Ingredients.
6) Cook for 8 minutes.
7) Serve and enjoy.

Nutrition information:
Calories per Serving: 311; Carbs: 22.0g; Protein: 31.0g; Fat: 11.0g

BBQ Chicken Recipe from Greece

Serves: 4, Cooking Time: 24 minutes
Ingredients
- 1 (8 ounce) container fat-free plain yogurt
- 2 tbsps. fresh lemon juice
- 2 tsps. dried oregano
- 1-pound skinless, boneless chicken breast halves - cut into 1-inch pieces
- 1 large red onion, cut into wedges
- 1/2 tsp. lemon zest
- 1/2 tsp. salt
- 1 large green bell pepper, cut into 1 1/2-inch pieces
- 1/3 cup crumbled feta cheese with basil and sun-dried tomatoes
- 1/4 tsp. ground black pepper
- 1/4 tsp. crushed dried rosemary

Instructions

1) In a shallow dish, mix well rosemary, pepper, salt, oregano, lemon juice, lemon zest, feta cheese, and yogurt. Add chicken and toss well to coat. Marinate in the ref for 3 hours.
2) Thread bell pepper, onion, and chicken pieces in skewers. Place on skewer rack.
3) For 12 minutes, cook on 360°F. Halfway through cooking time, turnover skewers. If needed, cook in batches.
4) Serve and enjoy.

Nutrition information:
Calories per Serving: 242; Carbs: 12.3g; Protein: 31.0g; Fat: 7.5g

BBQ Pineapple 'n Teriyaki Glazed Chicken

Serves: 4, Cooking Time: 23 minutes

Ingredients

- ¼ cup pineapple juice
- ¼ tsp. pepper
- ½ cup brown sugar
- ½ cup soy sauce
- ½ tsp. salt
- 1 green bell pepper, cut into 1-inch cubes
- 1 red bell pepper, cut into 1-inch cubes
- 1 red onion, cut into 1-inch cubes
- 1 Tbsp. cornstarch
- 1 Tbsp. water
- 1 yellow red bell pepper, cut into 1-inch cubes
- 2 boneless skinless chicken breasts, cut into 1-inch cubes
- 2 cups fresh pineapple cut into 1-inch cubes
- 2 garlic cloves, minced
- green onions, for garnish

Instructions

1) In a saucepan, bring to a boil salt, pepper, garlic, pineapple juice, soy sauce, and brown sugar. In a small bowl whisk well, cornstarch and water. Slowly stir in to mixture in pan while whisking constantly. Simmer until thickened, around 3 minutes. Save ¼ cup of the sauce for basting and set aside.
2) In shallow dish, mix well chicken and remaining thickened sauce. Toss well to coat. Marinate in the ref for a half hour.
3) Thread bell pepper, onion, pineapple, and chicken pieces in skewers. Place on skewer rack in air fryer.
4) For 10 minutes, cook on 360°F. Halfway through cooking time, turnover skewers and baste with sauce. If needed, cook in batches.
5) Serve and enjoy with a sprinkle of green onions.

Nutrition information:
Calories per Serving: 391; Carbs: 58.7g; Protein: 31.2g; Fat: 3.4g

BBQ Turkey Meatballs with Cranberry Sauce

Serves: 4, Cooking Time: 25 minutes

Ingredients

- 1 ½ tbsps. water
- 2 tsps. cider vinegar
- 1 tsp salt and more to taste
- 1-pound ground turkey
- 1 1/2 tbsps. barbecue sauce
- 1/3 cup cranberry sauce
- 1/4-pound ground bacon

Instructions

1) In a bowl, mix well with hands the turkey, ground bacon and a tsp of salt. Evenly form into 16 equal sized balls.
2) In a small saucepan boil cranberry sauce, barbecue sauce, water, cider vinegar, and a dash or two of salt. Mix well and simmer for 3 minutes.

3) Thread meatballs in skewers and baste with cranberry sauce. Place on skewer rack in air fryer.
4) For 15 minutes, cook on 360°F. Every after 5 minutes of cooking time, turnover skewers and baste with sauce. If needed, cook in batches.
5) Serve and enjoy.

Nutrition information:
Calories per Serving: 217; Carbs: 11.5g; Protein: 28.0g; Fat: 10.9g

Blueberry Overload French Toast

Serves: 5, Cooking Time: 45 minutes

Ingredients
- 1 (8 ounce) package cream cheese, cut into 1-inch cubes
- 1 cup fresh blueberries, divided
- 1 cup milk
- 1 tbsp. cornstarch
- 1/2 cup water
- 1/2 cup white sugar
- 1/2 tsp. vanilla extract
- 1-1/2 tsps. butter
- 2 tbsps. and 2 tsps. maple syrup
- 6 eggs, beaten
- 6 slices day-old bread, cut into 1-inch cubes

Instructions
1) Lightly grease baking pan of air fryer with cooking spray.
2) Evenly spread half of the bread on bottom of pan. Sprinkle evenly the cream cheese and ½ cup blueberries. Add remaining bread on top.
3) In a large bowl, whisk well eggs, milk, syrup, and vanilla extract. Pour over bread mixture.
4) Cover air fryer baking pan with foil and refrigerate overnight.
5) Preheat air fryer to 330°F.
6) Cook for 25 minutes covered in foil, remove foil and cook for another 20 minutes or until middle is set.
7) Meanwhile, make the sauce by mixing cornstarch, water, and sugar in a saucepan and bring to a boil. Stir in remaining blueberries and simmer until thickened and blueberries have burst.
8) Serve and enjoy with blueberry syrup.

Nutrition information:
Calories per Serving: 492; Carbs: 51.9g; Protein: 15.1g; Fat: 24.8g

Broccoli-Rice 'n Chees Casserole

Serves: 4, Cooking Time: 28 minutes

Ingredients

- 1 (10 ounce) can chunk chicken, drained
- 1 cup uncooked instant rice
- 1 cup water
- 1/2 (10.75 ounce) can condensed cream of chicken soup
- 1/2 (10.75 ounce) can condensed cream of mushroom soup
- 1/2 cup milk
- 1/2 small white onion, chopped
- 1/2-pound processed cheese food
- 2 tbsps. butter
- 8-ounce frozen chopped broccoli

Instructions

1) Lightly grease baking pan of air fryer with cooking spray. Add water and bring to a boil at 390°F. Stir in rice and cook for 3 minutes.
2) Stir in processed cheese, onion, broccoli, milk, butter, chicken soup, mushroom soup, and chicken. Mix well.
3) Cook for 15 minutes at 390°F, fluff mixture and continue cooking for another 10 minutes until tops are browned.
4) Serve and enjoy.

Nutrition information:
Calories per Serving: 752; Carbs: 82.7g; Protein: 36.0g; Fat: 30.8g

Buffalo Style Chicken Dip

Serves: 4, Cooking Time: 20 minutes

Ingredients

- 1 (8 ounce) package cream cheese, softened
- 1 tbsp. shredded pepper Jack cheese
- 1/2 pinch cayenne pepper, for garnish
- 1/2 pinch cayenne pepper, or to taste
- 1/4 cup and 2 tbsps. hot pepper sauce (such as Frank's Reshoot®)
- 1/4 cup blue cheese dressing
- 1/4 cup crumbled blue cheese
- 1/4 cup shredded pepper Jack cheese
- 1/4 tsp. seafood seasoning (such as Old Bay®)
- 1-1/2 cups diced cooked rotisserie chicken

Instructions

1) Lightly grease baking pan of air fryer with cooking spray. Mix in cayenne pepper, seafood seasoning, crumbled blue cheese, blue cheese dressing, pepper Jack, hot pepper sauce, cream cheese, and chicken.
2) For 15 minutes, cook on 390°F.
3) Let it stand for 5 minutes and garnish with cayenne pepper.
4) Serve and enjoy.

Nutrition information:
Calories per Serving: 405; Carbs: 3.2g; Protein: 17.1g; Fat: 35.9g

Buttered Spinach-Egg Omelet

Serves: 4, Cooking Time: 15 minutes

Ingredients
- ¼ cup coconut milk
- 1 tbsp. melted butter
- 1-pound baby spinach, chopped finely
- 3 tbsps. olive oil
- 4 eggs, beaten
- Salt and pepper to taste

Instructions
1) Preheat the air fryer for 5 minutes.
2) In a mixing bowl, combine the eggs, coconut milk, olive oil, and butter until well-combined.
3) Add the spinach and season with salt and pepper to taste.
4) Pour all ingredients in a baking dish that will fit in the air fryer.
5) Bake at 350°F for 15 minutes.

Nutrition information:
Calories per serving: 310; Carbohydrates: 3.6g; Protein: 13.6g; Fat: 26.8g

Caesar Marinated Grilled Chicken

Serves: 3, Cooking Time: 24 minutes

Ingredients
- ¼ cup crouton
- 1 tsp. lemon zest. Form into ovals, skewer and grill.
- 1/2 cup Parmesan
- 1/4 cup breadcrumbs
- 1-pound ground chicken
- 2 tbsps. Caesar dressing and more for drizzling
- 2-4 romaine leaves

Instructions
1) In a shallow dish, mix well chicken, 2 tbsps. Caesar dressing, parmesan, and breadcrumbs. Mix well with hands. Form into 1-inch oval patties.
2) Thread chicken pieces in skewers. Place on skewer rack in air fryer.
3) For 12 minutes, cook on 360°F. Halfway through cooking time, turnover skewers. If needed, cook in batches.
4) Serve and enjoy on a bed of lettuce and sprinkle with croutons and extra dressing.

Nutrition information:
Calories per Serving: 339; Carbs: 9.5g; Protein: 32.6g; Fat: 18.9g

Cheese Stuffed Chicken

Serves: 4, Cooking Time: 30 minutes

Ingredients

- 1 tbsp. creole seasoning
- 1 tbsp. olive oil
- 1 tsp. garlic powder
- 1 tsp. onion powder
- 4 chicken breasts, butterflied and pounded
- 4 slices Colby cheese
- 4 slices pepper jack cheese

Instructions

1) Preheat the air fryer to 390°F.
2) Place the grill pan accessory in the air fryer.
3) Create the dry rub by mixing in a bowl the creole seasoning, garlic powder, and onion powder. Season with salt and pepper if desired.
4) Rub the seasoning on to the chicken.
5) Place the chicken on a working surface and place a slice each of pepper jack and Colby cheese.
6) Fold the chicken and secure the edges with toothpicks.
7) Brush chicken with olive oil.
8) Grill for 30 minutes and make sure to flip the meat every 10 minutes.

Nutrition information:
Calories per serving: 727; Carbs:5.4 g; Protein: 73.1g; Fat: 45.9g

Cheesy Potato, Broccoli 'n Ham Bake

Serves: 3, Cooking Time: 35 minutes

Ingredients

- 1 1/2 tbsp. mayonnaise
- 1/3 cup canned condensed cream of mushroom soup
- 1/3 cup grated Parmesan cheese
- 1/3 cup milk
- 3/4 cup 3/cooked, cubed ham
- 6-ounce frozen chopped broccoli
- 6-ounce frozen French fries

Instructions

1) Lightly grease baking pan of air fryer with cooking spray.
2) Evenly spread French fries on bottom of pan. Place broccoli on top in a single layer. Evenly spread ham.
3) In a bowl, whisk well mayonnaise, milk, and soup. Pour over fries mixture.
4) Sprinkle cheese and over pan with foil.
5) For 25 minutes, cook on 390°F. Remove foil and continue cooking for another 10 minutes.
6) Serve and enjoy.

Nutrition information:
Calories per Serving: 511; Carbs: 34.7g; Protein: 22.8g; Fat: 31.2g

Cheesy Turkey-Rice with Broccoli

Serves: 4, Cooking Time: 40 minutes

Ingredients

- 1 cup cooked, chopped turkey meat
- 1 tbsp. and 1-1/2 tsps. butter, melted
- 1/2 (10 ounce) package frozen broccoli, thawed
- 1/2 (7 ounce) package whole wheat crackers, crushed
- 1/2 cup shredded Cheddar cheese
- 1/2 cup uncooked white rice

Instructions

1) Bring to a boil 2 cups of water in a saucepan. Stir in rice and simmer for 20 minutes. Turn off fire and set aside.
2) Lightly grease baking pan of air fryer with cooking spray. Mix in cooked rice, cheese, broccoli, and turkey. Toss well to mix.
3) Mix well melted butter and crushed crackers in a small bowl. Evenly spread on top of rice.
4) For 20 minutes, cook on 360°F until tops are lightly browned.
5) Serve and enjoy.

Nutrition information:
Calories per Serving: 269; Carbs: 23.7g; Protein: 17.0g; Fat: 11.8g

Chestnuts 'n Mushroom Chicken Casserole

Serves: 2, Cooking Time: 35 minutes

Ingredients

- 1 (10.75 ounce) can condensed cream of chicken soup
- 1 (4.5 ounce) can mushrooms, drained
- 1 1/2 tsps. melted butter
- 1 cup shredded, cooked chicken meat
- 1/2 (8 ounce) can water chestnuts, drained (optional)
- 1/2 cup mayonnaise
- 1/2 tsp. lemon juice
- 1/4 cup shredded Cheddar cheese
- 1/8 tsp. curry powder
- 1-1/4 cups cooked chopped broccoli

Instructions

1) Lightly grease baking pan of air fryer with cooking spray.
2) Evenly spread broccoli on bottom of pan. Sprinkle chicken on top, followed by water chestnuts and mushrooms.
3) In a bowl, whisk well melted butter, curry powder, lemon juice, mayonnaise, and soup. Pour over chicken mixture in pan. Cover pan with foil.
4) For 25 minutes, cook on 360°F.
5) Remove foil from pan and cook for another 10 minutes or until top is a golden brown.
6) Serve and enjoy.

Nutrition information:
Calories per Serving: 532; Carbs: 18.0g; Protein: 20.0g; Fat: 42.2g

Chicken BBQ on Kale Salad

Serves: 4, Cooking Time: 30 minutes

Ingredients
- ¼ cup Greek yogurt
- ¼ cup parmesan cheese, grated
- ½ cup cherry tomatoes, halved
- ½ tsp. Worcestershire sauce
- 1 clove of garlic, minced
- 1 large bunch Tuscan kale, cleaned and torn
- 3 tbsps. extra virgin olive oil
- 4 large chicken breasts, pounded
- Juice from 2 lemons, divided
- Salt and pepper to taste

Instructions
1) Place all Ingredients in a bowl except for the kale and tomatoes. Allow to marinate in the fridge for at least 2 hours.
2) Preheat the air fryer to 390°F.
3) Place the grill pan accessory in the air fryer.
4) Grill the chicken for 30 minutes.
5) Once cooked, slice the chicken and toss together with the kale and tomatoes.

Nutrition information:
Calories per serving: 500; Carbs: 5.9g; Protein: 82.3g; Fat: 16.3g

Chicken BBQ Recipe from Italy

Serves: 2, Cooking Time: 40 minutes

Ingredients
- 1 tbsp. fresh Italian parsley
- 1 tbsp. minced garlic
- 1-pound boneless chicken breasts
- 2 tbsps. tomato paste
- Salt and pepper to taste

Instructions
1) Place all Ingredients in a Ziploc bag except for the corn. Allow to marinate in the fridge for at least 2 hours.
2) Preheat the air fryer to 390°F.
3) Place the grill pan accessory in the air fryer.
4) Grill the chicken for 40 minutes.

Nutrition information:
Calories per serving: 292; Carbs: 6.6g; Protein: 52.6g; Fat: 6.1g

Chicken BBQ Recipe from Peru

Serves: 4, Cooking Time: 40 minutes

Ingredients
- ½ tsp. dried oregano
- 1 tsp. paprika
- 1/3 cup soy sauce
- 2 ½ pounds chicken, quartered
- 2 tbsps. fresh lime juice
- 2 tsps. ground cumin
- 5 cloves of garlic, minced

Instructions
1) Place all Ingredients in a Ziploc bag and shake to mix everything.
2) Allow to marinate for at least 2 hours in the fridge.
3) Preheat the air fryer to 390ºF.
4) Place the grill pan accessory in the air fryer.
5) Grill the chicken for 40 minutes making sure to flip the chicken every 10 minutes for even grilling.

Nutrition information:
Calories per serving: 377; Carbs: 7.9g; Protein: 59.7g; Fat: 11.8g

Chicken BBQ with Sweet 'n Sour Sauce

Serves: 6, Cooking Time: 40 minutes

Ingredients
- ¼ cup minced garlic
- ¼ cup tomato paste
- ¾ cup minced onion
- ¾ cup sugar
- 1 cup soy sauce
- 1 cup water
- 1 cup white vinegar
- 6 chicken drumsticks
- Salt and pepper to taste

Instructions
1) Place all Ingredients in a Ziploc bag
2) Allow to marinate for at least 2 hours in the fridge.
3) Preheat the air fryer to 390ºF.
4) Place the grill pan accessory in the air fryer.
5) Grill the chicken for 40 minutes.
6) Flip the chicken every 10 minutes for even grilling.
7) Meanwhile, pour the marinade in a saucepan and heat over medium flame until the sauce thickens.
8) Before serving the chicken, brush with the glaze.

Nutrition information:
Calories per serving: 407; Carbs:29.6 g; Protein: 27.8g; Fat: 19.7g

Chicken Fry Recipe from the Mediterranean

Serves: 2, Cooking Time: 21 minutes

Ingredients

- 2 boneless skinless chicken breast halves (6 ounces each)
- 3 tbsps. olive oil
- 6 pitted Greek or ripe olives, sliced
- 2 tbsps. capers, drained
- 1/2-pint grape tomatoes
- 1/4 tsp. salt
- 1/4 tsp. pepper

Instructions

1) Lightly grease baking pan of air fryer with cooking spray.
2) Add chicken and season with pepper and salt.
3) Brown for 3 minutes per side in preheated 390°F air fryer.
4) Stir in capers, olives, tomatoes, and oil.
5) Cook for 15 minutes at 330°F.
6) Serve and enjoy.

Nutrition information:
Calories per Serving: 330; Carbs: 6.0g; Protein: 36.0g; Fat: 18.0g

Chicken Grill Recipe from California

Serves: 4, Cooking Time: 40 minutes

Ingredients

- ¾ cup balsamic vinegar
- 1 tsp. garlic powder
- 2 tbsps. extra virgin olive oil
- 2 tbsps. honey
- 2 tsps. Italian seasoning
- 4 boneless chicken breasts
- 4 slices mozzarella
- 4 slices of avocado
- 4 slices tomato
- Balsamic vinegar for drizzling
- Salt and pepper to taste

Instructions

1) In a Ziploc bag, mix together the balsamic vinegar, garlic powder, honey, olive oil, Italian seasoning, salt, pepper, and chicken. Allow to marinate in the fridge for at least 2 hours.
2) Preheat the air fryer to 390°F.
3) Place the grill pan accessory in the air fryer.
4) Put the chicken on the grill and cook for 40 minutes.
5) Flip the chicken every 10 minutes to grill all sides evenly.
6) Serve the chicken with mozzarella, avocado, and tomato. Drizzle with balsamic vinegar.

Nutrition information:
Calories per serving: 853; Carbs: 43.2g; Protein:69.4 g; Fat: 44.7g

Chicken in Packets Southwest Style

Serves: 4, Cooking Time: 40 minutes

Ingredients

- 1 can black beans, rinsed and drained
- 1 cup cilantro, chopped
- 1 cup commercial salsa
- 1 cup corn kernels, frozen
- 1 cup Mexican cheese blend, shredded
- 4 chicken breasts
- 4 lime wedges
- 4 tsps. taco seasoning
- Salt and pepper to taste

Instructions

1) Preheat the air fryer to 390°F.
2) Place the grill pan accessory in the air fryer.
3) On a big aluminum foil, place the chicken breasts and season with salt and pepper to taste.
4) Add the corn, commercial salsa beans, and taco seasoning.
5) Close the foil and crimp the edges.
6) Place on the grill pan and cook for 40 minutes.
7) Before serving, top with cheese, cilantro and lime wedges.

Nutrition information:
Calories per serving: 837; Carbs: 47.5g; Protein: 80.1g; Fat: 36.2g

Chicken Kebab with Aleppo 'n Yogurt

Serves: 2, Cooking Time: 20 minutes

Ingredients

- 1 tbsp. Aleppo pepper
- 1 tbsp. extra-virgin olive oil
- 1 tbsp. red wine vinegar
- 1 tbsp. tomato paste
- 1 tsp. coarse kosher salt
- 1 tsp. freshly ground black pepper
- 3 garlic cloves, peeled, flattened
- 1-pound skinless boneless chicken (thighs and/or breast halves), cut into 1 1/4-inch cubes
- 1 unpeeled lemon; 1/2 thinly sliced into rounds, 1/2 cut into wedges for serving
- 1/3 cup plain whole-milk Greek-style yogurt

Instructions

1) Mix all Ingredients in a bowl. Marinate in the ref for at least an hour.
2) Thread chicken in skewers and place in air fryer skewer rack.
3) For 10 minutes, cook on 360°F. Halfway through cooking time, turnover skewers.
4) Serve and enjoy with lemon wedges.

Nutrition information:
Calories per Serving: 336; Carbs: 7.0g; Protein: 53.6g; Fat: 10.4g

Chicken Meatballs with Miso-Ginger

Serves: 4, Cooking Time: 10 minutes

Ingredients
- 1 1/2 tsps. white miso paste
- 1 large egg
- 1 tsp. finely grated ginger
- 1/4 cup panko (Japanese breadcrumbs), or fresh breadcrumbs
- 1/4 tsp. kosher salt
- 2 tbsps. sliced scallions
- 2 tsps. low-sodium soy sauce
- 3/4-pound ground chicken

Instructions
1) In a medium bowl, whisk well soy sauce, miso paste, and ginger. Set aside.
2) In a large bowl, mix well with hands ground chicken, large egg, scallions, and salt. Add panko and half of the sauce. Mix well.
3) Evenly divide into 12 balls. Thread into 4 skewers equally.
4) Place on skewer rack.
5) Cook for 2 minutes at 390°F. Baste with remaining sauce, turnover and cook for another 2 minutes. Baste with sauce on more time and cook for another minute.
6) Serve and enjoy.

Nutrition information:
Calories per Serving: 145; Carbs: 4.2g; Protein: 17.4g; Fat: 8.2g

Chicken Pot Pie with Coconut Milk

Serves: 8, Cooking Time: 30 minutes

Ingredients
- ¼ small onion, chopped
- ½ cup broccoli, chopped
- ¾ cup coconut milk
- 1 cup chicken broth
- 1/3 cup coconut flour
- 1-pound ground chicken
- 2 cloves of garlic, minced
- 2 tbsps. butter
- 4 ½ tbsps. butter, melted
- 4 eggs
- Salt and pepper to taste

Instructions
1) Preheat the air fryer for 5 minutes.
2) Place 2 tbsps. butter, broccoli, onion, garlic, coconut milk, chicken broth, and ground chicken in a baking dish that will fit in the air fryer. Season with salt and pepper to taste.
3) In a mixing bowl, combine the butter, coconut flour, and eggs.
4) Sprinkle evenly the top of the chicken and broccoli mixture with the coconut flour dough.
5) Place the dish in the air fryer.
6) Cook for 30 minutes at 325°F.

Nutrition information:
Calories per serving: 366; Carbohydrates: 3.4g; Protein: 21.8g; Fat: 29.5g

Chicken Roast with Pineapple Salsa

Serves: 2, Cooking Time: 45 minutes

Ingredients

- ¼ cup extra virgin olive oil
- ¼ cup freshly chopped cilantro
- 1 avocado, diced
- 1-pound boneless chicken breasts
- 2 cups canned pineapples
- 2 tsps. honey
- Juice from 1 lime
- Salt and pepper to taste

Instructions

1) Preheat the air fryer to 390°F.
2) Place the grill pan accessory in the air fryer.
3) Season the chicken breasts with lime juice, olive oil, honey, salt, and pepper.
4) Place on the grill pan and cook for 45 minutes.
5) Flip the chicken every 10 minutes to grill all sides evenly.
6) Once the chicken is cooked, serve with pineapples, cilantro, and avocado.

Nutrition information:
Calories per serving: 744; Carbs: 57.4g; Protein: 54.7g; Fat: 32.8g

Chicken Strips with Garlic

Serves: 4, Cooking Time: 25 minutes

Ingredients

- ¼ cup vegetable oil
- 1 cup coconut milk
- 1 tbsp. cayenne pepper
- 1 tsp. garlic powder
- 1 tsp. onion powder
- 1-pound chicken breast, cut into strips
- 2 cups almond flour
- 2 eggs
- 2 tbsps. paprika
- Salt and pepper to taste

Instructions

1) Season the chicken meat with salt and pepper to taste. Set aside.
2) In a mixing bowl, combine the eggs and coconut milk. Set aside.
3) In another bowl, mix the almond flour, paprika, garlic powder, and onion powder.
4) Soak the chicken meat in the egg mixture then dredge in the flour mixture.
5) Place in the air fryer basket.
6) Cook for 25 minutes at 350°F.
7) Meanwhile, prepare the hot sauce by combining the cayenne pepper and vegetable.
8) Drizzle over chicken once cooked.

Nutrition information:
Calories per serving: 539.7; Carbohydrates: 8.6g; Protein: 29.8g; Fat: 42.9g

Chicken Tikka Masala Kebab

Serves: 4, Cooking Time: 20 minutes

Ingredients

- 1 boneless, skinless chicken breast, cut into bite sized pieces
- 1 cup thick yogurt
- 1 medium bell pepper, cut into bite sized pieces
- 1 tbsp fresh ginger paste
- 1 tsp Garam masala
- 1 tsp turmeric powder
- 2 tbsp coriander powder
- 2 tbsp cumin powder
- 2 tbsp red chili powder
- 2 tsp olive oil
- 8 cherry tomatoes
- Salt to taste

Instructions

1) In a bowl, whisk well all Ingredients except for chicken breast, bell pepper, and tomatoes. Add chicken and marinate for at least 30 minutes.
2) With 4 steel skewers, skewer a piece of chicken, bell pepper, chicken, cherry tomato, chicken, and then tomato and pepper. Repeat for remaining skewers.
3) Place skewer in skewer rack, for 10 minutes, cook on 390°F. Halfway through cooking time, turnover skewer to cook evenly.
4) Serve and enjoy.

Nutrition information:
Calories per Serving: 273; Carbs: 17.4g; Protein: 20.3g; Fat: 13.5g

Chicken with Ginger-Cilantro Coconut

Serves: 5, Cooking Time: 20 minutes

Ingredients

- ¼ cup cilantro leaves, chopped
- ½ cup coconut milk
- 1 tbsp. grated ginger
- 1 tbsp. minced garlic
- 1 tsp. garam masala
- 1 tsp. smoked paprika
- 1 tsp. turmeric
- 1-pound chicken tenders, cut in half
- Salt and pepper to taste

Instructions

1) Place all ingredients in a bowl and stir to coat the chicken with all ingredients.
2) Allow to marinate in the fridge for 2 hours.
3) Preheat the air fryer for 5 minutes.
4) Place the chicken pieces in the air fryer basket.
5) Cook for 20 minutes at 400°F.

Nutrition information:
Calories per serving: 1198; Carbohydrates: 19.5g; Protein: 15.8g; Fat: 117.4g

Chicken with Peach Glaze

Serves: 4, Cooking Time: 40 minutes

Ingredients

- 1 jalapeno chopped
- 1 tbsp. chili powder
- 1 tbsp. minced garlic
- 1 tbsps. Dijon mustard
- 2 cups peach preserves
- 2 pounds chicken thighs
- 2 tbsps. soy sauce
- 3 tbsps. olive oil
- Salt and pepper to taste

Instructions

1) Place all Ingredients in a Ziploc bag and allow to rest in the fridge for at least 2 hours.
2) Preheat the air fryer to 390°F.
3) Place the grill pan accessory in the air fryer.
4) Grill for 40 minutes while flipping the chicken every 10 minutes.
5) Meanwhile, pour the marinade in a saucepan and allow to simmer for 5 minutes until the sauce thickens.
6) Brush the chicken with the glaze before serving.

Nutrition information:
Calories per serving: 730; Carbs: 31.7g; Protein: 39.4g; Fat: 49.5g

Chicken-Parm, Broccoli 'n Mushroom Bake

Serves: 2, Cooking Time: 40 minutes

Ingredients

- 1 (13.5 ounce) can spinach, drained
- 1 cup shredded mozzarella cheese
- 1/2 (10.75 ounce) can condensed cream of mushroom soup
- 1/3 cup bacon bits
- 1/4 cup grated Parmesan cheese
- 1/4 cup half-and-half
- 1-1/2 tsps. Italian seasoning
- 1-1/2 tsps. lemon juice
- 1-1/2 tsps. minced garlic
- 2 ounces fresh mushrooms, sliced
- 2 skinless, boneless chicken breast halves
- 2 tbsps. butter

Instructions

1) Lightly grease baking pan of air fryer with cooking spray. Add chicken breast and for 20 minutes, cook on 360°F. Halfway through cooking time, turnover chicken breast. Once done, transfer to a plate and set aside.
2) In same baking pan, melt butter. Stir in Parmesan cheese, half and half, Italian seasoning, mushroom soup, lemon juice, and garlic. Mix well and cook for 5 minutes or until heated through.
3) Stir in spinach and chicken. Tope with bacon bits and mozzarella cheese.
4) Cook for 15 minutes at 390°F until tops are lightly browned.
5) Serve and enjoy.

Nutrition information:
Calories per Serving: 659; Carbs: 17.6g; Protein: 61.6g; Fat: 38.0g

Chicken-Penne Pesto

Serves: 3, Cooking Time: 25 minutes

Ingredients

- 1 cup shredded Italian cheese blend
- 1/3 cup milk
- 1/4 (15 ounce) can crushed tomatoes
- 1/4 (15 ounce) jar Alfredo sauce
- 1/4 (15 ounce) jar pesto sauce
- 1-1/2 cups cubed cooked chicken
- 2 tbsps. grated Parmesan cheese
- 2 tbsps. seasoned bread crumbs
- 3/4 cup fresh baby spinach
- 3/4 tsp. olive oil
- 4-ounce penne pasta, cooked according to manufacturer's Instructions

Instructions

1) In a small bowl, whisk well olive oil, Parmesan, and bread crumbs. Set aside.
2) Lightly grease baking pan of air fryer with cooking spray. Mix in milk, pesto sauce, alfredo sauce, tomatoes, spinach, and Italian cheese blend. Mix well. Toss in cooked pasta and toss well to coat. Evenly sprinkle bread crumb mixture on top.
3) For 25 minutes, cook on 360°F until tops are lightly browned.
4) Serve and enjoy.

Nutrition information:
Calories per Serving: 729; Carbs: 40.7g; Protein: 45.4g; Fat: 47.2g

Chicken-Veggie Fusilli Casserole

Serves: 3, Cooking Time: 30 minutes

Ingredients

- 1 cup frozen mixed vegetables
- 1 tbsp. butter, melted
- 1 tbsp. grated Parmesan cheese
- 1 tbsp. olive oil
- 1/2 (10.75 ounce) can condensed cream of chicken soup
- 1/2 (10.75 ounce) can condensed cream of mushroom soup
- 1/2 cup dry bread crumbs
- 1/2 cup dry fusilli pasta, cooked according to manufacturer's instructions
- 1-1/2 tsps. dried basil
- 1-1/2 tsps. dried minced onion
- 1-1/2 tsps. dried parsley
- 3 chicken tenderloins, cut into chunks
- garlic powder to taste
- salt and pepper to taste

Instructions

1) Lightly grease baking pan of air fryer with olive oil. Add chicken. Season with parsley, basil, garlic

powder, pepper, salt, and minced onion.
2) For 10 minutes, cook on 360°F. Stir chicken halfway through cooking time.
3) Remove basket and toss the mixture a bit. Stir in mixed vegetables, cream of mushroom soup, cream of chicken soup, and cooked pasta. Mix well.
4) Mix melted butter, parmesan, and bread crumbs in a small bowl. Evenly spread on top of casserole.
5) Cook for 20 minutes at 390°F.
6) Serve and enjoy.

Nutrition information:
Calories per Serving: 399; Carbs: 35.4g; Protein: 19.8g; Fat: 19.8g

Chili, Lime & Corn Chicken BBQ

Serves: 4, Cooking Time: 40 minutes

Ingredients
- ½ tsp. cumin
- 1 tbsp. lime juice
- 1 tsp. chili powder
- 2 chicken breasts
- 2 chicken thighs
- 2 cups barbecue sauce
- 2 tsp. grated lime zest
- 4 ears of corn, cleaned
- Salt and pepper to taste

Instructions
1) Place all Ingredients in a Ziploc bag except for the corn. Allow to marinate in the fridge for at least 2 hours.
2) Preheat the air fryer to 390°F.
3) Place the grill pan accessory in the air fryer.
4) Grill the chicken and corn for 40 minutes.
5) Meanwhile, pour the marinade in a saucepan over medium heat until it thickens.
6) Before serving, brush the chicken and corn with the glaze.

Nutrition information:
Calories per serving: 849 ; Carbs: 87.7g; Protein: 52.3g; Fat: 32.1g

Chinese Five Spiced Marinated Chicken

Serves: 4, Cooking Time: 40 minutes

Ingredients

- ¼ cup hoisin sauce
- 1 ¼ tsps. sesame oil
- 1 ½ tsp. five spice powder
- 2 chicken breasts, halved
- 2 tbsps. rice vinegar
- 2 tsps. brown sugar
- 3 ½ tsp. grated ginger
- 3 ½ tsps. honey
- 3 cucumbers, sliced
- Salt and pepper to taste

Instructions

1) Place all Ingredients except for the cucumber in a Ziploc bag.
2) Allow to rest in the fridge for at least 2 hours.
3) Preheat the air fryer to 390°F.
4) Place the grill pan accessory in the air fryer.
5) Grill for 40 minutes and make sure to flip the chicken often for even cooking.
6) Serve chicken with cucumber once cooked.

Nutrition information:
Calories per serving: 330; Carbs:16.7 g; Protein: 31.2g; Fat: 15.4g

Chipotle Chicken ala King

Serves: 4, Cooking Time: 40 minutes

Ingredients

- 1 tbsp. sour cream
- 1 tsp. ground cumin
- 4 corn tortillas, cut into quarters
- 1/2 (10.75 ounce) can condensed cream of mushroom soup
- 1/2 (10.75 ounce) can condensed cream of chicken soup
- 1-1/2 tsps. vegetable oil
- 1/2 white onion, diced
- 1/2 red bell pepper, diced
- 1/2 green bell pepper, diced
- 1/2 (10 ounce) can diced tomatoes with green chile peppers (such as RO*TEL®)
- 1/2 cup chicken broth
- 1/2 tsp. ancho chile powder
- 1/2 cooked chicken, torn into shreds or cut into chunks
- 1/4 tsp. dried oregano
- 1/4-pound shredded Cheddar cheese
- 1/8 tsp. chipotle chile powder

Instructions

1) Lightly grease baking pan of air fryer with vegetable oil. Add bell pepper, red bell pepper, and onion. For 5 minutes, cook on 360°F.
2) Meanwhile, in a large bowl, whisk well chipotle chile powder, oregano, ancho chile powder, cumin, sour

cream, chicken broth, diced tomatoes, cream of chicken soup, and cream of mushroom soup.
3) Once bell peppers are done cooking, pour into bowl of sauce and mix well.
4) Add a few scoops of sauce on bottom of air fryer baking pan. Place ½ of chicken on top of sauce, top with 1/3 cheese, cover with a layer of torn tortilla. Repeat process until all ingredients are used up.
5) Cover pan with foil.
6) Cook for 25 minutes. Uncover and continue cooking for another 10 minutes.
7) Serve and enjoy.

Nutrition information:
Calories per Serving: 482; Carbs: 25.1g; Protein: 32.1g; Fat: 28.1g

Chipotle-Garlic Smoked Wings
Serves: 8, Cooking Time: 30 minutes
Ingredients
- ½ cup barbecue sauce
- 1 tbsp. chili powder
- 1 tbsp. garlic powder
- 1 tbsp. liquid smoke seasoning
- 1 tsp. chipotle chili powder
- 1 tsp. mustard powder
- 3 tbsps. paprika
- 4 pounds chicken wings
- 4 tsps. salt

Instructions
1) Place all Ingredients in a Ziploc bag
2) Allow to marinate for at least 2 hours in the fridge.
3) Preheat the air fryer to 390°F.
4) Place the grill pan accessory in the air fryer.
5) Grill the chicken for 30 minutes.
6) Flip the chicken every 10 minutes for even grilling.
7) Meanwhile, pour the marinade in a saucepan and heat over medium flame until the sauce thickens.
8) Before serving the chicken, brush with the glaze.

Nutrition information:
Calories per serving: 324; Carbs: 10.8g; Protein: 50.7g; Fat: 8.6g

Chives, Eggs 'n Ham Casserole

Serves: 4, Cooking Time: 15 minutes

Ingredients
- 1 egg, whole
- 2 tbsps. butter, unsalted
- 2 tbsps. coconut cream
- 2 tsp. fresh chives, chopped
- 3 uncured ham, chopped
- 4 large eggs, beaten
- Salt and pepper to taste

Instructions
1) Preheat the air fryer for 5 minutes.
2) In a mixing bowl, combine the beaten eggs, coconut cream, butter, and chives. Season with salt and pepper to taste.
3) Pour into a baking dish that will fit in the air fryer and sprinkle ham on top.
4) Crack 1 egg on top.
5) Place in the air fryer.
6) Cook for 15 minutes at 350°F.

Nutrition information:
Calories per serving: 178; Carbohydrates: 2.6g; Protein: 6.4g; Fat: 15.8g

Chorizo-Oregano Frittata

Serves: 6, Cooking Time: 15 minutes

Ingredients
- ½ chorizo sausage, sliced
- ½ zucchini, sliced
- 3 large eggs, beaten
- 3 tbsps. olive oil
- A dash of oregano
- A dash of Spanish paprika

Instructions
1) Preheat the air fryer for 5 minutes.
2) Combine all ingredients in a mixing bowl until well-incorporated.
3) Pour into a greased baking dish that will fit in the air fryer basket.
4) Place the baking dish in the air fryer.
5) Close and cook for 15 minutes at 350°F.

Nutrition information:
Calories per serving: 94; Carbohydrates: 0.5g; Protein: 1.8g; Fat: 9.4g

Cilantro-Lime 'n Liquid Smoke Chicken Grill

Serves: 4, Cooking Time: 40 minutes

Ingredients

- 1 ½ tsp. honey
- 1 tbsp. lime zest
- 1 tsp. liquid smoke
- 1/3 cup chopped cilantro
- 1/3 cup fresh lime juice
- 2 tbsps. olive oil
- 3 cloves of garlic, minced
- 4 chicken breasts, halved
- Salt and pepper to taste

Instructions

1) Place all Ingredients in a bowl and allow to marinate in the fridge for at least 2 hours.
2) Preheat the air fryer to 390°F.
3) Place the grill pan accessory in the air fryer.
4) Grill in the chicken for 40 minutes and make sure to flip the chicken every 10 minutes for even grilling.

Nutrition information:
Calories per serving: 571; Carbs: 6.1g; Protein: 60.9g; Fat: 33.6g

Coco Milk -Oregano Marinated Drumsticks

Serves: 6, Cooking Time: 30 minutes

Ingredients

- ½ cup almond flour
- ½ cup coconut milk
- ½ tsp. oregano
- ½ tsp. paprika
- ½ tsp. salt
- 3 tbsps. melted butter
- 6 chicken drumsticks

Instructions

1) Preheat the air fryer for 5 minutes
2) Soak the chicken drumsticks in coconut milk.
3) In a mixing bowl, combine the almond flour, salt, paprika, and oregano.
4) Dredge the chicken in the almond flour mixture.
5) Place the chicken pieces in the air fryer basket.
6) Air fry for 30 minutes at 325°F.
7) Halfway through the cooking time, give the fryer basket a shape.
8) Drizzle with melted butter once cooked.

Nutrition information:
Calories per serving: 305; Carbohydrates: 1.4g; Protein: 24.1g; Fat: 22.5g

Copycat KFC Chicken Strips

Serves: 8, Cooking Time: 20 minutes

Ingredients
- 1 chicken breast, cut into strips
- 1 egg, beaten
- 2 tbsps. almond flour
- 2 tbsps. desiccated coconut
- A dash of oregano
- A dash of paprika
- A dash of thyme
- Salt and pepper to taste

Instructions
1) Soak the chicken in egg.
2) In a mixing bowl, combine the rest of the ingredients until well-combined.
3) Dredge the chicken in the dry ingredients.
4) Place in the air fryer basket.
5) Cook for 20 minutes at 350°F.

Nutrition information:
Calories per serving: 100; Carbohydrates: 0.9g; Protein: 4.8g; Fat: 8.6g

Creamy Chicken 'n Pasta Tetrazzini

Serves: 3, Cooking Time: 30 minutes

Ingredients
- 1 cup chopped cooked chicken breast
- 1/2 (10.75 ounce) can condensed cream of mushroom soup
- 1/2 cup chicken broth
- 1/2 cup shredded sharp Cheddar cheese
- 1/4 (10 ounce) package frozen green peas
- 1/4 cup grated Parmesan cheese
- 1/4 cup minced green bell pepper
- 1/4 cup minced onion
- 1/4 tsp. salt
- 1/4 tsp. Worcestershire sauce
- 1/8 tsp. ground black pepper
- 2 tbsps. butter
- 2 tbsps. cooking sherry
- 3/4 cup sliced fresh mushrooms
- 4-ounce linguine pasta, cooked following manufacturer's instructions

Instructions
1) Lightly grease baking pan of air fryer and melt butter for 2 minutes at 360°F. Stir in bell pepper, onion, and mushrooms. Cook for 5 minutes.
2) Add chicken broth and mushroom soup, mix well. Cook for 5 minutes.
3) Mix in chicken, pepper, salt, Worcestershire sauce, sherry, peas, cheddar cheese, and pasta. Sprinkle paprika and Parmesan on top.
4) Cook for 15 minutes at 390°F until tops are lightly browned.
5) Serve and enjoy.

Nutrition information:
Calories per Serving: 494; Carbs: 39.0g; Protein: 28.8g; Fat: 24.7g

Creamy Chicken 'n Rice

Serves: 3, Cooking Time: 45 minutes

Ingredients

- 1 (10.75 ounce) can cream of celery soup
- 1 (10.75 ounce) can cream of chicken soup
- 1 (10.75 ounce) can cream of mushroom soup
- 1/2 cup butter, sliced into pats
- 2 cups instant white rice
- 2 cups water
- 3 chicken breasts, cut into cubes
- salt and ground black pepper to taste

Instructions

1) Lightly grease baking pan of air fryer with cooking spray.
2) In pan, mix cream of mushroom, celery soup, chicken soup, rice, water and chicken. Mix well.
3) Season with pepper and salt. Top with butter pats.
4) Cover pan with foil and for 35 minutes, cook on 360°F.
5) Let it stand for 10 minutes.
6) Serve and enjoy.

Nutrition information:

Calories per Serving: 439; Carbs: 36.7g; Protein: 16.8g; Fat: 25.0g

Creamy Chicken Breasts with crumbled Bacon

Serves: 4, Cooking Time: 25 minutes

Ingredients

- ¼ cup olive oil
- 1 block cream cheese
- 4 chicken breasts
- 8 slices of bacon, fried and crumbled
- Salt and pepper to taste

Instructions

1) Preheat the air fryer for 5 minutes.
2) Place the chicken breasts in a baking dish that will fit in the air fryer.
3) Add the olive oil and cream cheese. Season with salt and pepper to taste.
4) Place the baking dish with the chicken and cook for 25 minutes at 350°F.
5) Sprinkle crumbled bacon after.

Nutrition information:

Calories per serving: 827; Carbohydrates: 1.7g; Protein: 61.2g; Fat: 67.9g

Creamy Chicken-Veggie Pasta

Serves: 3, Cooking Time: 30 minutes

Ingredients

- 3 chicken tenderloins, cut into chunks
- salt and pepper to taste
- garlic powder to taste
- 1 cup frozen mixed vegetables
- 1 tbsp. grated Parmesan cheese
- 1 tbsp. butter, melted
- 1/2 (10.75 ounce) can condensed cream of chicken soup
- 1/2 (10.75 ounce) can condensed cream of mushroom soup
- 1/2 cup dry fusilli pasta, cooked according to manufacturer's Instructions
- 1 tbsp. and 1-1/2 tsps. olive oil
- 1-1/2 tsps. dried minced onion
- 1-1/2 tsps. dried basil
- 1-1/2 tsps. dried parsley
- 1/2 cup dry bread crumbs

Instructions

1) Lightly grease baking pan of air fryer with oil. Add chicken and season with parsley, basil, garlic powder, pepper, salt, and minced onion. For 10 minutes, cook on 360°F. Stirring halfway through cooking time.
2) Then stir in mixed vegetables, mushroom soup, chicken soup, and cooked pasta. Mix well.
3) Mix well butter, Parmesan cheese, and bread crumbs in a small bowl and spread on top of casserole.
4) Cook for 20 minutes or until tops are lightly browned.
5) Serve and enjoy.

Nutrition information:
Calories per Serving: 399; Carbs: 35.4g; Protein: 19.8g; Fat: 19.8g

Creamy Coconut Egg 'n Mushroom Bake

Serves: 4, Cooking Time: 20 minutes

Ingredients

- ½ cup mushrooms, chopped
- 1 cup coconut cream
- 1 tsp. onion powder
- 2 tbsps. butter
- 8 eggs, beaten
- Salt and pepper to taste

Instructions

1) Preheat the air fryer for 5 minutes.
2) In a mixing bowl, combine the eggs, butter, and coconut cream.
3) Pour in a baking dish together with the mushrooms and onion powder.
4) Season with salt and pepper to taste.
5) Place in the air fryer chamber and cook for 20 minutes at 310°F.

Nutrition information:
Calories per serving: 512; Carbohydrates: 3.8g; Protein: 20.8g; Fat: 45.9g

Creamy Scrambled Eggs with Broccoli

Serves: 2, Cooking Time: 20 minutes

Ingredients

- 3 Eggs
- 2 tbsp Cream
- 2 tbsp Parmesan Cheese grated or cheddar cheese
- Salt to taste
- Black Pepper to taste
- 1/2 cup Broccoli small florets
- 1/2 cup Bell Pepper cut into small pieces

Instructions

1) Lightly grease baking pan of air fryer with cooking spray. Spread broccoli florets and bell pepper on bottom and for 7 minutes, cook on 360°F.
2) Meanwhile, in a bowl whisk eggs. Stir in cream. Season with pepper and salt.
3) Remove basket and toss the mixture a bit. Pour egg mixture over.
4) Cook for another 10 minutes.
5) Sprinkle cheese and let it rest for 3 minutes.
6) Serve and enjoy.

Nutrition information:
Calories per Serving: 273; Carbs: 5.6g; Protein: 16.1g; Fat: 20.6g

Creamy Turkey Bake

Serves: 5, Cooking Time: 30 minutes

Ingredients

- 1 can (10-3/4 ounces) condensed cream of chicken soup, undiluted
- 1 can (4 ounces) mushroom stems and pieces, drained
- 1 cup chopped cooked turkey or chicken
- 1 tube (12 ounces) refrigerated buttermilk biscuits, cut into 4 equal slices
- 1/2 cup frozen peas
- 1/4 cup 2% milk
- Dash each ground cumin, dried basil and thyme

Instructions

1) Lightly grease baking pan of air fryer with cooking spray. Add all ingredients and toss well to mix except for biscuits.
2) Top with biscuits. Cover pan with foil.
3) For 15 minutes, cook on 390°F.
4) Remove foil and cook for 15 minutes at 330°F or until biscuits are lightly browned.
5) Serve and enjoy.

Nutrition information:
Calories per Serving: 325; Carbs: 38.0g; Protein: 14.0g; Fat: 13.0g

Crispy 'n Salted Chicken Meatballs

Serves: 6, Cooking Time: 20 minutes

Ingredients
- ½ cup almond flour
- ¾ pound skinless boneless chicken breasts, ground
- 1 ½ tsp. herbs de Provence
- 1 tbsp. coconut milk
- 2 eggs, beaten
- Salt and pepper to taste

Instructions
1) Mix all ingredient in a bowl.
2) Form small balls using the palms of your hands.
3) Place in the fridge to set for at least 2 hours.
4) Preheat the air fryer for 5 minutes.
5) Place the chicken balls in the fryer basket.
6) Cook for 20 minutes at 325°F.
7) Halfway through the cooking time, give the fryer basket a shake to cook evenly on all sides.

Nutrition information:
Calories per serving: 116.1; Carbohydrates: 1.2g; Protein: 15.9g; Fat: 5.3g

Crispy Fried Buffalo Chicken Breasts

Serves: 4, Cooking Time: 30 minutes

Ingredients
- ¼ cup sugar-free hot sauce
- ¼ tsp. cayenne pepper
- ¼ tsp. paprika
- 1 clove of garlic, minced
- 1 cup almond flour
- 1 large egg, beaten
- 1 tsp. stevia powder
- 1-pound chicken breasts, cut into thick strips
- 3 tbsps. butter
- Salt and pepper to taste

Instructions
1) Preheat the air fryer for 5 minutes.
2) Season the chicken breasts with salt and pepper to taste.
3) Dredge first in beaten egg then in flour mixture.
4) Arrange neatly in the air fryer basket.
5) Close and cook for 30 minutes at 350°F.
6) Halfway through the cooking time, shake the air fryer basket to cook evenly.
7) Meanwhile, prepare the sauce by combine the rest of the ingredients. Season the sauce with salt and pepper to taste. Set aside.
8) Once the chicken tenders are cooked, place in a bowl with the sauce and toss to coat.

Nutrition information:
Calories per serving: 312; Carbohydrates: 1.7g; Protein: 20.4g; Fat: 24.8g

Crispy Tender Parmesan Chicken

Serves: 2, Cooking Time: 20 minutes

Ingredients

- 1 tbsp. butter, melted
- 2 chicken breasts
- 2 tbsps. parmesan cheese
- 6 tbsps. almond flour

Instructions

1) Preheat the air fryer for 5 minutes.
2) Combine the almond flour and parmesan cheese in a plate.
3) Drizzle the chicken breasts with butter.
4) Dredge in the almond flour mixture.
5) Place in the fryer basket.
6) Cook for 20 minutes at 350ºF.

Nutrition information:

Calories per serving: 712; Carbohydrates: 1.4g; Protein: 35.7g; Fat: 62.6g

Curried Rice 'n Chicken Bake

Serves: 3, Cooking Time: 45 minutes

Ingredients

- 1 clove garlic, minced
- 6 ounces skinless, boneless chicken breast halves - cut into 1-inch cubes
- 1/2 cup water
- 1/2 (8 ounce) can stewed tomatoes
- 1-1/2 tsps. lemon juice
- 1-1/2 tsps. curry powder
- 1/2 cube chicken bouillon
- 1/2 bay leaf (optional)
- 1/4 cup and 2 tbsps. quick-cooking brown rice
- 1/4 cup raisins
- 1/4 tsp. ground cinnamon
- 1/8 tsp. salt

Instructions

1) Lightly grease baking pan of air fryer with cooking spray.
2) Stir in bay leaf, garlic, salt, cinnamon, bouillon, curry powder, lemon juice, raisins, brown rice, stewed tomatoes, and water. For 20 minutes, cook on 360ºF. Halfway through cooking time, stir in chicken and mix well.
3) Cover pan with foil.
4) Cook for 15 minutes at 390ºF, remove foil, cook for 10 minutes until tops are lightly browned.
5) Serve and enjoy.

Nutrition information:

Calories per Serving: 247; Carbs: 34.5g; Protein: 22.7g; Fat: 2.0g

Curry-Peanut Butter Rubbed Chicken

Serves: 3, Cooking Time: 12 minutes

Ingredients
- ½-lb boneless and skinless chicken thigh meat, cut into 2-inch chunks
- 1 medium bell pepper, seeded and cut into chunks
- 1 tbsp. lime juice
- 1 tbsp. Thai curry paste
- 1 tsp. salt
- 2/3 cup coconut milk
- 3 tbsps. peanut butter

Instructions
1) In a shallow dish, mix well all Ingredients except for chicken and bell pepper. Transfer half of the sauce in a small bowl for basting.
2) Add chicken to dish and toss well to coat. Marinate in the ref for 3 hours.
3) Thread bell pepper and chicken pieces in skewers. Place on skewer rack in air fryer.
4) For 12 minutes, cook on 360°F. Halfway through cooking time, turnover skewers and baste with sauce. If needed, cook in batches.
5) Serve and enjoy.

Nutrition information:
Calories per Serving: 282; Carbs: 10.0g; Protein: 20.0g; Fat: 18.0g

Dijon-Garlic Thighs

Serves: 6, Cooking Time: 25 minutes

Ingredients
- 1 tbsp. cider vinegar
- 1 tbsp. Dijon mustard
- 1-pound chicken thighs
- 2 tbsp. olive oil
- 2 tsps. herbs de Provence
- Salt and pepper to taste

Instructions
1) Place all ingredients in a Ziploc bag.
2) Allow to marinate in the fridge for at least 2 hours.
3) Preheat the air fryer for 5 minutes.
4) Place the chicken in the fryer basket.
5) Cook for 25 minutes at 350°F.

Nutrition information:
Calories per serving: 214; Carbohydrates: 1.1g; Protein: 12.7g; Fat: 17.6g

Drunken Chicken Jerk Spiced

Serves: 8, Cooking Time: 60 minutes

Ingredients
- ¾ ground cloves
- ¾ malt vinegar
- ¾ soy sauce
- 1 ½ tsps. ground nutmeg
- 2 ½ tsps. ground allspice
- 2 tbsps. rum
- 2tbsp. salt
- 4 habanero chilies
- 5 cloves of garlic, minced
- 8 pieces chicken legs

Instructions

1) Place all Ingredients in a Ziploc bag and give a good shake. Allow to marinate in the fridge for at least 2 hours.
2) Preheat the air fryer to 390°F.
3) Place the grill pan accessory in the air fryer.
4) Grill the chicken for 60 minutes and flip the chicken every 10 minutes for even grilling.

Nutrition information:
Calories per serving: 193; Carbs: 1.2g; Protein: 28.7 g; Fat: 8.1g

Easy Chicken Fried Rice

Serves: 3, Cooking Time: 20 minutes

Ingredients
- 1 cup frozen peas & carrots
- 1 packed cup cooked chicken, diced
- 1 tbsp vegetable oil
- 1/2 cup onion, diced
- 3 cups cold cooked white rice
- 6 tbsp soy sauce

Instructions

1) Lightly grease baking pan of air fryer with vegetable oil. Add frozen carrots and peas.
2) For 5 minutes, cook on 360°F.
3) Stir in chicken and cook for another 5 minutes.
4) Add remaining ingredients and toss well to mix.
5) Cook for another 10 minutes, while mixing halfway through.
6) Serve and enjoy.

Nutrition information:
Calories per Serving: 445; Carbs: 59.4g; Protein: 20.0g; Fat: 14.1g

Easy Fried Chicken Southern Style

Serves: 6, Cooking Time: 30 minutes

Ingredients
- 1 cup coconut flour
- 1 tsp. garlic powder
- 1 tsp. paprika
- 1 tsp. pepper
- 1 tsp. salt
- 5 pounds chicken leg quarters

Instructions
1) Preheat the air fryer for 5 minutes.
2) Combine all ingredients in a bowl. Give a good stir.
3) Place ingredients in the air fryer.
4) Cook for 30 minutes at 350°F.

Nutrition information:
Calories per serving:611; Carbohydrates: 2.8g; Protein: 92.7g; Fat: 25.4g

Easy How-To Hard Boil Egg in Air Fryer

Serves: 6, Cooking Time: 15 minutes

Ingredients
- 6 eggs

Instructions
1) Preheat the air fryer for 5 minutes.
2) Place the eggs in the air fryer basket.
3) Cook for 15 minutes at 360°F.
4) Remove from the air fryer basket and place in cold water.

Nutrition information:
Calories per serving: 140; Carbohydrates: 0g; Protein: 12g; Fat: 10g

Eggs 'n Turkey Bake

Serves: 4, Cooking Time: 15 minutes

Ingredients
- ½ tsp. garlic powder
- ½ tsp. onion powder
- 1 cup coconut milk
- 1-pound leftover turkey, shredded
- 2 cups kale, chopped
- 4 eggs, beaten
- Salt and pepper to taste

Instructions
1) Preheat the air fryer for 5 minutes.
2) In a mixing bowl, combine the eggs, coconut milk, garlic powder, and onion powder. Season with salt and pepper to taste.
3) Place the turkey meat and kale in a baking dish.
4) Pour over the egg mixture.
5) Place in the air fryer.
6) Cook for 15 minutes at 350°F.

Nutrition information:
Calories per serving: 817; Carbohydrates: 3.6g; Protein: 32.9g; Fat: 74.5g

Eggs Benedict on English Muffins

Serves: 5, Cooking Time: 40 minutes

Ingredients
- ½ tsp onion powder
- 1 cup milk
- 1 stalk green onions, chopped
- 1/2 (.9 ounce) package hollandaise sauce mix
- 1/2 cup milk
- 1/2 tsp. salt
- 1/4 tsp. paprika
- 2 tbsps. margarine
- 3 English muffins, cut into 1/2-inch dice
- 4 large eggs
- 6-ounces Canadian bacon, cut into 1/2-inch dice

Instructions
1) Lightly grease baking pan of air fryer with cooking spray.
2) Place half of the bacon on bottom of pan, evenly spread died English muffins on top. Evenly spread remaining bacon on top.
3) In a large bowl, whisk well eggs, 1 cup milk, green onions, onion powder, and salt. Pour over English muffin mixture. Sprinkle top with paprika. Cover with foil and refrigerate overnight.
4) Preheat air fryer to 390°F.
5) Cook in air fryer covered in foil for 25 minutes. Remove foil and continue cooking for another 15 minutes or until set.
6) Meanwhile, make the hollandaise sauce by melting margarine in a sauce pan. Mix remaining milk and hollandaise sauce in a small bowl and whisk into melted margarine. Simmer until thickened while continuously stirring.
7) Serve and enjoy with sauce.

Nutrition information:
Calories per Serving: 282; Carbs: 21.2g; Protein: 17.5g; Fat: 14.1g

Eggs, Cauliflower 'n Broccoli Brekky

Serves: 3, Cooking Time: 20 minutes

Ingredients
- ½ cup milk
- ½ cup shredded Cheddar cheese
- 1 cup broccoli, cut into little bits or riced
- 1 cup cauliflower, riced
- 1 tsps. salt
- 1/2 tsp. ground black pepper
- 1/2-pound hot pork sausage, diced
- 3 large eggs

Instructions
1) Lightly grease baking pan of air fryer with cooking spray. And cook pork sausage for 5 minutes at 360°F.

2) Remove basket and toss the mixture a bit. Stir in riced cauliflower and broccoli. Cook for another 5 minutes.
3) Meanwhile, whisk well eggs, salt, pepper, and milk. Stir in cheese.
4) Remove basket and pour in egg mixture.
5) Cook for another 10 minutes.
6) Serve and enjoy.

Nutrition information:
Calories per Serving: 434; Carbs: 6.5g; Protein: 27.3g; Fat: 33.2g

French Toast with Apples 'n Raisins

Serves: 6, Cooking Time: 40 minutes

Ingredients
- ½ cup diced peeled apples
- ½-lb loaf cinnamon raisin bread, cubed
- 1 ¼ cups half-and-half cream
- 2 tbsp maple syrup
- 3 tbsp butter, melted
- 4 eggs
- 4-oz cream cheese, diced

Instructions
1) Lightly grease baking pan of air fryer with cooking spray.
2) Evenly spread half of the bread on bottom of pan. Sprinkle evenly the cream cheese and apples. Add remaining bread on top.
3) In a large bowl, whisk well eggs, cream, butter, and maple syrup. Pour over bread mixture.
4) Cover air fryer baking pan with plastic wrap and refrigerate for two hours.
5) Preheat air fryer to 325°F.
6) Cook for 40 minutes.
7) Serve and enjoy while warm.

Nutrition information:
Calories per Serving: 362; Carbs: 28.3g; Protein: 10.1g; Fat: 23.1g

Garam Masala 'n Yogurt Marinated Chicken

Serves: 3, Cooking Time: 40 minutes

Ingredients
- ½ cup whole milk yogurt
- ½ tsp. ground cumin
- 1 ½ pounds skinless chicken thighs
- 1 ½ tsp. garam masala
- 1 tbsp. ground coriander
- 1 tbsp. smoked paprika
- 1-inch ginger, peeled and chopped
- 2 tbsps. prepared mustard
- 3 tbsps. fresh lime juice
- 4 cloves of garlic, minced
- 7 dried chilies, seeds removed and broken into pieces
- Salt and pepper to taste

Instructions

1. Place all ingredients in a Ziploc bag and give a good shake to combine everything.
2. Allow to marinate for at least 2 hours in the fridge.
3. Preheat the air fryer to 390°F.
4. Place the grill pan accessory in the air fryer.
5. Grill for at least 40 minutes.
6. Make sure to flip the chicken every 10 minutes.

Nutrition information:
Calories per serving: 589; Carbs: 25.5g; Protein:54.6 g; Fat: 29.8g

Garlic Paprika Rubbed Chicken Breasts

Serves: 4, Cooking Time: 30 minutes
Ingredients
- 1 tbsp. stevia powder
- 2 tbsps. lemon juice, freshly squeezed
- 2 tbsps. Spanish paprika
- 2 tsp. minced garlic
- 3 tbsps. olive oil
- 4 boneless chicken breasts
- Salt and pepper to taste

Instructions
1) Preheat the air fryer for 5 minutes.
2) Place all ingredients in a baking dish that will fit in the air fryer. Stir to combine.
3) Place the chicken pieces in the air fryer.
4) Cook for 30 minutes at 325°F.

Nutrition information:
Calories per serving:424; Carbohydrates: 3.9g; Protein: 62.2g; Fat: 17.7g

Garlic Rosemary Roasted Chicken

Serves: 6, Cooking Time: 50 minutes
Ingredients
- 1 tsp rosemary
- 2 pounds whole chicken
- 4 cloves of garlic, minced
- Salt and pepper to taste

Instructions
1) Season the whole chicken with garlic, salt, and pepper.
2) Place in the air fryer basket.
3) Cook for 30 minutes at 330°F.
4) Flip the chicken in the other side and cook for another 20 minutes.

Nutrition information:
Calories per serving: 328; Carbohydrates: 30.8g; Protein: 14.5g; Fat: 16.3g

Ginger Garam Masala Rubbed Chicken

Serves: 4, Cooking Time: 50 minutes

Ingredients

- 1 bell pepper, seeded and julienned
- 1 cup coconut milk
- 1 tsp. coriander powder
- 1 tsp. garam masala
- 1 tsp. turmeric powder
- 1 thumb-size ginger, grated
- 1 whole chicken, sliced into
- 2 tbsps. olive oil

Instructions

1) Preheat the air fryer for 5 minutes.
2) Place all ingredients in a baking dish that will fit in the air fryer.
3) Stir to combine.
4) Place in the air fryer.
5) Cook for 50 minutes at 350°F.

Nutrition information:

Calories per serving: 699; Carbohydrates: 4.9 g; Protein: 44.5g; Fat: 55.7g

Greens 'n Turkey sausage Frittata

Serves: 2, Cooking Time: 20 minutes

Ingredients

- ½ cup cheddar cheese finely grated, extra sharp
- ½ cup milk skimmed
- 1/2-pound breakfast turkey sausage
- 1/4 tsp cayenne pepper
- 1/4 tsp garlic powder
- 2-oz hash browns frozen, shredded
- 3 eggs
- 5-oz pre-cut mixed greens (kale, spinach, swiss chard or whatever else you can find)
- green onions for serving
- salt to taste

Instructions

1) Lightly grease baking pan of air fryer with cooking spray and add turkey sausage.
2) For 5 minutes, cook on 360°F. Open halfway and break up sausage.
3) Meanwhile in a bowl whisk well eggs. Season with salt, cayenned, and garlic powder. Add milk and whisk well.
4) Remove basket and break sausage some more. Stir in frozen hash brown and continue cooking for 5 minutes.
5) Toss in mixed greens and cheese.
6) Pour egg mixture over hash brown mixture.
7) Cook for another 10 minutes until eggs are set to desired doneness.
8) Sprinkle green onions and let it rest for a minute.
9) Serve and enjoy.

Nutrition information:

Calories per Serving: 616; Carbs: 39.8g; Protein: 39.7g; Fat: 33.1g

Grilled Chicken Pesto

Serves: 8, Cooking Time: 30 minutes

Ingredients
- 1 ¾ cup commercial pesto
- 8 chicken thighs
- Salt and pepper to taste

Instructions
1) Place all Ingredients in the Ziploc bag and allow to marinate in the fridge for at least 2 hours.
2) Preheat the air fryer to 390°F.
3) Place the grill pan accessory in the air fryer.
4) Grill the chicken for at least 30 minutes.
5) Make sure to flip the chicken every 10 minutes for even grilling.

Nutrition information:
Calories per serving: 477; Carbs: 3.8g; Protein: 32.6g; Fat: 36.8g

Grilled Chicken Recipe From Jamaica

Serves: 2, Cooking Time: 30 minutes

Ingredients
- ¼ cup pineapple chunks
- 1 tbsp. vegetable oil
- 2 whole chicken thighs
- 3 tsps. lime juice
- 4 tbsps. jerk seasoning

Instructions
1) In a shallow dish, mix well all Ingredients. Marinate in the ref for 3 hours.
2) Thread chicken pieces and pineapples in skewers. Place on skewer rack in air fryer.
3) For 30 minutes, cook on 360°F. Halfway through cooking time, turnover skewers.
4) Serve and enjoy.

Nutrition information:
Calories per Serving: 579; Carbs: 36.3g; Protein: 25.7g; Fat: 36.7g

Grilled Chicken Recipe from Korea

Serves: 4, Cooking Time: 30 minutes

Ingredients
- ½ cup gochujang
- ½ tsp. fresh ground black pepper
- 1 scallion, sliced thinly
- 1 tsp. salt
- 2 pounds chicken wings

Instructions
1) Place in a Ziploc bag the chicken wings, salt, pepper, and gochujang sauce.
2) Allow to marinate in the fridge for at least 2 hours.
3) Preheat the air fryer to 390°F.

4) Place the grill pan accessory in the air fryer.
5) Grill the chicken wings for 30 minutes making sure to flip the chicken every 10 minutes.
6) Top with scallions and serve with more gochujang.

Nutrition information:
Calories per serving: 278; Carbs: 0.8g; Protein: 50.1g; Fat: 8.2g

Grilled Chicken Recipe from Morocco

Serves: 4, Cooking Time: 20 minutes

Ingredients
- 1-pound skinless, boneless chicken thighs, cut into 2" pieces
- 2 garlic cloves, chopped
- 2 tsps. ground cumin
- 2 tsps. paprika
- 3 tbsps. plain yogurt
- 4 garlic cloves, finely chopped
- Kosher salt
- Kosher salt
- Vegetable oil (for grilling)
- Warm pita bread, labneh (Lebanese strained yogurt), chopped tomatoes, and fresh mint leaves (for serving)
- 1/2 cup finely chopped fresh flat-leaf parsley
- 1/3 cup olive oil
- 1/4 tsp. crushed red pepper flakes

Instructions

1) In food processor, process garlic, salt, and oil until creamy. Add yogurt and continue pulsing until emulsified. Transfer to a bowl, set aside in the ref.
2) In a large bowl, marinate chicken in red pepper flakes, paprika, cumin, parsley, and garlic. Marinate for at least two hours in the ref.
3) Thread chicken in skewers and place in skewer rack of air fryer.
4) For 10 minutes, cook on 390°F. Halfway through cooking time, turnover skewers.
5) Serve and enjoy with the dip on the side.

Nutrition information:
Calories per Serving: 343; Carbs: 8.1g; Protein: 28.0g; Fat: 22.0g

Grilled Chicken Wings with Curry-Yogurt

Serves: 4, Cooking Time: 35 minutes

Ingredients
- ½ cup plain yogurt
- 1 tbsps. curry powder
- 2 pounds chicken wings
- Salt and pepper to taste

Instructions

1) Season the chicken wings with yogurt, curry powder, salt and pepper. Toss to combine everything.
2) Allow to marinate in the fridge for at least 2 hours.

3) Preheat the air fryer to 390°F.
4) Place the grill pan accessory in the air fryer.
5) Grill the chicken for 35 minutes and make sure to flip the chicken halfway through the cooking time.

Nutrition information:
Calories per serving: 301; Carbs: 3.3g; Protein: 51.3g; Fat: 9.2g

Grilled Thighs with Honey Balsamic

Serves: 8, Cooking Time: 40 minutes

Ingredients
- 1/3 cup honey
- 2 tbsps. balsamic vinegar
- 2 tbsps. butter
- 3 cloves of garlic, minced
- 8 bone-in chicken thighs
- Chopped chives for garnish
- Lemon wedges for garnish
- Salt and pepper to taste

Instructions
1) In a mixing bowl, season the chicken with salt and pepper to taste. Add the butter, balsamic vinegar, honey, and garlic. Allow to marinate for 2 hours in the fridge.
2) Preheat the air fryer to 390°F.
3) Place the grill pan accessory in the air fryer.
4) Put the chicken on the grill pan and cook for 40 minutes. Flip the chicken every 10 minutes to grill evenly.
5) Meanwhile, place the remaining marinade in a saucepan and allow to simmer until thickened.
6) Once cooked, brush the chicken with the sauce and garnish with chives and lemon wedges.

Nutrition information:
Calories per serving: 524; Carbs: 32.4g; Protein: 25.1g; Fat: 32.7g

Healthy Turkey Shepherd's Pie

Serves: 2, Cooking Time: 50 minutes

Ingredients
- 1 tbsp. butter, room temperature
- 1/2 clove garlic, minced
- 1/2 large carrot, shredded
- 1/2 onion, chopped
- 1/2 tsp. chicken bouillon powder
- 1/2-pound ground turkey
- 1/8 tsp. dried thyme
- 1-1/2 large potatoes, peeled
- 1-1/2 tsps. all-purpose flour
- 1-1/2 tsps. chopped fresh parsley

- 1-1/2 tsps. olive oil
- 2 tbsps. warm milk
- 4.5-ounce can sliced mushrooms
- ground black pepper to taste
- salt to taste

Instructions
1) Until tender, boil potatoes. Drain and transfer to a bowl. Mash with milk and butter until creamy. Set aside.
2) Lightly grease baking pan of air fryer with olive oil. Add onion and for 5 minutes, cook on 360°F. Add chicken bouillon, garlic, thyme, parsley, mushrooms, carrot, and ground turkey. Cook for 10 minutes while stirring and crumbling halfway through cooking time.
3) Season with pepper and salt. Stir in flour and mix well. Cook for 2 minutes.
4) Evenly spread turkey mixture. Top with mashed potatoes, evenly.
5) Cook for 20 minutes or until potatoes are lightly browned.
6) Serve and enjoy.

Nutrition information:
Calories per Serving: 342; Carbs: 38.0g; Protein: 18.3g; Fat: 12.9g

Honey & Sriracha Over Chicken

Serves: 4, Cooking Time: 40 minutes

Ingredients
- ½ tsp. garlic powder
- ½ tsp. paprika
- 1 tbsp. honey
- 1 tsp. Dijon mustard
- 2 tbsps. sriracha
- 3 tbsps. rice vinegar
- 4 chicken breasts
- Salt and pepper to taste

Instructions
1) Place all Ingredients in a Ziploc bag and allow to marinate for at least 2 hours in the fridge.
2) Preheat the air fryer to 390°F.
3) Place the grill pan accessory in the air fryer.
4) Grill the chicken for at least 40 minutes and flip the chicken every 10 minutes for even cooking.

Nutrition information:
Calories per serving: 510; Carbs: 6.1g; Protein: 60.8g; Fat: 26.9g

Honey, Lime, And Garlic Chicken BBQ

Serves: 4, Cooking Time: 40 minutes

Ingredients
- ¼ cup lime juice, freshly squeezed
- ½ cup cilantro, chopped finely
- ½ cup honey
- 1 tbsp. olive oil
- 2 cloves of garlic, minced
- 2 pounds boneless chicken breasts
- 2 tbsps. soy sauce
- Salt and pepper to taste

Instructions
1) Place all Ingredients in a Ziploc bag and give a good shake. Allow to marinate in the fridge for at least 2 hours.
2) Preheat the air fryer to 390°F.
3) Place the grill pan accessory in the air fryer.
4) Grill the chicken for 40 minutes making sure to flip the chicken every 10 minutes to grill evenly on all sides.

Nutrition information:
Calories per serving: 458; Carbs: 38.9g; Protein: 52.5 g; Fat: 10.2g

Honey-Balsamic Orange Chicken

Serves: 3, Cooking Time: 40 minutes

Ingredients
- ½ cup balsamic vinegar
- ½ cup honey
- 1 ½ pounds boneless chicken breasts, pounded
- 1 tbsp. orange zest
- 1 tsp. fresh oregano, chopped
- 2 tbsps. extra virgin olive oil
- Salt and pepper to taste

Instructions
1) Put the chicken in a Ziploc bag and pour over the rest of the Ingredients. Shake to combine everything. Allow to marinate in the fridge for at least 2 hours.
2) Preheat the air fryer to 390°F.
3) Place the grill pan accessory in the air fryer.
4) Grill the chicken for 40 minutes.

Nutrition information:
Calories per serving: 521; Carbs: 56.1g; Protein: 51.8g; Fat: 9.9g

Lebanese Style Grilled Chicken

Serves: 3, Cooking Time: 20 minutes

Ingredients

- 1 onion, cut into large chunks
- 1 small green bell pepper, cut into large chunks
- 1 tsp. tomato paste
- 1/2 cup chopped fresh flat-leaf parsley
- 1/2 tsp. dried oregano
- 1/3 cup plain yogurt
- 1/8 tsp. ground allspice
- 1/8 tsp. ground black pepper
- 1/8 tsp. ground cardamom
- 1/8 tsp. ground cinnamon
- 1-pound skinless, boneless chicken breast halves cut into 2-inch pieces
- 2 cloves garlic, minced
- 2 tbsps. lemon juice
- 2 tbsps. vegetable oil
- 3/4 tsp. salt

Instructions

1) In a resealable plastic bag, mix cardamom, cinnamon, allspice, pepper, oregano, salt, tomato paste, garlic, yogurt, vegetable oil, and lemon juice. Add chicken, remove excess air, seal, and marinate in the ref for at least 4 hours.
2) Thread chicken into skewers, place on skewer rack and cook in batches.
3) For 10 minutes, cook on 360°F. Halfway through cooking time, turnover skewers.
4) Serve and enjoy with a sprinkle of parsley.

Nutrition information:
Calories per Serving: 297; Carbs: 9.8g; Protein: 34.3g; Fat: 13.4g

Leftovers 'n Enchilada Bake

Serves: 3, Cooking Time: 45 minutes

Ingredients

- 1 egg
- 1/2 (15 ounce) can black beans, drained
- 1/2 (15 ounce) can tomato sauce
- 1/2 (7.5 ounce) package corn bread mix
- 1/2 cup shredded Mexican-style cheese blend, or more to taste
- 1/2 envelope taco seasoning mix
- 1/2-pound chicken breast tenderloins
- 1-1/2 tsps. vegetable oil
- 2 tbsps. cream cheese
- 2 tbsps. water
- 2-1/4 tsps. chili powder
- 3 tbsps. milk

Instructions

1) Lightly grease baking pan of air fryer with vegetable oil. Add chicken and cook for 5 minutes per side at 360°F.

2) Stir in chili powder, taco seasoning mix, water, and tomato sauce. Cook for 10 minutes, while stirring and turning chicken halfway through cooking time.
3) Remove chicken from pan and shred with two forks. Return to pan and stir in cream cheese and black beans. Mix well.
4) Top with Mexican cheese.
5) In a bowl, whisk well egg and milk. Add corn bread mix and mix well. Pour over chicken.
6) Cover pan with foil.
7) Cook for another 15 minutes. Remove foil and cook for 10 minutes more or until topping is lightly browned.
8) Let it rest for 5 minutes.
9) Serve and enjoy.

Nutrition information:
Calories per Serving: 487; Carbs: 45.9g; Protein: 31.2g; Fat: 19.8g

Lemon-Aleppo Chicken

Serves: 4, Cooking Time: 1 hour

Ingredients
- ¼ cup Aleppo-style pepper
- ¼ cup fresh lemon juice
- ¼ cup oregano
- 1 cup green olives, pitted and cracked
- 1.4 cup chopped rosemary
- 2 pounds whole chicken, backbones removed and butterflied
- 6 cloves of garlic, minced
- Salt and pepper to taste

Instructions
1) Place the chicken breast side up and slice through the breasts. Using your palms, press against the breastbone to flatten the breasts or you may remove the bones altogether.
2) Once the bones have been removed, season the chicken with salt, pepper, garlic, pepper, rosemary, lemon juice, and oregano.
3) Allow to marinate in the fridge for at least 12 hours.
4) Preheat the air fryer to 390°F.
5) Place the grill pan accessory in the air fryer.
6) Place the chicken on the grill pan and place the olives around the chicken.
7) Grill for 1 hour and make sure to flip the chicken every 10 minutes for even grilling.

Nutrition information:
Calories per serving: 502; Carbs:50.4 g; Protein:37.6 g; Fat: 16.6g

Lemon-Butter Battered Thighs

Serves: 8, Cooking Time: 35 minutes

Ingredients

- ½ cup chicken stock
- 1 cup almond flour
- 1 egg, beaten
- 1 onion, diced
- 2 pounds chicken thighs
- 2 tbsps. capers
- 3 tbsps. olive oil
- 4 tbsps. butter
- Juice from 2 lemons, freshly squeezed
- Salt and pepper to taste

Instructions

1) Preheat the air fryer for 5 minutes.
2) Combine all ingredients in a baking dish. Make sure that all lumps are removed.
3) Place the baking dish in the air fryer chamber.
4) Cook for 35 minutes at 325°F.

Nutrition information:
Calories per serving: 386; Carbohydrates: 3.7g; Protein: 20.6g; Fat: 32.1g

Lemon-Oregano Chicken BBQ

Serves: 6, Cooking Time: 40 minutes

Ingredients

- 1 tbsp. grated lemon zest
- 2 tbsps. fresh lemon juice
- 2 tbsps. oregano, chopped
- 3 pounds chicken breasts
- 4 cloves of garlic, minced
- Salt and pepper to taste

Instructions

1) Preheat the air fryer to 390°F.
2) Place the grill pan accessory in the air fryer.
3) Season the chicken with oregano, garlic, lemon zest, lemon juice, salt and pepper.
4) Grill for 40 minutes and flip every 10 minutes to cook evenly.

Nutrition information:
Calories per serving: 388; Carbs: 1.9g; Protein: 47.5g; Fat: 21.2g

Lemon-Parsley Chicken Packets

Serves: 4, Cooking Time: 45 minutes

Ingredients

- ¼ cup smoked paprika
- ½ cup parsley leaves
- ½ tsp. liquid smoke seasoning
- 1 ½ tbsp. cayenne pepper
- 2 pounds chicken thighs
- 4 lemons, halved

- Salt and pepper to taste

Instructions
1) Preheat the air fryer to 390°F.
2) Place the grill pan accessory in the air fryer.
3) In a large foil, place the chicken and season with paprika, liquid smoke seasoning, salt, pepper, and cayenne pepper.
4) Top with lemon and parsley.
5) Instructions
6) Place on the grill and cook for 45 minutes.

Nutrition information:
Calories per serving: 551; Carbs: 10.4g; Protein: 39.2g; Fat: 39.1g

Malaysian Chicken Satay with Peanut Sauce

Serves: 4, Cooking Time: 25 minutes

Ingredients
- 1 tbsp. fish sauce
- 1 tbsp. lime juice
- 1 tbsp. white sugar
- 1 tbsp. yellow curry powder
- 1 tsp. fish sauce
- 1 tsp. white sugar
- 1/2 cup chicken broth
- 1/2 cup unsweetened coconut milk
- 1/2 tsp. granulated garlic
- 1/4 cup creamy peanut butter
- 1-pound skinless, boneless chicken breasts, cut into strips
- 2 tbsps. olive oil
- 2 tsps. yellow curry powder
- 3/4 cup unsweetened coconut milk

Instructions
1) In resealable bag, mix well garlic, 1 tsp fish sauce, 1 tsp sugar, 2 tsps. curry powder, and ½ cup coconut milk. Add chicken and toss well to coat. Remove excess air and seal bag. Marinate for 2 hours.
2) Thread chicken into skewer and place on skewer rack.
3) For 10 minutes, cook on 390°F. Halfway through cooking time, turnover skewers.
4) Meanwhile, make the peanut sauce by bringing remaining coconut milk to a simmer in a medium saucepan. Stir in curry powder and cook for 4 minutes. Add 1 tbsp fish sauce, lime juice, 1 tbsp sugar, peanut butter, and chicken broth. Mix well and cook until heated through. Transfer to a small bowl.
5) Serve and enjoy with the peanut sauce.

Nutrition information:
Calories per Serving: 482; Carbs: 12.1g; Protein: 31.7g; Fat: 34.0g

Meat-Covered Boiled Eggs

Serves: 7, Cooking Time: 25 minutes

Ingredients
- ¼ cup coconut flour
- 1-pound ground beef
- 2 eggs, beaten
- 2 tbsps. butter, melted
- 7 large eggs, boiled and peeled
- Cooking spray
- Salt and pepper to taste

Instructions
1) Preheat the air fryer for 5 minutes.
2) Place the beaten eggs, ground beef, butter, and coconut flour in a mixing bowl. Season with salt and pepper to taste.
3) Coat the boiled eggs with the meat mixture and place in the fridge to set for 2 hours.
4) Grease with cooking spray.
5) Place in the air fryer basket.
6) Cook at 350°F for 25 minutes.

Nutrition information:
Calories per serving: 325; Carbohydrates: 1.8g; Protein: 21.4g; Fat: 25.8g

Middle Eastern Chicken BBQ with Tzatziki Sauce

Serves: 6, Cooking Time: 24 minutes

Ingredients
- 1 1/2 pounds skinless, boneless chicken breast halves - cut into bite-sized pieces
- 1 tsp. dried oregano
- 1/2 tsp. salt
- 1/4 cup olive oil
- 2 cloves garlic, minced
- 2 tbsps. lemon juice

Tzatziki Dip Ingredients
- 1 (6 ounce) container plain Greek-style yogurt
- 1 tbsp. olive oil
- 2 tsps. white vinegar
- 1 clove garlic, minced
- 1 pinch salt
- 1/2 cucumber - peeled, seeded, and grated

Instructions
1) In a medium bowl mix well, all Tzatziki dip Ingredients. Refrigerate for at least 2 hours to allow flavors to blend.
2) In a resealable bag, mix well salt, oregano, garlic, lemon juice, and olive oil. Add chicken, squeeze excess air, seal, and marinate for at least 2 hours.
3) Thread chicken into skewers and place on skewer rack. Cook in batches.
4) For 12 minutes, cook on 360°F. Halfway through cooking time, turnover skewers and baste with marinade from resealable bag.
5) Serve and enjoy with Tzatziki dip.

Nutrition information:
Calories per Serving: 264; Carbs: 2.6g; Protein: 25.5g; Fat: 16.8g

Mixed Vegetable Breakfast Frittata

Serves: 6, Cooking Time: 45 minutes

Ingredients

- ½-pound breakfast sausage
- 1 cup cheddar cheese shredded
- 1 tsp. kosher salt
- 1/2 cup milk or cream
- 1/2 tsp. black pepper
- 6 eggs
- 8-ounces frozen mixed vegetables (bell peppers, broccoli, etc.), thawed

Instructions

1) Lightly grease baking pan of air fryer with cooking spray. For 10 minutes, cook on 360°F the breakfast sausage and crumble. Halfway through cooking time, crumble sausage some more until it looks like ground meat. Once done cooking, discard excess fat.
2) Stir in thawed mixed vegetables and cook for 7 minutes or until heated through, stirring halfway through cooking time.
3) Meanwhile, in a bowl, whisk well eggs, cream, salt, and pepper.
4) Remove basket, evenly spread vegetable mixture, and pour in egg mixture. Cover pan with foil.
5) Cook for another 15 minutes, remove foil and continue cooking for another 5-10 minutes or until eggs are set to desired doneness.
6) Serve and enjoy.

Nutrition information:
Calories per Serving: 187; Carbs: 7.0g; Protein: 15.0g; Fat: 11.0g

Mushroom 'n Coconut Cream Quiche

Serves: 8, Cooking Time: 20 minutes

Ingredients

- ¼ cup coconut cream
- ½ cup almond flour
- ½ cup mushroom, sliced
- ½ onion, chopped
- 1 tbsp. chives, chopped
- 2 tbsps. coconut oil
- 4 eggs, beaten
- Salt and pepper to taste

Instructions

1) Preheat the air fryer for 5 minutes.
2) In a mixing bowl, combine the almond flour and coconut oil.
3) Press the almond flour mixture at the bottom of a heat-proof baking dish.
4) Place in the air fryer and cook for 5 minutes.
5) Meanwhile, combine the rest of the ingredients in a mixing bowl.
6) Take the crust out and pour over the egg mixture.
7) Put the baking dish back into the air fryer and cook for 15 minutes at 350°F.

Nutrition information:
Calories per serving: 125; Carbohydrates: 2.2g; Protein: 4.8g; Fat: 10.8g

Naked Cheese, Chicken Stuffing

Serves: 3, Cooking Time: 20 minutes

Ingredients

- 1 cup cooked, cubed chicken breast meat
- 1/2 (10.75 ounce) can condensed cream of chicken soup
- 1/2 (14.5 ounce) can green beans, drained
- 1/2 cup shredded Cheddar cheese
- 6-ounce unseasoned dry bread stuffing mix
- salt and pepper to taste

Instructions

1) Mix well pepper, salt, soup, and chicken in a medium bowl.
2) Make the stuffing according to package Directions for Cooking.
3) Lightly grease baking pan of air fryer with cooking spray. Evenly spread chicken mixture on bottom of pan. Top evenly with stuffing. Sprinkle cheese on top.
4) Cover pan with foil.
5) For 15 minutes, cook on 390°F.
6) Remove foil and cook for 5 minutes at 390°F until tops are lightly browned.
7) Serve and enjoy.

Nutrition information:
Calories per Serving: 418; Carbs: 48.8g; Protein: 27.1g; Fat: 12.7g

Non-Fattening Breakfast Frittata

Serves: 2, Cooking Time: 15 minutes

Ingredients

- ¼ cup sliced mushrooms
- ¼ cup sliced tomato
- 1 cup egg whites
- 2 Tbsp chopped fresh chives
- 2 Tbsp skim milk
- Salt and Black pepper, to taste

Instructions

1) Lightly grease baking pan of air fryer with cooking spray.
2) Spread mushrooms and tomato on bottom of pan.
3) In a bowl, whisk well egg whites, milk, chives, pepper and salt. Pour into baking pan.
4) For 15 minutes, cook on 330°F.
5) Remove basket and let it sit for a minute.
6) Serve and enjoy.

Nutrition information:
Calories per Serving: 231; Carbs: 35.1g; Protein: 21.5g; Fat: 0.5g

Orange-Tequila Glazed Chicken

Serves: 6, Cooking Time: 40 minutes

Ingredients
- ¼ cup tequila
- 1 shallot, minced
- 1/3 cup orange juice
- 2 tbsps. brown sugar
- 2 tbsps. honey
- 2 tbsps. whole coriander seeds
- 3 cloves of garlic, minced
- 3 pounds chicken breasts
- Salt and pepper to taste

Instructions
1) Place all Ingredients in a Ziploc bag and allow to marinate for at least 2 hours in the fridge.
2) Preheat the air fryer to 390°F.
3) Place the grill pan accessory in the air fryer.
4) Grill the chicken for at least 40 minutes
5) Flip the chicken every 10 minutes for even cooking.
6) Meanwhile, pour the marinade in a saucepan and simmer until the sauce thickens.
7) Brush the chicken with the glaze before serving.

Nutrition information:
Calories per serving: 440; Carbs: 11.2g; Protein: 48.1g; Fat: 22.5g

Oregano-Thyme Rubbed Thighs

Serves: 4, Cooking Time: 11 minutes

Ingredients
- 4 bone-in chicken thighs with skin
- 1/8 tsp. garlic salt
- 1/8 tsp. onion salt
- 1/8 tsp. dried oregano
- 1/8 tsp. ground thyme
- 1/8 tsp. paprika
- 1/8 tsp. ground black pepper

Instructions
1) Lightly grease baking pan of air fryer with cooking spray. Place chicken with skin side touching the bottom of pan.
2) In a small bowl whisk well pepper, paprika, thyme, oregano, onion salt, and garlic salt. Sprinkle all over chicken.
3) For 1 minute, cook on 390°F.
4) Turnover chicken while rubbing on bottom and sides of pan for more seasoning.
5) Cook for 10 minutes at 390°F.
6) Serve and enjoy.

Nutrition information:
Calories per Serving: 185; Carbs: 0.2g; Protein: 19.2g; Fat: 11.9g

Over the Top Chicken Enchiladas

Serves: 3, Cooking Time: 50 minutes

Ingredients
- 1/2 (1.25 ounce) package mild taco seasoning mix
- 1/2 (10 ounce) can enchilada sauce
- 1/2 (10.75 ounce) can condensed cream of chicken soup
- 1/2 (4 ounce) can chopped green chilies, drained
- 1/2 (6 ounce) can sliced black olives
- 1/2 bunch green onions, chopped, divided
- 1/2 cup sour cream
- 1/2 cup water
- 1/2 small onion, chopped
- 1/2 tsp. lime juice
- 1/4 tsp. garlic powder
- 1/4 tsp. onion powder
- 1/8 tsp. chili powder
- 1-1/2 cups Cheddar cheese, shredded, divided
- 1-1/2 tsps. butter
- 1-pound skinless, boneless chicken breast meat, cooked and shredded
- 3 (12 inch) flour tortillas

Instructions
1) Lightly grease baking pan of air fryer with butter. Add onion and for 5 minutes, cook on 360°F.
2) Stir in water, green onions, taco seasoning, green chilies, and shredded chicken. Cook for another 10 minutes.
3) Stir in garlic powder, onion powder, and lime juice. Cook for 5 minutes more.
4) In a bowl whisk well chili powder, sour cream, and cream of chicken soup. Pour a cup of the mixture in the baking pan and mix well.
5) Evenly divide the chicken mixture into the flour tortillas, sprinkle with ½ of the cheese and roll.
6) Pour remaining soup mixture into air fryer baking pan. Place tortillas seam side down. Pour enchilada sauce on top and sprinkle remaining cheese.
7) Cover pan with foil.
8) Cook for another 20 minutes, remove foil and continue cooking another 10 minutes.
9) Serve and enjoy.

Nutrition information:
Calories per Serving: 706; Carbs: 52.5g; Protein: 42.2g; Fat: 36.3g

Paprika-Cumin Rubbed Chicken Tenderloin

Serves: 6, Cooking Time: 25 minutes

Ingredients
- ¼ cup coconut flour
- ¼ cup olive oil
- ½ tsp. garlic powder
- ½ tsp. ground cumin
- ½ tsp. onion powder
- ½ tsp. smoked paprika
- 1-pound chicken tenderloins
- Salt and pepper to taste

Instructions
1) Preheat the air fryer for 5 minutes.
2) Soak the chicken tenderloins in olive oil.
3) Mix the rest of the ingredients and stir using your hands to combine everything.
4) Place the chicken pieces in the air fryer basket.
5) Cook for 25 minutes at 325°F.

Nutrition information:
Calories per serving: 430; Carbohydrates: 4.1g; Protein:27.3g; Fat: 33.8g

Pasta with Turkey-Basil Red Sauce

Serves: 3, Cooking Time: 35 minutes

Ingredients
- 1 tsp. white sugar
- 1/2 cup tomato sauce
- 1/2-pound lean ground turkey
- 1/4 tsp. dried basil
- 2 cloves garlic, minced
- 7-ounce can stewed, diced tomatoes
- 8-ounce bow tie pasta, cooked according to manufacturer's Instructions

Instructions
1) Lightly grease baking pan of air fryer with cooking spray. Add ground turkey and garlic.
2) For 10 minutes, cook on 360°F. Halfway through cooking time stir and crumble ground turkey.
3) Stir in basil, sugar, tomato sauce, and stewed tomatoes. Mix well.
4) Cook for another 10 minutes, mixing well halfway through cooking time.
5) Stir in cooked pasta and mix well.
6) Cook for another 5 minutes, mix well.
7) Serve and enjoy.

Nutrition information:
Calories per Serving: 316; Carbs: 46.9g; Protein: 18.3g; Fat: 6.1g

Pepper-Salt Egg 'n Spinach Casserole

Serves: 6, Cooking Time: 20 minutes

Ingredients
- ½ cup red onion, chopped
- 1 cup mushrooms, sliced
- 1 red bell pepper, seeded and julienned
- 3 cups frozen spinach, chopped
- 3 egg whites, beaten
- 4 eggs, beaten
- Salt and pepper to taste

Instructions
1) Preheat the air fryer for 5 minutes.
2) In a mixing bowl, combine the eggs and egg whites. Whisk until fluffy.
3) Place the rest of the ingredients in a baking dish and pour the egg mixture.
4) Place in the air fryer chamber.
5) Cook for 20 minutes at 310°F.

Nutrition information:
Calories per serving: 170; Carbohydrates: 4.8g; Protein: 9.3g; Fat: 12.6g

Peppery Lemon-Chicken Breast

Serves: 1, Cooking Time:

Ingredients
- 1 chicken breast
- 1 tsp. minced garlic
- 2 lemons, rinds and juice reserved
- Salt and pepper to taste

Instructions
1) Preheat the air fryer.
2) Place all ingredients in a baking dish that will fit in the air fryer.
3) Place in the air fryer basket.
4) Close and cook for 20 minutes at 400°F.

Nutrition information:
Calories per serving: 539; Carbohydrates: 11.8g; Protein: 61.8g; Fat: 27.2g

Pineapple Juice-Soy Sauce Marinated Chicken

Serves: 5, Cooking Time: 20 minutes

Ingredients
- 3 tbsps. light soy sauce
- 1-pound chicken breast tenderloins or strips
- 1/2 cup pineapple juice
- 1/4 cup packed brown sugar

Instructions
1) In a small saucepan bring to a boil pineapple juice, brown sugar, and soy sauce. Transfer to a large bowl. Stir in chicken and pineapple. Let it marinate in the fridge for an hour.

2) Thread pineapple and chicken in skewers. Place on skewer rack.
3) For 10 minutes, cook on 360°F. Halfway through cooking time, turnover chicken and baste with marinade.
4) Serve and enjoy.

Nutrition information:
Calories per Serving: 157; Carbs: 14.7g; Protein: 19.4g; Fat: 2.2g

Quick 'n Easy Brekky Eggs 'n Cream

Serves: 2, Cooking Time: 15 minutes

Ingredients
- 2 eggs
- 2 tbsps. coconut cream
- A dash of Spanish paprika
- Salt and pepper to taste

Instructions
1) Preheat the air fryer for 5 minutes.
2) Place the eggs and coconut cream in a bowl. Season with salt and pepper to taste then whisk until fluffy
3) Pour into greased ramekins and sprinkle with Spanish paprika.
4) Place in the air fryer.
5) Bake for 15 minutes at 350°F.

Nutrition information:
Calories per serving:178.1; Carbohydrates: 1.1g; Protein: 9.9g; Fat: 14.9g

Quick 'n Easy Garlic Herb Wings

Serves: 4, Cooking Time: 35 minutes

Ingredients
- ¼ cup chopped rosemary
- 2 pounds chicken wings
- 6 medium garlic cloves, grated
- Salt and pepper to taste

Instructions
1) Season the chicken with garlic, rosemary, salt and pepper.
2) Preheat the air fryer to 390°F.
3) Place the grill pan accessory in the air fryer.
4) Grill for 35 minutes and make sure to flip the chicken every 10 minutes.

Nutrition information:
Calories per serving: 287; Carbs: 2.9g; Protein: 50.4g; Fat: 8.2g

Radish Hash Browns with Onion-Paprika Spice

Serves: 6, Cooking Time: 10 minutes

Ingredients

- ¼ tsp. ground black pepper
- ½ tsp. paprika
- ¾ tsp. salt
- 1 onion, chopped
- 1 tsp. garlic powder
- 1 tsp. onion powder
- 1-pound radish, peeled and grated
- 3 tbsp. coconut oil

Instructions

1) Preheat the air fryer for 5 minutes.
2) Place all ingredients in a mixing bowl.
3) Form patties using your hands and place individual patties in the air fryer basket.
4) Grease with cooking spray before closing the air fryer.
5) Cook for 10 minutes at 350°F until crispy.

Nutrition information:
Calories per serving: 81; Carbohydrates: 5.7g; Protein: 0.9g; Fat: 6.1g

Reuben Style Chicken Roll-up

Serves: 2, Cooking Time: 15 minutes

Ingredients

- 1/4 tsp. garlic salt
- 1/4 tsp. pepper
- 2 boneless skinless chicken breast halves (4 ounces each)
- 2 slices deli corned beef
- 2 slices swirled rye and pumpernickel bread
- 2 slices Swiss cheese
- 2 tbsps. Thousand Island salad dressing
- Additional Thousand Island salad dressing, optional

Instructions

1) Tear bread into 2-inch pieces and place in blender. Pulse until crumbly. Transfer to a shallow bowl.
2) With meal mallet, pound chicken to ¼*inch thick. Season with pepper and salt. Top chicken with corned beef and cheese. Roll chicken and secure ends with toothpick.
3) Brush chicken with dressing and dip in crumbs until covered totally.
4) Lightly grease baking pan of air fryer with cooking spray. Place rollups.
5) For 15 minutes, cook on 330°F preheated air fryer.
6) Turnover rollups and continue cooking for another 10 minutes.
7) Serve and enjoy with extra dressing.

Nutrition information:
Calories per Serving: 317; Carbs: 18.0g; Protein: 32.0g; Fat: 13.0g

Roast Chicken Recipe from Africa

Serves: 6, Cooking Time: 45 minutes

Ingredients
- ¼ cup fresh lemon juice
- ½ cup piri piri sauce
- 1 large shallots, quartered
- 1-inch fresh ginger, peeled and sliced thinly
- 3 cloves of garlic, minced
- 3 pounds chicken breasts
- Salt and pepper to taste

Instructions
1) Preheat the air fryer to 390°F.
2) Place the grill pan accessory in the air fryer.
3) On a large foil, place the chicken top with the rest of the Ingredients.
4) Fold the foil and crimp the edges.
5) Grill for 45 minutes.

Nutrition information:
Calories per serving: 395; Carbs: 3.4g; Protein: 47.9g; Fat: 21.1g

Salsa on Chicken-Rice Bake

Serves: 4, Cooking Time: 65 minutes

Ingredients
- 2 skinless, boneless chicken breast halves
- 1 cup shredded Monterey Jack cheese
- 1 cup shredded Cheddar cheese
- 1/2 (10.75 ounce) can condensed cream of chicken soup
- 1/2 (10.75 ounce) can condensed cream of mushroom soup
- 1/2 onion, chopped
- 1-1/3 cups water
- 2/3 cup uncooked white rice
- 3/4 cup mild salsa

Instructions
1) Lightly grease baking pan of air fryer with cooking spray. Add water, rice, and chicken. Cover with foil and for 25 minutes, cook on 360°F.
2) Remove foil and remove chicken and cut into bite sized pieces. Fluff rice and transfer to plate.
3) In a bowl mix well, cheeses. In another bowl whisk well salsa, onion, cream of mushroom, and cream of chicken.
4) In same air fryer baking pan evenly spread ½ of rice on bottom, top with ½ of chicken, ½ of soup mixture, and then ½ of cheese. Repeat layering process.
5) Cover with foil and cook for another 25 minutes. Remove foil and cook until top is browned, around 15 minutes.
6) Serve and enjoy.

Nutrition information:
Calories per Serving: 475; Carbs: 34.8g; Protein: 30.0g; Fat: 23.9g

Salsa Verde Over Grilled Chicken

Serves: 2, Cooking Time: 40 minutes

Ingredients

- ½ red onion, chopped
- ½ tsp. chili powder
- 1 jalapeno thinly sliced
- 1 jar salsa verde, divided
- 1-pound boneless skinless chicken breasts
- 2 cloves of garlic, minced
- 2 tbsps. chopped cilantro
- 2 tbsps. extra virgin olive oil
- 4 slices Monterey Jack cheese
- Juice from ½ lime
- Lime wedges for serving

Instructions

1) In a Ziploc bag, add half of the salsa verde, olive oil, lime juice, garlic, chili powder and chicken. Allow to marinate in the fridge for at least 2 hours.
2) Preheat the air fryer to 390°F.
3) Place the grill pan accessory in the air fryer.
4) Grill the chicken for 40 minutes.
5) Flip the chicken every 10 minutes to cook evenly.
6) Serve the chicken with the cheese, jalapeno, red onion, cilantro, and lime wedges.

Nutrition information:
Calories per serving: 541; Carbs: 4.5g; Protein: 65.3g; Fat: 29.1g

Salted Meaty Egg Frittata

Serves: 3, Cooking Time: 20 minutes

Ingredients

- ½ pound ground beef
- 1 onion, chopped
- 3 cloves of garlic, minced
- 3 eggs, beaten
- 3 tbsps. olive oil
- Salt and pepper to taste

Instructions

1) Heat oil in a skillet under medium heat.
2) Sauté the garlic and onion until fragrant.
3) Add the ground beef and sauté for 5 minutes or until lightly golden. Set aside.
4) Preheat the air fryer for 5 minutes.
5) In a mixing bowl, combine the rest of the ingredients
6) Place the sautéed beef in a baking dish that will fit in the air fryer chamber.
7) Pour over the egg mixture.
8) Cook for 20 minutes at 320°F.

Nutrition information:
Calories per serving: 461; Carbohydrates: 6.8g; Protein: 28.9g; Fat: 35.4g

Savory Chives 'n Bacon Frittata

Serves: 4, Cooking Time: 15 minutes

Ingredients
- 1 tbsp. chives
- 6 eggs, beaten
- 6 uncured bacon, fried and crumbled
- Salt and pepper to taste

Instructions
1) Preheat the air fryer for 5 minutes.
2) Mix all ingredients in a mixing bowl.
3) Pour the mixture in a greased baking dish that will fit in the air fryer.
4) Close and cook for 15 minutes at 350°F.

Nutrition information:
Calories per serving: 255; Carbohydrates: 3.6g; Protein: 15.6g; Fat: 19.8g

Shishito Pepper Rubbed Wings

Serves: 6, Cooking Time: 30 minutes

Ingredients
- 1 ½ cups shishito peppers, pureed
- 2 tbsps. sesame oil
- 3 pounds chicken wings
- Salt and pepper to taste

Instructions
1) Place all Ingredients in a Ziploc bowl and allow to marinate for at least 2 hours in the fridge.
2) Preheat the air fryer to 390°F.
3) Place the grill pan accessory in the air fryer.
4) Grill for at least 30 minutes flipping the chicken every 5 minutes and basting with the remaining sauce.

Nutrition information:
Calories per serving: 321; Carbs: 1.7g; Protein: 50.2g; Fat: 12.6g

Soy-Honey Glaze Chicken Kebabs

Serves: 8, Cooking Time: 36 minutes

Ingredients
- 1 clove garlic
- 1 red bell peppers, cut into 2-inch pieces
- 1/8 tsp. ground black pepper
- 2 tbsps. and 2 tsps. honey
- 2 tbsps. and 2 tsps. soy sauce
- 2 tbsps. vegetable oil
- 2-1/2 small onions, cut into 2-inch pieces
- 4 skinless, boneless chicken breast halves cut into 1-inch cubes

Instructions

1) Whisk well pepper, soy sauce, honey, and oil. Transfer ¼ of the marinade to a small bowl for basting. Add chicken to bowl and toss well to coat. Add pepper, onion, and garlic. Toss well to mix. Let it marinate for 2 hours.
2) Thread vegetables and chicken into skewers and place on sewer rack in air fryer.
3) For 12 minutes, cook on 360°F. Halfway through cooking time, baste with marinade sauce and turnover skewers.
4) Serve and enjoy.

Nutrition information:
Calories per Serving: 179; Carbs: 12.4g; Protein: 17.4g; Fat: 6.6g

Spinach 'n Bacon Egg Cups

Serves: 4, Cooking Time: 10 minutes

Ingredients
- ¼ cup spinach, chopped finely
- 1 bacon strip, fried and crumbled
- 3 tbsps. butter
- 4 eggs, beaten
- Salt and pepper to taste

Instructions
1) Preheat the air fryer for 5 minutes.
2) In a mixing bowl, combine the eggs, butter, and spinach. Season with salt and pepper to taste.
3) Grease a ramekin with cooking spray and pour the egg mixture inside.
4) Sprinkle with bacon bits.
5) Place the ramekin in the air fryer.
6) Cook for 10 minutes at 350°F.

Nutrition information:
Calories per serving: 214; Carbohydrates: 2.2g; Protein: 9.4g; Fat: 18.6g

Spinach-Egg with Coconut Milk Casserole

Serves: 6, Cooking Time: 20 minutes

Ingredients
- ¼ cup coconut milk
- 1 onion, chopped
- 1 tsp. garlic powder
- 12 large eggs, beaten
- 2 tbsps. coconut oil
- 3 cups spinach, chopped
- Salt and pepper to taste

Instructions
1) Preheat the air fryer for 5 minutes.
2) In a mixing bowl, combine all ingredients except for the spinach. Whisk until well-incorporated.
3) Place the spinach in a baking dish and pour over the egg mixture
4) Place in the air fryer chamber and cook for 20 minutes at 310°F.

Nutrition information:
Calories per serving:185; Carbohydrates: 3.2g; Protein: 6.9g; Fat: 16.1g

Sriracha-Ginger Chicken

Serves: 3, Cooking Time: 25 minutes

Ingredients
- ¼ cup fish sauce
- ¼ cup sriracha
- ½ cup light brown sugar
- ½ cup rice vinegar
- 1 ½ pounds chicken breasts, pounded
- 1/3 cup hot chili paste
- 2 tsps. grated and peeled ginger

Instructions
1) Place all Ingredients in a Ziploc bag and allow to marinate for at least 2 hours in the fridge.
2) Preheat the air fryer to 390°F.
3) Place the grill pan accessory in the air fryer.
4) Grill the chicken for 25 minutes.
5) Flip the chicken every 10 minutes for even grilling.
6) Meanwhile, pour the marinade in a saucepan and heat over medium flame until the sauce thickens.
7) Before serving the chicken, brush with the sriracha glaze.

Nutrition information:
Calories per serving: 415; Carbs: 5.4g; Protein: 49.3g; Fat: 21.8g

Sriracha-vinegar Marinated Chicken

Serves: 4, Cooking Time: 40 minutes

Ingredients
- ¼ cup Thai fish sauce
- ¼ cups sriracha sauce
- ½ cup rice vinegar
- 1 tbsps. sugar
- 2 garlic cloves, minced
- 2 pounds chicken breasts
- Juice from 1 lime, freshly squeezed
- Salt and pepper to taste

Instructions
1) Place all Ingredients in a Ziploc bag except for the corn. Allow to marinate in the fridge for at least 2 hours.
2) Preheat the air fryer to 390°F.
3) Place the grill pan accessory in the air fryer.
4) Grill the chicken for 40 minutes and make sure to flip the chicken to grill evenly.
5) Meanwhile, place the marinade in a saucepan and heat over medium flame until it thickens.
6) Brush the chicken with the glaze and serve with cucumbers if desired.

Nutrition information:
Calories per serving: 427; Carbs: 6.7g; Protein: 49.1g; Fat: 22.6g

Sticky-Sweet Chicken BBQ

Serves: 2, Cooking Time: 40 minutes

Ingredients

- ½ cup balsamic vinegar
- ½ cup soy sauce
- 1-pound chicken drumsticks
- 2 cloves of garlic, minced
- 2 green onion, sliced thinly
- 2 tbsps. sesame seeds
- 3 tbsps. honey

Instructions

1) In a Ziploc bag, combine the soy sauce, balsamic vinegar, honey, garlic, and chicken. Allow to marinate in the fridge for at least 30 minutes.
2) Preheat the air fryer to 330°F.
3) Place the grill pan accessory in the air fryer.
4) Place on the grill and cook for 30 to 40 minutes. Make sure to flip the chicken every 10 minutes to cook evenly.
5) Meanwhile, use the remaining marinade and put it in a saucepan. Simmer until the sauce thickens.
6) Once the chicken is cooked, brush with the thickened marinade and garnish with sesame seeds and green onions.

Nutrition information:
Calories per serving: 594; Carbs: 43.7g; Protein: 48.7g; Fat: 24.9g

Sweet Lime 'n Chili Chicken Barbecue

Serves: 2, Cooking Time: 40 minutes

Ingredients

- ¼ cup soy sauce
- 1 cup sweet chili sauce
- 1-pound chicken breasts
- Juice from 2 limes, freshly squeezed

Instructions

1) In a Ziploc bag, combine all Ingredients and give a good shake. Allow to marinate for at least 2 hours in the fridge.
2) Preheat the air fryer to 390°F.
3) Place the grill pan accessory in the air fryer.
4) Place chicken on the grill and cook for 30 to 40 minutes. Make sure to flip the chicken every 10 minutes to cook evenly.
5) Meanwhile, use the remaining marinade and put it in a saucepan. Simmer until the sauce thickens.
6) Once the chicken is cooked, brush with the thickened marinade.

Nutrition information:
Calories per serving: 563; Carbs: 39.2g; Protein: 43.6g; Fat: 25.7g

Teriyaki Glazed Chicken Bake

Serves: 2, Cooking Time: 25 minutes

Ingredients

- 2 tbsps. cider vinegar
- 4 skinless chicken thighs
- 1-1/2 tsps. cornstarch
- 1-1/2 tsps. cold water
- 1/2 clove garlic, minced
- 1/4 cup white sugar

- 1/4 cup soy sauce
- 1/4 tsp. ground ginger
- 1/8 tsp. ground black pepper

Instructions
1) Lightly grease baking pan of air fryer with cooking spray. Add all Ingredients and toss well to coat. Spread chicken in a single layer on bottom of pan.
2) For 15 minutes, cook on 390°F.
3) Turnover chicken while brushing and covering well with the sauce.
4) Cook for 15 minutes at 330°F.
5) Serve and enjoy.

Nutrition information:
Calories per Serving: 267; Carbs: 19.9g; Protein: 24.7g; Fat: 9.8g

Tomato, Cheese 'n Broccoli Quiche

Serves: 2, Cooking Time: 24 minutes

Ingredients
- ½ cup Cheddar Cheese grated
- ½ cup Whole Milk
- 1 Large Carrot, peeled and diced
- 1 Large Tomato, chopped
- 1 small Broccoli, cut into florets
- 1 Tsp Parsley
- 1 Tsp Thyme
- 2 Large Eggs
- 2 tbsp Feta Cheese
- Salt & Pepper

Instructions
1) Lightly grease baking pan of air fryer with cooking spray.
2) Spread carrots, broccoli, and tomato in baking pan.
3) For 10 minutes, cook on 330°F.
4) Meanwhile, in a medium bowl whisk well eggs and milk. Season generously with pepper and salt. Whisk in parsley and thyme.
5) Remove basket and toss the mixture a bit. Sprinkle cheddar cheese. Pour egg mixture over vegetables and cheese.
6) Cook for another 12 minutes or until set to desired doneness.
7) Sprinkle feta cheese and let it sit for 2 minutes.
8) Serve and enjoy.

Nutrition information:
Calories per Serving: 363; Carbs: 23.7g; Protein: 21.0g; Fat: 20.4g

Tomato, Eggplant 'n Chicken Skewers

Serves: 4, Cooking Time: 25 minutes

Ingredients
- ¼ tsp. cayenne pepper
- ¼ tsp. ground cardamom
- 1 ½ tsp. ground turmeric
- 1 can coconut milk
- 1 cup cherry tomatoes
- 1 medium eggplant, cut into cubes

- 1 onion, cut into wedges
- 1-inch ginger, grated
- 2 pounds boneless chicken breasts, cut into cubes
- 2 tbsps. fresh lime juice
- 2 tbsps. tomato paste
- 3 tsps. lime zest
- 4 cloves of garlic, minced
- Salt and pepper to taste

Instructions
1) Place in a bowl the garlic, ginger, coconut milk, lime zest, lime juice, tomato paste, salt, pepper, turmeric, cayenne pepper, cardamom, and chicken breasts. Allow to marinate in the fridge for at least for 2 hours.
2) Preheat the air fryer to 390°F.
3) Place the grill pan accessory in the air fryer.
4) Skewer the chicken cubes with eggplant, onion, and cherry tomatoes on bamboo skewers.
5) Place on the grill pan and cook for 25 minutes making sure to flip the chicken every 5 minutes for even cooking.

Nutrition information:
Calories per serving: 485; Carbs:19.7 g; Protein: 55.2g; Fat: 20.6g

Turmeric and Lemongrass Chicken Roast

Serves: 6, Cooking Time: 40 minutes

Ingredients
- 1 tsp. turmeric
- 2 lemongrass stalks
- 2 tbsps. fish sauce
- 3 cloves of garlic, minced
- 3 pounds whole chicken
- 3 shallots, chopped
- Salt and pepper to taste

Instructions
1) Place all Ingredients in a Ziploc bag and allow to marinate for at least 2 hours in the fridge.
2) Preheat the air fryer to 390°F.
3) Place the grill pan accessory in the air fryer.
4) Grill the chicken for 40 minutes making sure to flip every 10 minutes for even grilling.

Nutrition information:
Calories per serving: 495; Carbs: 49.1g; Protein: 38.5g; Fat: 16.1g

Chapter 6 Air Fryer Dessert Recipes

Angel Food Cake

Serves: 12, Cooking Time: 30 minutes

Ingredients
- ¼ cup butter, melted
- 1 cup powdered erythritol
- 1 tsp. strawberry extract
- 12 egg whites
- 2 tsps. cream of tartar
- A pinch of salt

Instructions
1) Preheat the air fryer for 5 minutes.
2) Mix the egg whites and cream of tartar.
3) Use a hand mixer and whisk until white and fluffy.
4) Add the rest of the ingredients except for the butter and whisk for another minute.
5) Pour into a baking dish.
6) Place in the air fryer basket and cook for 30 minutes at 400°F or if a toothpick inserted in the middle comes out clean.
7) Drizzle with melted butter once cooled.

Nutrition information:
Calories per serving: 65; Carbohydrates: 1.8g; Protein: 3.1g; Fat: 5g

Apple Pie in Air Fryer

Serves: 4, Cooking Time: 35 minutes

Ingredients
- ½ tsp. vanilla extract
- 1 beaten egg
- 1 large apple, chopped
- 1 Pillsbury Refrigerator pie crust
- 1 tbsp. butter
- 1 tbsp. ground cinnamon
- 1 tbsp. raw sugar
- 2 tbsp. sugar
- 2 tsps. lemon juice
- Baking spray

Instructions
1) Lightly grease baking pan of air fryer with cooking spray. Spread pie crust on bottom of pan up to the sides.
2) In a bowl, mix vanilla, sugar, cinnamon, lemon juice, and apples. Pour on top of pie crust. Top apples with butter slices.
3) Cover apples with the other pie crust. Pierce with knife the tops of pie.
4) Spread beaten egg on top of crust and sprinkle sugar.
5) Cover with foil.
6) For 25 minutes, cook on 390°F.
7) Remove foil cook for 10 minutes at 330°F until tops are browned.
8) Serve and enjoy.

Nutrition information:
Calories per Serving: 372; Carbs: 44.7g; Protein: 4.2g; Fat: 19.6g

Apple-Toffee Upside-Down Cake

Serves: 9, Cooking Time: 30 minutes

Ingredients
- ¼ cup almond butter
- ¼ cup sunflower oil
- ½ cup walnuts, chopped
- ¾ cup + 3 tbsp. coconut sugar
- ¾ cup water
- 1 ½ tsp. mixed spice
- 1 cup plain flour
- 1 lemon, zest
- 1 tsp. baking soda
- 1 tsp. vinegar
- 3 baking apples, cored and sliced

Instructions
1) Preheat the air fryer to 390°F.
2) In a skillet, melt the almond butter and 3 tbsps. sugar. Pour the mixture over a baking dish that will fit in the air fryer. Arrange the slices of apples on top. Set aside.
3) In a mixing bowl, combine flour, ¾ cup sugar, and baking soda. Add the mixed spice.
4) In another bowl, mix the oil, water, vinegar, and lemon zest. Stir in the chopped walnuts.
5) Combine the wet ingredients to the dry ingredients until well combined.
6) Pour over the tin with apple slices.
7) Bake for 30 minutes or until a toothpick inserted comes out clean.

Nutrition information:
Calories per serving: 335; Carbohydrates: 39.6g; Protein: 3.8g; Fat: 17.9g

Banana-Choco Brownies

Serves: 12, Cooking Time: 30 minutes

Ingredients
- 2 cups almond flour
- 2 tsps. baking powder
- ½ tsp. baking powder
- ½ tsp. baking soda
- ½ tsp. salt
- 1 over-ripe banana
- 3 large eggs
- ½ tsp. stevia powder
- ¼ cup coconut oil
- 1 tbsp. vinegar
- 1/3 cup almond flour
- 1/3 cup cocoa powder

Instructions
1) Preheat the air fryer for 5 minutes.
2) Combine all ingredients in a food processor and pulse until well-combined.
3) Pour into a baking dish that will fit in the air fryer.
4) Place in the air fryer basket and cook for 30 minutes at 350°F or if a toothpick inserted in the middle comes out clean.

Nutrition information:
Calories per serving: 75; Carbohydrates: 2.1g; Protein: 1.7g; Fat: 6.6g

Blueberry & Lemon Cake

Serves: 4, Cooking Time: 17 minutes

Ingredients
- 2 eggs
- 1 cup blueberries
- zest from 1 lemon
- juice from 1 lemon
- 1 tsp. vanilla
- brown sugar for topping (a little sprinkling on top of each muffin-less than a tsp.)
- 2 1/2 cups self-rising flour
- 1/2 cup Monk Fruit (or use your preferred sugar)
- 1/2 cup cream
- 1/4 cup avocado oil (any light cooking oil)

Instructions
1) In mixing bowl, beat well wet Ingredients. Stir in dry ingredients and mix thoroughly.
2) Lightly grease baking pan of air fryer with cooking spray. Pour in batter.
3) For 12 minutes, cook on 330oF.
4) Let it stand in air fryer for 5 minutes.
5) Serve and enjoy.

Nutrition information:
Calories per Serving: 589; Carbs: 76.7g; Protein: 13.5g; Fat: 25.3g

Bread Pudding with Cranberry

Serves: 4, Cooking Time: 45 minutes

Ingredients
- 1-1/2 cups milk
- 2-1/2 eggs
- 1/2 cup cranberries1 tsp. butter
- 1/4 cup and 2 tbsps. white sugar
- 1/4 cup golden raisins
- 1/8 tsp. ground cinnamon
- 3/4 cup heavy whipping cream
- 3/4 tsp. lemon zest
- 3/4 tsp. kosher salt
- 3/4 French baguettes, cut into 2-inch slices
- 3/8 vanilla bean, split and seeds scraped away

Instructions
1) Lightly grease baking pan of air fryer with cooking spray. Spread baguette slices, cranberries, and raisins.
2) In blender, blend well vanilla bean, cinnamon, salt, lemon zest, eggs, sugar, and cream. Pour over baguette slices. Let it soak for an hour.
3) Cover pan with foil.
4) For 35 minutes, cook on 330oF.
5) Let it rest for 10 minutes.
6) Serve and enjoy.

Nutrition information:
Calories per Serving: 581; Carbs: 76.1g; Protein: 15.8g; Fat: 23.7g

Cherries 'n Almond Flour Bars

Serves: 12, Cooking Time: 35 minutes

Ingredients
- ¼ cup water
- ½ cup butter, softened
- ½ tsp. salt
- ½ tsp. vanilla
- 1 ½ cups almond flour
- 1 cup erythritol
- 1 cup fresh cherries, pitted
- 1 tbsp. xanthan gum
- 2 eggs

Instructions
1) In a mixing bowl, combine the first 6 ingredients until you form a dough.
2) Press the dough in a baking dish that will fit in the air fryer.
3) Place in the air fryer and bake for 10 minutes at 375°F.
4) Meanwhile, mix the cherries, water, and xanthan gum in a bowl.
5) Take the dough out and pour over the cherry mixture.
6) Return to the air fryer and cook for 25 minutes more at 375°F.

Nutrition information:
Calories per serving: 99; Carbohydrates: 2.1g; Protein: 1.8g; Fat: 9.3g

Cherry-Choco Bars

Serves: 8, Cooking Time: 15 minutes

Ingredients
- ¼ tsp. salt
- ½ cup almonds, sliced
- ½ cup chia seeds
- ½ cup dark chocolate, chopped
- ½ cup dried cherries, chopped
- ½ cup prunes, pureed
- ½ cup quinoa, cooked
- ¾ cup almond butter
- 1/3 cup honey
- 2 cups old-fashioned oats
- 2 tbsp. coconut oil

Instructions
1) Preheat the air fryer to 375°F.
2) In a mixing bowl, combine the oats, quinoa, chia seeds, almond, cherries, and chocolate.
3) In a saucepan, heat the almond butter, honey, and coconut oil.
4) Pour the butter mixture over the dry mixture. Add salt and prunes.
5) Mix until well combined.
6) Pour over a baking dish that can fit inside the air fryer.
7) Cook for 15 minutes.
8) Let it cool for an hour before slicing into bars.

Nutrition information: Calories per serving: 321; Carbohydrates: 35g; Protein: 7g; Fat: 17g

Chocolate Chip in a Mug

Serves: 6, Cooking Time: 20 minutes

Ingredients
- ¼ cup walnuts, shelled and chopped
- ½ cup butter, unsalted
- ½ cup dark chocolate chips
- ½ cup erythritol
- ½ tsp. baking soda
- ½ tsp. salt
- 1 tbsp. vanilla extract
- 2 ½ cups almond flour
- 2 large eggs, beaten

Instructions
1) Preheat the air fryer for 5 minutes.
2) Combine all ingredients in a mixing bowl.
3) Place in greased mugs.
4) Bake in the air fryer for 20 minutes at 375°F.

Nutrition information:
Calories per serving: 234; Carbohydrates: 4.9g; Protein: 2.3g; Fat: 22.8g

Choco-Peanut Mug Cake

Serves: 1, Cooking Time: 20 minutes

Ingredients
- ¼ tsp. baking powder
- ½ tsp. vanilla extract
- 1 egg
- 1 tbsp. heavy cream
- 1 tbsp. peanut butter
- 1 tsp. butter, softened
- 2 tbsp. erythritol
- 2 tbsps. cocoa powder, unsweetened

Instructions
1) Preheat the air fryer for 5 minutes.
2) Combine all ingredients in a mixing bowl.
3) Pour into a greased mug.
4) Place in the air fryer basket and cook for 20 minutes at 400°F or if a toothpick inserted in the middle comes out clean.

Nutrition information:
Calories per serving: 293; Carbohydrates: 8.5g; Protein: 12.4g; Fat: 23.3g

Coco-Lime Bars

Serves: 3, Cooking Time: 20 minutes

Ingredients
- ¼ cup almond flour
- ¼ cup coconut oil
- ¼ cup dried coconut flakes
- ¼ tsp. salt

- ½ cup lime juice
- ¾ cup coconut flour
- 1 ¼ cup erythritol powder
- 1 tbsp. lime zest
- 4 eggs

Instructions
1) Preheat the air fryer for 5 minutes.
2) Combine all ingredients in a mixing bowl.
3) Place in greased mug.
4) Bake in the air fryer for 20 minutes at 375°F.

Nutrition information:
Calories per serving: 506; Carbohydrates: 21.9g; Protein: 19.3g; Fat: 37.9g

Coconut 'n Almond Fat Bombs

Serves: 12, Cooking Time: 15 minutes

Ingredients
- ¼ cup almond flour
- ½ cup shredded coconut
- 1 tbsp. coconut oil
- 1 tbsp. vanilla extract
- 2 tbsps. liquid stevia
- 3 egg whites

Instructions
1) Preheat the air fryer for 5 minutes.
2) Combine all ingredients in a mixing bowl.
3) Form small balls using your hands.
4) Place in the air fryer basket and cook for 15 minutes at 400°F.

Nutrition information:
Calories per serving: 23; Carbohydrates: 0.7g; Protein: 1.1g; Fat: 1.8g

Coconutty Lemon Bars

Serves: 12, Cooking Time: 25 minutes

Ingredients
- ¼ cup cashew
- ¼ cup fresh lemon juice, freshly squeezed
- ¾ cup coconut milk
- ¾ cup erythritol
- 1 cup desiccated coconut
- 1 tsp. baking powder
- 2 eggs, beaten
- 2 tbsps. coconut oil
- A dash of salt

Instructions
1) Preheat the air fryer for 5 minutes.
2) In a mixing bowl, combine all ingredients.
3) Use a hand mixer to mix everything.
4) Pour into a baking dish that will fit in the air fryer.
5) Bake for 25 minutes at 350°F or until a toothpick inserted in the middle comes out clean.

Nutrition information:
Calories per serving: 118; Carbohydrates: 3.9g; Protein: 2.6g; Fat:10.2g

Coffee 'n Blueberry Cake

Serves: 6, Cooking Time: 35 minutes

Ingredients
- 1 cup white sugar
- 1 egg
- 1/2 cup butter, softened
- 1/2 cup fresh or frozen blueberries
- 1/2 cup sour cream
- 1/2 tsp. baking powder
- 1/2 tsp. ground cinnamon
- 1/2 tsp. vanilla extract
- 1/4 cup brown sugar
- 1/4 cup chopped pecans
- 1/8 tsp. salt
- 1-1/2 tsps. confectioners' sugar for dusting
- 3/4 cup and 1 tbsp. all-purpose flour

Instructions
1) In a small bowl, whisk well pecans, cinnamon, and brown sugar.
2) In a blender, blend well all wet Ingredients. Add dry Ingredients except for confectioner's sugar and blueberries. Blend well until smooth and creamy.
3) Lightly grease baking pan of air fryer with cooking spray.
4) Pour half of batter in pan. Sprinkle half of pecan mixture on top. Pour the remaining batter. And then topped with remaining pecan mixture.
5) Cover pan with foil.
6) For 35 minutes, cook on 330°F.
7) Serve and enjoy with a dusting of confectioner's sugar.

Nutrition information:
Calories per Serving: 471; Carbs: 59.5g; Protein: 4.1g; Fat: 24.0g

Coffee Flavored Cookie Dough

Serves: 12, Cooking Time: 20 minutes

Ingredients
- ¼ cup butter
- ¼ tsp. xanthan gum
- ½ tsp. coffee espresso powder
- ½ tsp. stevia powder
- ¾ cup almond flour
- 1 egg
- 1 tsp. vanilla
- 1/3 cup sesame seeds
- 2 tbsps. cocoa powder
- 2 tbsps. cream cheese, softened

Instructions
1) Preheat the air fryer for 5 minutes.
2) Combine all ingredients in a mixing bowl.
3) Press into a baking dish that will fit in the air fryer.
4) Place in the air fryer basket and cook for 20 minutes at 400°F or if a toothpick inserted in the middle comes out clean.

Nutrition information:
Calories per serving: 88; Carbohydrates: 1.3g; Protein: 1.9g; Fat: 8.3g

Coffee Flavored Doughnuts

Serves: 6, Cooking Time: 6 minutes

Ingredients
- ¼ cup coconut sugar
- ¼ cup coffee
- ½ tsp. salt
- 1 cup white all-purpose flour
- 1 tbsp. sunflower oil
- 1 tsp. baking powder
- 2 tbsp. aquafaba

Instructions
1) In a mixing bowl mix together the dry Ingredients flour, sugar, salt, and baking powder.
2) In another bowl, combine the aquafaba, sunflower oil, and coffee.
3) Mix to form a dough.
4) Let the dough rest inside the fridge.
5) Preheat the air fryer to 400ºF.
6) Knead the dough and create doughnuts.
7) Arrange inside the air fryer in single layer and cook for 6 minutes.
8) Do not shake so that the donut maintains its shape.

Nutrition information:
Calories per serving: 113; Carbohydrates: 20.45g; Protein: 2.16g; Fat:2.54g

Crisped 'n Chewy Chonut Holes

Serves: 6, Cooking Time: 10 minutes

Ingredients
- ¼ cup almond milk
- ¼ cup coconut sugar
- ¼ tsp. cinnamon
- ½ tsp. salt
- 1 cup white all-purpose flour
- 1 tbsp. coconut oil, melted
- 1 tsp. baking powder
- 2 tbsp. aquafaba or liquid from canned chickpeas

Instructions
1) In a mixing bowl, mix the flour, sugar, and baking powder. Add the salt and cinnamon and mix well.
2) In another bowl, mix together the coconut oil, aquafaba, and almond milk.
3) Gently pour the dry ingredients to the wet ingredients. Mix together until well combined or until you form a sticky dough.
4) Place the dough in the refrigerator to rest for at least an hour.
5) Preheat the air fryer to 370ºF.
6) Create small balls of the dough and place inside the air fryer and cook for 10 minutes. Do not shake the air fryer.
7) Once cooked, sprinkle with sugar and cinnamon.
8) Serve with your breakfast coffee.

Nutrition information:
Calories per serving: 120; Carbohydrates: 21.62g; Protein: 2.31g; Fat:2.76g

Crispy Good Peaches

Serves: 4, Cooking Time: 30 minutes

Ingredients
- 1 tsp. cinnamon
- 1 tsp. sugar, white
- 1/3 cup oats, dry rolled
- 1/4 cup Flour, white
- 2 tbsp. Flour, white
- 3 tbsp. butter, unsalted
- 3 tbsp. sugar
- 3 tbsp. pecans, chopped
- 4 cup sliced peaches, frozen

Instructions
1) Lightly grease baking pan of air fryer with cooking spray. Mix in a tsp cinnamon, 2 tbsp flour, 3 tbsp sugar, and peaches.
2) For 20 minutes, cook on 300oF.
3) Mix the rest of the Ingredients in a bowl. Pour over peaches.
4) Cook for 10 minutes at 330oF.
5) Serve and enjoy.

Nutrition information:
Calories per Serving: 435; Carbs: 74.1g; Protein: 4.3g; Fat: 13.4g

Easy Baked Chocolate Mug Cake

Serves: 3, Cooking Time: 15 minutes

Ingredients
- ½ cup cocoa powder
- ½ cup stevia powder
- 1 cup coconut cream
- 1 package cream cheese, room temperature
- 1 tbsp. vanilla extract
- 4 tbsps. butter

Instructions
1) Preheat the air fryer for 5 minutes.
2) In a mixing bowl, combine all ingredients.
3) Use a hand mixer to mix everything until fluffy.
4) Pour into greased mugs.
5) Place the mugs in the fryer basket.
6) Bake for 15 minutes at 350oF.
7) Place in the fridge to chill before serving.

Nutrition information:
Calories per serving: 744; Carbohydrates:15.3 g; Protein: 13.9g; Fat: 69.7g

Hot Coconut 'n Cocoa Buns

Serves: 8
Preparation Time: 8 minutes, Cooking Time: 15 minutes

Ingredients
- ¼ cup cacao nibs
- 1 cup coconut milk
- 1/3 cup coconut flour
- 3 tbsps. cacao powder
- 4 eggs, beaten

Instructions
1) Preheat the air fryer for 5 minutes.
2) Combine all ingredients in a mixing bowl.
3) Form buns using your hands and place in a baking dish that will fit in the air fryer.
4) Bake for 15 minutes for 375°F.
5) Once air fryer turns off, leave the buns in the air fryer until it cools completely.

Nutrition information:
Calories per serving: 161; Carbohydrates: 4g; Protein: 5.7g; Fat: 13.6g

Keto-Friendly Doughnut Recipe

Serves: 4, Cooking Time: 20 minutes

Ingredients
- ¼ cup coconut milk
- ¼ cup erythritol
- ¼ cup flaxseed meal
- ¾ cup almond flour
- 1 tbsp. cocoa powder
- 1 tsp. vanilla extract
- 2 large eggs, beaten
- 3 tbsps. coconut oil

Instructions
1) Place all ingredients in a mixing bowl.
2) Mix until well-combined.
3) Scoop the dough into individual doughnut molds.
4) Preheat the air fryer for 5 minutes.
5) Cook for 20 minutes at 350°F.
6) Bake in batches if possible.

Nutrition information:
Calories per serving: 222; Carbohydrates: 5.1g; Protein: 3.9g; Fat: 20.7g

Lava Cake in A Mug

Serves: 4, Cooking Time: 15 minutes

Ingredients
- ¼ cup coconut oil, melted
- ¼ tsp. vanilla powder
- 1 cup dark chocolate powder
- 1 tbsp. almond flour
- 2 tbsps. stevia powder
- 3 large eggs, beaten

Instructions
1) Preheat the air fryer for 5 minutes.
2) Combine all ingredients in a mixing bowl.
3) Grease ramekins with coconut oil and dust with chocolate powder.
4) Pour the batter into the ramekins and place in the fryer basket.
5) Close and bake at 375°F for 15 minutes.

Nutrition information:
Calories per serving: 251; Carbohydrates: 14.5g; Protein: 4.1g; Fat: 19.6g

Leche Flan Filipino Style

Serves: 4, Cooking Time: 30 minutes

Ingredients
- 1 cup heavy cream
- 1 tsp. vanilla extract
- 1/2 (14 ounce) can sweetened condensed milk
- 1/2 cup milk
- 2-1/2 eggs
- 1/3 cup white sugar

Instructions
1) In blender, blend well vanilla, eggs, milk, cream, and condensed milk.
2) Lightly grease baking pan of air fryer with cooking spray. Add sugar and heat for 10 minutes at 370°F until melted and caramelized. Lower heat to 300°F and continue melting and swirling.
3) Pour milk mixture into caramelized sugar. Cover pan with foil.
4) Cook for 20 minutes at 330°F.
5) Let it cool completely in the fridge.
6) Place a plate on top of pan and invert pan to easily remove flan.
7) Serve and enjoy.

Nutrition information:
Calories per Serving: 498; Carbs: 46.8g; Protein: 10.0g; Fat: 30.0g

Lusciously Easy Brownies

Serves: 8, Cooking Time: 20 minutes

Ingredients
- 1 egg
- 2 tbsps. and 2 tsps. unsweetened cocoa powder
- 1/2 cup white sugar
- 1/2 tsp. vanilla extract
- 1/4 cup butter
- 1/4 cup all-purpose flour
- 1/8 tsp. salt
- 1/8 tsp. baking powder

Frosting Ingredients
- 1 tbsp. and 1-1/2 tsps. butter, softened
- 1 tbsp. and 1-1/2 tsps. unsweetened cocoa powder
- 1-1/2 tsps. honey
- 1/2 tsp. vanilla extract
- 1/2 cup confectioners' sugar

Instructions
1) Lightly grease baking pan of air fryer with cooking spray. Melt ¼ cup butter for 3 minutes. Stir in vanilla, eggs, and sugar. Mix well.
2) Stir in baking powder, salt, flour, and cocoa mix well. Evenly spread.
3) For 20 minutes, cook on 300oF.
4) In a small bowl, make the frosting by mixing well all Ingredients. Frost brownies while still warm.
5) Serve and enjoy.

Nutrition information:
Calories per Serving: 191; Carbs: 25.7g; Protein: 1.8g; Fat: 9.0g

Maple Cinnamon Buns

Serves: 9, Cooking Time: 30 minutes

Ingredients
- ¼ cup icing sugar
- ½ cup pecan nuts, toasted
- ¾ cup tbsp. unsweetened almond milk
- 1 ½ cup plain white flour, sifted
- 1 ½ tbsp. active yeast
- 1 cup wholegrain flour, sifted
- 1 tbsp. coconut oil, melted
- 1 tbsp. ground flaxseed
- 2 ripe bananas, sliced
- 2 tsps. cinnamon powder
- 4 Medjool dates, pitted
- 4 tbsps. maple syrup

Instructions
1) Heat the ¾ cup almond milk to lukewarm and add the maple syrup and yeast. Allow the yeast to activate for 5 to 10 minutes.
2) Meanwhile, mix together flaxseed and 3 tbsps. of water to make the egg replacement. Allow flaxseed to

soak for 2 minutes. Add the coconut oil.
3) Pour the flaxseed mixture to the yeast mixture.
4) In another bowl, combine the two types of flour and the 1 tbsp. cinnamon powder. Pour the yeast-flaxseed mixture and combine until dough forms.
5) Knead the dough on a floured surface for at least 10 minutes.
6) Place the kneaded dough in a greased bowl and cover with a kitchen towel. Leave in a warm and dark area for the bread to rise for 1 hour.
7) While the dough is rising, make the filling by mixing together the pecans, banana slices, and dates. Add 1 tbsp. of cinnamon powder.
8) Preheat the air fryer to 390°F.
9) Roll the risen dough on a floured surface until it is thin. Spread the pecan mixture on to the dough.
10) Roll the dough and cut into nine slices.
11) Place inside a dish that will fit in the air fryer and cook for 30 minutes.
12) Once cooked, sprinkle with icing sugar.

Nutrition information:
Calories per serving: 293; Carbohydrates: 44.9g; Protein: 5.6g; Fat:10.1 g

Melts in Your Mouth Caramel Cheesecake

Serves: 8, Cooking Time: 40 minutes

Ingredients
- 1 Can Dulce de Leche
- 1 Tbsp Melted Chocolate
- 1 Tbsp Vanilla Essence
- 250 g Caster Sugar
- 4 Large Eggs
- 50 g Melted Butter
- 500 g Soft Cheese
- 6 Digestives, crumbled

Instructions
1) Lightly grease baking pan of air fryer with cooking spray. Mix and press crumbled digestives and melted butter on pan bottom. Spread dulce de leche.
2) In bowl, beat well soft cheese and sugar until fluffy. Stir in vanilla and egg. Pour over dulce de leche.
3) Cover pan with foil. For 15 minutes, cook on 390°F.
4) Cook for 10 minutes at 330°F. And then 15 minutes at 300°F.
5) Let it cool completely in air fryer. Refrigerate for at least 4 hours before slicing.
6) Serve and enjoy.

Nutrition information:
Calories per Serving: 463; Carbs: 44.1g; Protein: 17.9g; Fat: 23.8g

Mouth-Watering Strawberry Cobbler

Serves: 4, Cooking Time: 25 minutes

Ingredients

- 1 tbsp. butter, diced
- 1 tbsp. and 2 tsps. butter
- 1-1/2 tsps. cornstarch
- 1/2 cup water
- 1-1/2 cups strawberries, hulled
- 1/2 cup all-purpose flour
- 1-1/2 tsps. white sugar
- 1/4 cup white sugar
- 1/4 tsp. salt
- 1/4 cup heavy whipping cream
- 3/4 tsp. baking powder

Instructions

1) Lightly grease baking pan of air fryer with cooking spray. Add water, cornstarch, and sugar. Cook for 10 minutes 390oF or until hot and thick. Add strawberries and mix well. Dot tops with 1 tbsp butter.
2) In a bowl, mix well salt, baking powder, sugar, and flour. Cut in 1 tbsp and 2 tsp butter. Mix in cream. Spoon on top of berries.
3) Cook for 15 minutes at 390oF, until tops are lightly browned.
4) Serve and enjoy.

Nutrition information:
Calories per Serving: 255; Carbs: 32.0g; Protein: 2.4g; Fat: 13.0g

Oriental Coconut Cake

Serves: 8, Cooking Time: 40 minutes

Ingredients

- 1 cup gluten-free flour
- 2 eggs
- 1/2 cup flaked coconut
- 1-1/2 tsps. baking powder
- 1/2 tsp. baking soda
- 1/2 tsp. xanthan gum
- 1/2 tsp. salt
- 1/2 cup coconut milk
- 1/2 cup vegetable oil
- 1/2 tsp. vanilla extract
- 1/4 cup chopped walnuts
- 3/4 cup white sugar

Instructions

1) In blender blend all wet Ingredients. Add dry ingredients and blend thoroughly.
2) Lightly grease baking pan of air fryer with cooking spray.
3) Pour in batter. Cover pan with foil.
4) For 30 minutes, cook on 330oF.
5) Let it rest for 10 minutes
6) Serve and enjoy.

Nutrition information:
Calories per Serving: 359; Carbs: 35.2g; Protein: 4.3g; Fat: 22.3g

Pecan-Cranberry Cake

Serves: 6, Cooking Time: 25 minutes

Ingredients
- 1 1/2 cups Almond Flour
- 1 tsp baking powder
- 1/2 cup fresh cranberries
- 1/2 tsp vanilla extract
- 1/4 cup cashew milk (or use any dairy or non-dairy milk you prefer)
- 1/4 cup chopped pecans
- 1/4 cup Monk fruit (or use your preferred sweetener)
- 1/4 tsp cinnamon
- 1/8 tsp salt
- 2 large eggs

Instructions
1) In blender, add all wet Ingredients and mix well. Add all dry Ingredients except for cranberries and pecans. Blend well until smooth.
2) Lightly grease baking pan of air fryer with cooking spray. Pour in batter. Drizzle cranberries on top and then followed by pecans.
3) For 20 minutes, cook on 330ºF.
4) Let stand for 5 minutes.
5) Serve and enjoy.

Nutrition information:
Calories per Serving: 98; Carbs: 11.7g; Protein: 1.7g; Fat: 4.9g

Poppy Seed Pound Cake

Serves: 8, Cooking Time: 20 minutes

Ingredients
- ¼ cup erythritol powder
- ¼ tsp. vanilla extract
- ½ cup coconut milk
- 1 ½ cups almond flour
- 1 ½ tsp. baking powder
- 1/3 cup butter, unsalted
- 2 large eggs, beaten
- 2 tbsp. psyllium husk powder
- 2 tbsps. poppy seeds

Instructions
1) Preheat the air fryer for 5 minutes.
2) In a mixing bowl, combine all ingredients.
3) Use a hand mixer to mix everything.
4) Pour into a small loaf pan that will fit in the air fryer.
5) Bake for 20 minutes at 375ºF or until a toothpick inserted in the middle comes out clean.

Nutrition information:
Calories per serving: 145; Carbohydrates: 3.6; Protein: 2.1g; Fat: 13.6g

Pound Cake with Fresh Apples

Serves: 6, Cooking Time: 60 minutes

Ingredients

- 1 cup white sugar
- 1 tsp. vanilla extract
- 1 medium Granny Smith apples - peeled, cored and chopped
- 1-1/2 eggs
- 1-1/2 cups all-purpose flour
- 1/2 tsp. baking soda
- 1/2 tsp. salt
- 1/4 tsp. ground cinnamon
- 2/3 cup and 1 tbsp. chopped walnuts
- 3/4 cup vegetable oil

Instructions
1) In blender, blend all Ingredients except for apples and walnuts. Blend thoroughly. Fold in apples and walnuts.
2) Lightly grease baking pan of air fryer with cooking spray. Pour batter.
3) Cover pan with foil.
4) For 30 minutes, cook on preheated 330oF air fryer.
5) Remove foil and cook for another 20 minutes.
6) Let it stand for 10 minutes.
7) Serve and enjoy.

Nutrition information:
Calories per Serving: 696; Carbs: 71.1g; Protein: 6.5g; Fat: 42.8g

Quick 'n Easy Pumpkin Pie

Serves: 8, Cooking Time: 35 minutes

Ingredients

- 1 (14 ounce) can sweetened condensed milk
- 1 (15 ounce) can pumpkin puree
- 1 9-inch unbaked pie crust
- 1 large egg
- 1 tsp. ground cinnamon
- 1/2 tsp. fine salt
- 1/2 tsp. ground ginger
- 1/4 tsp. freshly grated nutmeg
- 1/8 tsp. Chinese 5-spice powder
- 3 egg yolks

Instructions
1) Lightly grease baking pan of air fryer with cooking spray. Press pie crust on bottom of pan, stretching all the way up to the sides of the pan. Pierce all over with fork.
2) In blender, blend well egg, egg yolks, and pumpkin puree. Add Chinese 5-spice powder, nutmeg, salt, ginger, cinnamon, and condensed milk. Pour on top of pie crust.
3) Cover pan with foil.
4) For 15 minutes, cook on preheated 390oF air fryer.
5) Remove foil and continue cooking for 20 minutes at 330oF until middle is set.
6) Allow to cool in air fryer completely.
7) Serve and enjoy.

Nutrition information:
Calories per Serving: 326; Carbs: 41.9g; Protein: 7.6g; Fat: 14.2g

Raspberry-Coco Desert

Serves: 12, Cooking Time: 20 minutes

Ingredients
- ¼ cup coconut oil
- 1 cup coconut milk
- 1 cup raspberries, pulsed
- 1 tsp. vanilla bean
- 1/3 cup erythritol powder
- 3 cups desiccated coconut

Instructions
1) Preheat the air fryer for 5 minutes.
2) Combine all ingredients in a mixing bowl.
3) Pour into a greased baking dish.
4) Bake in the air fryer for 20 minutes at 375°F.

Nutrition information:
Calories per serving: 132; Carbohydrates: 9.7g; Protein: 1.5g; Fat: 9.7g

Raspberry-Coconut Cupcake

Serves: 6, Cooking Time: 30 minutes

Ingredients
- ½ cup butter
- ½ tsp. salt
- ¾ cup erythritol
- 1 cup almond milk, unsweetened
- 1 cup coconut flour
- 1 tbsp. baking powder
- 3 tsps. vanilla extract
- 7 large eggs, beaten

Instructions
1) Preheat the air fryer for 5 minutes.
2) Mix all ingredients using a hand mixer.
3) Pour into hard cupcake molds.
4) Place in the air fryer basket.
5) Bake for 30 minutes at 350°F or until a toothpick inserted in the middle comes out clean.
6) Bake by batches if possible.
7) Allow to chill before serving.

Nutrition information:
Calories per serving: 235; Carbohydrates: 7.4g; Protein: 3.8g; Fat: 21.1g

Strawberry Pop Tarts

Serves: 6, Cooking Time: 25 minutes

Ingredients

- 1 oz reduced-fat Philadelphia cream cheese
- 1 tsp cornstarch
- 1 tsp stevia
- 1 tsp sugar sprinkles
- 1/2 cup plain, non-fat vanilla Greek yogurt
- 1/3 cup low-sugar strawberry preserves
- 2 refrigerated pie crusts
- olive oil or coconut oil spray

Instructions

1) Cut pie crusts into 6 equal rectangles.
2) In a bowl, mix cornstarch and preserves. Add preserves in middle of crust. Fold over crust. Crimp edges with fork to seal. Repeat process for remaining crusts.
3) Lightly grease baking pan of air fryer with cooking spray. Add pop tarts in single layer. Cook in batches for 8 minutes at 370oF.
4) Meanwhile, make the frosting by mixing stevia, cream cheese, and yogurt in a bowl. Spread on top of cooked pop tart and add sugar sprinkles.
5) Serve and enjoy.

Nutrition information:
Calories per Serving: 317; Carbs: 34.8g; Protein: 4.7g; Fat: 17.6g

Strawberry Shortcake Quickie

Serves: 4, Cooking Time: 25 minutes

Ingredients

- ¼ tsp. liquid stevia
- ¼ tsp. salt
- ½ cup butter
- ½ tsp. baking powder
- 1 cup strawberries, halved
- 1 tsp. vanilla extract
- 1/3 cup erythritol
- 2/3 cup almond flour
- 3 large eggs, beaten

Instructions

1) Preheat the air fryer for 5 minutes.
2) In a mixing bowl, combine all ingredients except for the strawberries.
3) Use a hand mixer to mix everything.
4) Pour into greased mugs.
5) Top with sliced strawberries
6) Place the mugs in the fryer basket.
7) Bake for 25 minutes at 350oF.
8) Place in the fridge to chill before serving.

Nutrition information:
Calories per serving: 265; Carbohydrates: 3.7g; Protein:2.5 g; Fat: 26.7g

Vanilla Pound Cake

Serves: 12, Cooking Time: 30 minutes

Ingredients
- ¼ tsp. salt
- ½ cup erythritol powder
- 1 vanilla bean, scraped
- 1/3 cup water
- 2/3 cup butter, melted
- 4 large eggs

Instructions
1) Preheat the air fryer for 5 minutes.
2) Combine all ingredients in a mixing bowl.
3) Pour into a greased baking dish.
4) Bake in the air fryer for 30 minutes at 375°F.

Nutrition information:
Calories per serving: 126; Carbohydrates: 2.3g; Protein: 1.6g; Fat: 12.3g

Yummy Banana Cookies

Serves: 6, Cooking Time: 10 minutes

Ingredients
- 1 cup dates, pitted and chopped
- 1 tsp. vanilla
- 1/3 cup vegetable oil
- 2 cups rolled oats
- 3 ripe bananas

Instructions
1) Preheat the air fryer to 350°F.
2) In a bowl, mash the bananas and add in the rest of the ingredients.
3) Let it rest inside the fridge for 10 minutes.
4) Drop a tsp.ful on cut parchment paper.
5) Place the cookies on parchment paper inside the air fryer basket. Make sure that the cookies do not overlap.
6) Cook for 20 minutes or until the edges are crispy.
7) Serve with almond milk.

Nutrition information:
Calories per serving: 382; Carbohydrates: 50.14g; Protein: 6.54g; Fat: 17.2g

Zucchini-Choco Bread

Serves: 12, Cooking Time: 20 minutes

Ingredients
- ¼ tsp. salt
- ½ cup almond milk
- ½ cup maple syrup
- ½ cup sunflower oil
- ½ cup unsweetened cocoa powder
- 1 cup oat flour
- 1 cup zucchini, shredded and squeezed
- 1 tbsp. flax egg (1 tbsp. flax meal + 3 tbsps. water)
- 1 tsp. apple cider vinegar
- 1 tsp. baking soda
- 1 tsp. vanilla extract
- 1/3 cup chocolate chips

Instructions
1) Preheat the air fryer to 350°F.
2) Line a baking dish that will fit the air fryer with parchment paper.
3) In a bowl, combine the flax meal, zucchini, sunflower oil, maple, vanilla, apple cider vinegar and milk.
4) Stir in the oat flour, baking soda, cocoa powder, and salt. Mix until well combined.
5) Add the chocolate chips.
6) Pour over the baking dish and cook for 15 minutes or until a toothpick inserted in the middle comes out clean.

Nutrition information:
Calories per serving: 213; Carbohydrates: 24.2 g; Protein: 4.6g; Fat: 10.9g

Made in the USA
Middletown, DE
04 November 2019